THE FINE COTTON FIASCO

THE FINE COTTON FIASCO

PETER HOYSTED & PAT SHEIL

EBURY
PRESS

EBURY PRESS

UK | USA | Canada | Ireland | Australia
India | New Zealand | South Africa | China

Ebury Press is part of the Penguin Random House group of companies whose
addresses can be found at global.penguinrandomhouse.com.

Penguin
Random House
Australia

First published by Ebury Press in 2019
Copyright © Peter Hoysted and Pat Sheil 2019

The moral right of the authors has been asserted.

Cover photograph by eastern light photography/Shutterstock
Cover design by James Rendall © Penguin Random House Australia Pty Ltd
Typeset in Adobe Garamond Pro by Midland Typesetters, Australia

Printed and bound in Australia by Griffin Press, an accredited
ISO AS/NZS 14001 Environmental Management Systems printer

A catalogue record for this
book is available from the
National Library of Australia

ISBN 978 0 14379 370 0

penguin.com.au

*This work is dedicated to the memory of Fine Cotton,
Bold Personality and Dashing Soltaire – the only characters
in the entire story who were truly innocent.*

CONTENTS

FOREWORD

'Racing's Darkest Day'. So screamed the headline on Queensland's *Sunday Mail* on 19 August 1984, less than 24 hours after Bold Personality's dismal impersonation of Fine Cotton was rumbled. The jig was up, the conspirators had fled, tyres screeching from the car park at the Eagle Farm racecourse and out of the state, with the cops in hot pursuit.

Punters were left angrily holding betting tickets that had less value than the cost of the ink printed upon them. Some, including members of the Queensland Fraud Squad, had had 'the mail' – inside information that Fine Cotton would prevail in the Second Division Commerce Novice Handicap. Others were simply duped into betting on the nine-year-old picnic racing nag, drawn into shelling out their hard earned on the back of a betting plunge that was without precedent for such a modest event.

The phrase still hangs over the Fine Cotton fiasco. Old salts in the racing caper still refer to it as 'racing's darkest day'. They furrow their brows at the audacity of it and the acute embarrassment that fell upon the industry when the forensic examinations of racing authorities and the criminal justice system commenced in earnest.

The truth of it is that there were many darker days in thoroughbred racing before the Fine Cotton fiasco and there have been many others since. Where the Fine Cotton fiasco stands in terms of superlatives is the funniest, most farcical effort to strip bookmakers of their money ever seen in this country and, we wager, any other.

The entire episode constitutes arguably the silliest moment in Australian history. The sheer incompetence of the men on the ground, their seemingly inexplicable persistence in the face of irrefutable evidence that their scam was never going to work – and would certainly end catastrophically – is hilarious.

This book has its genesis in a radio interview conducted between one of its authors, Peter Hoysted, and Richard Fidler, the then host of ABC Radio's *Conversations*. Over the course of several alcohol-fuelled lunches, Hoysted had taken to telling the Fine Cotton story as a long-form anecdote. More so than Hoysted, Fidler understood the fiasco's exalted place in Australian history as a comic farce of the highest order that desperately needed to find its way from the anecdotal to the more permanent medium of print.

The interview was scheduled with the author confident that Australians would not be intrigued by, nor much interested in, a story of a 35-year-old horse race. Indeed, when the interview concluded, the author figured its hour-long audio artefact would sit gathering dust up on the highest shelf in a bleak corner of the national broadcaster, to be dragged out only when normal broadcasting experienced technical conniptions.

It is a matter of record that the interview ran the very next day and would be downloaded more than a million times.

This brought about a review of the intrinsic worth of the Fine Cotton story. It certainly was a tale of a 35-year-old horse race, but more so, it was a caper. And people love a caper. It was a reckless journey gone haywire from the very point of planning and design to the shattering inevitably of abject failure.

It was also, it seemed, universally amusing. We have here an epic tale of optimism and self-delusion, a slapstick magma of greed and desperation worthy of the Marx Brothers – where the prat-falling was not of the type where one might fall heavily on one's posterior only to get up, give it a good rub and acknowledge the laughter from those who had witnessed it.

In the background of this doomed comic criminal conspiracy were men who threatened to inflict more than a minor bruising of one's rear end. They were cold-hearted killers, violent sociopaths who for years had murdered, tortured and terrified anyone who got in their way. These fellows were not funny guys, and the pawns in their game only ignored the looming inevitability of failure under the threat of extreme violence if they pulled out.

Some things are inherently comical. A duck is always funnier than a chicken, and a criminal making a fool of himself is the kind of comedy that can be laughed at without fear of hurting anyone's feelings. But this wacky Punch and Judy show was played out against the background of a very nasty criminal conspiracy, and the fact remains that the only people who got it in the neck were the poor bloody infantry, while the generals sat in their chateaus and sipped champagne.

Or, in this case, hit up pethidine, chomped on cigars, gorged themselves on party pies or perched their enormous arses on the

Treasury benches of the Queensland parliament. It doesn't much matter. The point is that the further away a participant was from the trenches, the less likely he was to get covered in shit.

If this book, at times, reads like a violent true crime story overflowing with ludicrous vaudeville, it is because that's what it is.

The Fine Cotton fiasco occurred at the junction of two great events: the looming collapse of the Queensland state government led by Sir Joh Bjelke-Petersen, in a shower of fetid corruption that could no longer be ignored, and the Sydney gang wars of 1984–85 where a new group of villains, cashed up on drug distribution and armed to the back teeth, challenged the existing order who had dominated organised crime in the city for almost three decades by ruthlessly murdering anyone who got in their way.

As it turns out, you can't tell the Fine Cotton story without the ugliness – not the whole story, anyway.

As we were putting this book together, we were constantly struck by one thing – that just about everyone we told about the project had heard some version or another of the Fine Cotton story, or at least knew about the ill-fated ring-in in Queensland. What's more, they would invariably raise their eyebrows and laugh aloud at the memory of it, and wanted to know more.

In short, Australians whose involvement in racing might be owning a stable of champion thoroughbreds, or simply buying a two-dollar ticket in the office Melbourne Cup sweep, at least know the name Fine Cotton.

The Fine Cotton story is embedded in Australian folklore for good, because it stands proudly amidst the pantheon of immortals when it comes to idiocy writ large. At Eagle Farm, a horse that wasn't Fine Cotton wins a race and for a moment, just a moment, a deranged criminal conspiracy had reaped unspeakable riches, only for the whole caper to implode in anarchic scenes across the country. It just goes to show that from the great and the good to the greedy and the grotesque, there's no such thing as a sure thing.

Welcome to Queensland, 1984. We hope you enjoy your day at the races.

Peter Hoysted and Pat Sheil
Sydney 2019

CHAPTER ONE
A Day at the Races

'We need a miracle. And a hose.'
— Hayden Haitana

Race Day: 18 August 1984. Brisbane, Queensland. Dawn.

THE THREE OF them, Hayden Haitana, John Gillespie and Bobby North, peeled themselves off a lumpy couch (Hayden), a decrepit armchair (John) and the floor (Bobby) at around 6 am.

John was the first to stir, which had nothing to do with diligence and everything to do with a bladder about to burst its stopcocks, and a tongue as dry as a Wilcannia nature strip on New Year's Day.

He woke the others when he staggered to the kitchen, pissed for an eternity into the sink and, groaning with relief, pulled one of the few remaining beers out of the fridge and ripped it open.

After swallowing most of it in one cacophonous gargle, his half-strangled, half-burped 'Fuckin' hell!' and the suppressed gastric heave that followed were more than even the terminally hungover Hayden and Bobby could ignore.

Haitana opened his eyes, one after the other, and immediately wished he hadn't. The place was a wreck, but it had never been pretty. Then again, it looked much worse than he remembered it the morning before. It stank of stale beer and two or three hundred cheap cigarettes.

Grisly as it was, it wasn't the state of the house that filled him with horror. It was the unfolding realisation of what being in the place meant, why they were there, and what the day ahead held in store.

He closed his eyes in a vain, desperate attempt to transport himself to a motel room in Bendigo where, if there was a God, he'd wake in a minute or two and get ready to take a couple of second-rate runners to a midweek meeting and maybe even turn a few quid, all on the up and up.

On any other day, that would have been a tedious prospect. Right now it sounded like paradise.

The mirage couldn't last, and it didn't. Hayden's desperate reverie was shattered as Bobby lifted his torso off the floorboards on one elbow and croaked, 'Fuck's sake, John, if ya gonna make that much racket, ya can get me a beer too. How many we got left, anyway?'

Hayden opened his eyes once more and inhaled deeply, a reverse sigh that clutched at the fetid miasma for a trace of oxygen. Attempting to sit, he was paralysed for a moment as an awful tectonic throb shuddered through his skull. His lungs emptied over parched lips in a wordless lament for what had become of him. He shook his head, regretted it, and made himself stand up.

Starting toward the window, Hayden hesitated as his face moved into direct sunshine and his brain screamed in protest at the sensory overload, but his desperate need to breathe urged him on. He gritted his teeth, squinted his eyes, took two more steps into the glare and lifted the window open. The cool fresh air, for a moment or two, gave solace. Hayden's instinctive, animal response was relief.

But with the clean air came a flash of clarity, and his conscious mind rebelled. The sweet fragrance was an illusion, or, worse, a reminder that the three of them were a desecration of nature. Turning to look back at his companions he felt, for the first time since this fiasco had begun, a surge of self-loathing.

He leaned his elbows on the windowsill, gulped more fresh air, and rallied the dregs of his resolve. Regret was pointless. He would simply have to make the best of this. There could be a way through it, maybe even a way out, if he could make people, even very dangerous people, see sense.

But right now, there was a horse to deal with.

The horse. The horse in the paddock behind the house, the horse that wasn't his horse, that wasn't even the horse that was meant to substitute for his horse. No, this was not the animal that might just about have passed for Fine Cotton in a mounting yard, the one that was a dead ringer, they'd said. Could have been his twin brother, they'd told him.

Maybe it was, but so what, even if it was bloody identical? That horse was fucked, crippled, useless, not even worth thinking about now.

No, out the back was the third bloody horse. The one that was going to be a ring-in for a ring-in, a beast that allegedly might be able to run the distance in quick time – if they hadn't already half killed it – but one that looked nothing at all like Fine Cotton.

'Oh God,' Hayden mumbled under his breath, remembering the hairdressing farce of the night before. 'What the fuck does it look like now?'

Gillespie and North were in the kitchen, both already well into their second beers, telling each other at great length how fuckin' dreadful they felt. Haitana joined them, and for a moment thought about having a drink himself, but knew that any vestige of authority he might still have would dissolve in it if he did.

'Come on, you two,' he growled, herding them to the back door. 'Let's check this out.'

They stumbled onto the creaking verandah, squinting in the cruel daylight as they took tentative steps down into the shabby yard. A 44-gallon drum overflowed with rubbish, mostly beer and whisky bottles, leavened with the odd pizza box and a foil bag of stinking chicken bones. Disorderly squadrons of flies hovered and buzzed over it all, in a lazy celebration of rot and decay.

But the three men paid no attention to the state of the yard. It was the creature that stood before them on the other side of a rusting barbed-wire fence that held their gaze.

It was John who reacted first. 'Fuck me! Jesus, get a look at that, will ya?'

Bobby said nothing, his hysterical laughter making words redundant.

Hayden, his lower jaw having dropped far enough to please the most demanding dentist, and his eyes like saucers, was silent, though a thought flashed through his mind, one of those flippant, tangential notions that the brain can conjure up to protect itself from a vision of catastrophe.

'Bold Personality. Good name for it. You'd bloody well need a bold personality to walk around in public looking like that.'

The horse was orange.

Not just 'a kind of orangey shade of red', or 'a striking tinge of russet', but bright, radiant orange. Like something you'd see in a fruit bowl. Call it an orange, a tangelo or a tangerine. That sort of orange. Like an amber traffic light Hayden often regarded as a sign to speed up and plough on through. But this orange offered more than a casual warning. It screamed: 'Danger. Disgrace and jail await. Stop. Stop at once.'

For more than a month Hayden had dreaded this day, and its arrival bursting with orange portents of doom made his already queasy stomach turn. He sucked in a sharp burst of air and began sweating that dreadful cold sweat that almost always preceded the violent expulsion of the contents of his stomach.

But Bobby beat him to it. His hilarity had got the better of his beery breakfast, and he'd fallen to his knees and hurled up the lot.

'We need a miracle,' Hayden said, looking at the horse, then at Bobby.

'And a hose.'

*

At Warwick Farm Racecourse in south-west Sydney, the bookies' pencillers were looking at a bad case of carpal-tunnel syndrome from scribbling bets.

Prominent rails bookie Mark Read watched the mayhem. He turned to his offsider who was fiddling at the betting board, cranking Fine Cotton up one more notch skywards. Read had studied the form. Fine Cotton was a nine-year-old try-hard with nothing to suggest it could win. He'd noted the owner/trainer, Hayden Haitana, had flogged the horse. Ten starts in three weeks. It hadn't run a drum.

'Shut it down.'

Read's penciller was happy to hear that he could stop scrawling, but gave his boss the upturned eyebrow all the same.

'If this isn't a ring-in, I'll walk bare-arsed down Pitt Street,' Read said.

Read looked across at Bill Waterhouse, whose stand was an island of calm in an ocean of turmoil and shrieking chaos. Bill wasn't taking a bet on Race 4 at Eagle Farm. The punters had given him a wide berth. Across the way, Bill's son, Robbie, was having a quiet time of it, too. He must have shut down Fine Cotton as well.

Punters around Australia were thinking the same thing. In the morning's betting, Fine Cotton had come in from 33/1 to 4/1, moving up the line on the bookies' scales from the bottom line of betting, where the old picnic race meet nag belonged.

It was preposterous. The biggest betting plunge Australia had ever seen. Desperate punters with inside mail were circling. Thousands were invested in betting agencies in Papua New Guinea, Fiji and over the phone in Darwin. On the tote in pubs and at TABs around the country, the Queensland screen blinked Fine Cotton's price, and with just about every electronic blip the price came in. Thirty-three dollars to $30, then $25, all the way in to a lousy 4.50.

In Hobart, investment banker Ian Murray was laying bets. He was known as a big-time punter in Sydney, and was often seen hobnobbing in the Members' at Randwick, Rosehill Gardens and Warwick Farm. Wherever they were running, he'd be there. He earned good money, so he bet large. Five thousand here, ten thousand there. He took his punting very seriously.

When his friends heard he was taking the weekend off, they didn't quite believe him. The spring carnival was a month away, and some of the best horses in the country were getting form and fitness in the big meets at Melbourne and Sydney. Perhaps he was going to the casino to hit the tables and work the odds?

'Just a weekend away,' he'd said. 'A break. Relax for a couple of days, a lazy weekend off the punt.'

But Murray was going to have a bet. A big bet, or a series of big bets. Just not with his own money this time. Murray was doing a friend a favour. Laying bets in smaller wagers through a range of bookmakers at a race meet in Hobart.

There was nothing particularly fascinating about the Hobart races. Murray didn't even glance at the form on the eight-race card. He wasn't betting on any of them. He was going there to lay bets in Brisbane. Big ones. Fine Cotton to win.

The attraction of betting in Hobart was that it was almost as far away as anyone could get from Brisbane while still being in the betting loop, and any mail or hint of a fix was going to take some time to get down there.

Murray circled the betting ring before placing two bets. The first was $5000 to win $100,000. The second, $12,000 to win $120,000. Hobart may have been isolated from the good mail on the mainland but the bookies communicate with one another, often in code and with little more than a nod or the raising of an eyebrow. They took Murray's money, but with bets that large they could sense that something was going on. He had to keep going, get it all done in quick time while the window of opportunity was still open. Before these blokes twigged. They would soon enough.

At the Appin dogs in Sydney's south-west, a priest bearing the dog collar and the sign of the cross on his breast shuffled through the paltry crowd. Father Ted O'Dwyer, a whisky priest with little spiritual guidance to offer, finding his own in a bottle, and a hapless punter whose racing advice was just as useful, was sweating profusely. He often did. Thirty-five years of rotgut and Rothmans had left him with the aerobic capacity of a slug.

But today his sweat wasn't squeezed out of him by his inevitable Saturday morning hangover, though that wasn't any fun either. No, this was the clammy, nervous sweat he'd suffer when delivering mass at a funeral for some poor bastard he didn't know, didn't give a screaming shit about. The sweat that poured out of him whenever he knew there was a high probability that he was about to fuck up in a big way.

He knew that what he was doing wasn't exactly by the book. Certainly not the Good Book, though he hadn't read that one for a long time. Years ago he'd photocopied 20-odd sheets of it, had the print blown up to the point he could read it aloud in just about any condition, and not glanced at a Bible since.

The readings he'd selected covered just about every contingency from baptisms to weddings, Easter to Christmas. It was without doubt the only truly brilliant move of his otherwise unsatisfactory ecclesiastical career.

At home he read paperback BDSM porn novels. He had hundreds of them.

But deep down, under the wreckage of a dissolute and transparently fraudulent pretence at representing God on earth, Ted O'Dwyer wasn't such a bad bloke. He could never turn down a friend in need. And anyway, laying bets wasn't a crime.

Well, it might have been the way he was doing it. But having a lash at this shithole was a masterstroke. No-one would cotton on.

Ha! 'Cotton on'. If he didn't feel so dreadful he might have chuckled to himself. But all he wanted to do was get out of there.

Appin. Jesus Christ. He was a long way from his well-heeled, but ever-diminishing flock in Sydney's eastern suburbs. He'd never heard of the Appin greyhound track until this week, but after a baffling drive down the Hume Highway, and missing the obscure turn-off twice, here he was.

It's fair to say that the Appin dogs is not the most salubrious sporting arena in Australia. It is not a place where dreams go to die. They'd died long before they wound up in this place.

O'Dwyer manoeuvred his ancient vehicle though the car park, his tyres crushing empty pay packets, torn open in vain by desperate men. The place stank of despair, neglect and the sickly perfume of last hopes.

Father Edward O'Dwyer, man of God, emptied the contents of his briefcase onto the seat of his car. Four thousand dollars in cash. All 50s, gathered together in four equal bundles.

He made his way to the betting ring and gingerly sidled up to one of the bookies.

'Are you taking bets on Eagle Farm?'

'All the major metropolitan races here, Father. Waddya like?'

'I'll have a thousand the win, Brisbane race four, horse five,' the priest said quietly.

The penciller glanced at the bookmaker for permission to proceed.

'You been into the collection plate, Father?' the bookie grinned.

The priest glared back, saying nothing but keenly aware of the glob of sweat that was dripping off his nose.

'All right, you're on. A thousand to twenty thousand the win. Brisbane race four, horse five. Fine Cotton to win.'

In all, O'Dwyer made four bets at Appin, each identical to the first. A thousand to win on Fine Cotton. By the time he came to the last bookie, he delved into his back pocket for the first time and put a hundred of his own money on Fine Cotton. After all, he'd been told it couldn't lose.

With his betting tickets in his hand, he dashed out to the car park, jumped into his car and took off for the safety of Warwick Farm. Appin dogs. What a ghastly, God-forsaken place it was. Yet he felt almost cleansed by having been there, like an imperfect man who has endured purgatory in order to wash away his sins.

He liked a drink, loved smutty books. Sure, he was not a model priest by any means, no shining advertisement for the true faith. But he felt positively angelic after spending an hour amidst the tortured souls of the Appin dog track. Men who can't just drive away. The trapped. The condemned.

By the time this flawed man of the cloth was nearing Warwick Farm, it was getting right out of hand. In all, the bookies were looking at a two million dollar bath. They were betting against a huge plunge. If the punters were right, it may well have sent more than a few into early retirement, replete with ugly orders from the Federal Court.

Anguished regret, bankruptcy, the sheriff's relentless knock at the door. Forced out of the game forever.

Oh, no. Father Edward O'Dwyer wasn't the only one sweating. Not by a long shot.

The hose could wait. Hayden had a hangover he could have rendered in oil on canvas. The only cure at his disposal was another beer. He peered into the fridge and jostled a stubby of Queensland's alleged finest, XXXX, out of its cardboard prison and into his hand. Even through the calluses and nicks, cuts and bruises on his hand, he could tell it wasn't cold. Or not cold enough.

'Fuck's sake,' he murmured before banging the top off the small bottle with the flat of his hand and gulping deeply, more than half of the bottle's contents surging down his throat and into his grumbling stomach. He burped volcanically, a cacophonous clatter of digestive impertinence, expelling the stench of last night's drinking along with a stale reminder of the 30-odd cigarettes he'd smoked.

This was a one-way ticket to the slammer, and being given the arse from racing forever into the bargain. Racing was all he knew, all he had. Christ, what a fuck-up.

He had an orange horse due to race in less than four hours. The vision of Bold Personality turning into the straight at Eagle Farm ahead of the pack, a blazing, incandescent orange blur, made him gasp with horror before he took another chug on his beer and realised it would be a miracle if it ever got that far.

A bright orange horse in the mounting yards was bound to catch the eye of the punters. But it wouldn't even get to that point of abject humiliation. The steward's inspection half an hour before the race would be when the shit hit the fan. An orange horse in the stables, glowing like a traffic light that screamed, 'Warning, warning, ring-in!' That would be the end of it, right there.

The stewards were stupid, but they weren't that fuckin' dumb.

Hayden knew how it would go down. Within minutes of the steward poking his nose into the stable, the track PA would blare out, 'Mr Hayden Haitana, to the stewards' room, please.' That would be it. Ignominy, failure, despair. Warned off the tracks for years. Maybe life.

And that wouldn't be the worst of it. The wallopers were bound to be next on the scene and he'd be frogmarched out of Eagle Farm in a pair of matching stainless-steel bracelets. He still had Fine Cotton up his sleeve but Gillespie wouldn't let it run.

Haitana referred to Gillespie as 'The Phantom', both while conversing with other mutual acquaintances and directly to the man himself. The moniker was apt on two counts.

Gillespie regarded himself as capable of super heroics without possessing any actual superpowers, in much the same way as the Lee Falk comic-book character. Rather than powers of flight, speed or herculean strength, he relied on his wits, subterfuge and ability to think two, three and sometimes 10 steps ahead of any troublemakers.

Haitana had gleaned that the appellation was derived from Gillespie's substantial body of criminal work, knocked up during one of his many stints in prison. He presumed, rightly, that Gillespie had been given his nickname as a testament to his trademark fickleness while banged away, and he briefly worried that Gillespie may suffer some discomfort if it became a universal replacement for his real name.

But Haitana's partner in deception seemed neither embarrassed nor annoyed by it. In time, Haitana could only think of Gillespie as The Phantom, a spectre who cast the longest of shadows and even during long absences never seemed very far away.

The Phantom gave Fine Cotton no hope, but Hayden thought otherwise. If he could get one of his trademark speed balls into the animal an hour before the race, he'd run the grandstand down.

He slurped away at the stubby. Right. Time to move. If he was turning into the final straight to disaster, he may as well do it at a full gallop. He marched back into the living room where North and The Phantom were involved in whispered discussion.

'Bobby, we're going to your joint,' Haitana said. 'We'll hose the ringer down there.'

North protested. His mind was instantly summoning up the ghastly image of two horses standing on his manicured front lawn, one a flaming orange, while he and Haitana went to work with the hose. The neighbours would shit.

'Bobby, it's on the fuckin' way and we've got to get moving.'

Gillespie was sanguine, but as usual wanted to know all the ins and outs. Every fucking detail.

'Positive thoughts, Hayden. Good stuff, mate. We'll get the ringer over to Bobby's and get him ready. We're just taking him, right?'

'No. We're taking Fine Cotton as well.'

Gillespie knew in an instant what was on Haitana's mind. 'Mate, what's the point? Your nag's going to be standing around like a stale bottle all day.'

It was a decent analogy. There were more than a few half-empty, stale bottles around the room – two plonked on the coffee table, a couple on the floor beside the sofa and another three on the mantelpiece.

'John, we're taking Fine Cotton for insurance. I'm not going to Eagle Farm with only an orange horse on the bridle and me balls exposed in me left hand.'

'Your nag's not going to race, Hayden. Don't pull a swifty on me.'

'I fuckin' know that, John. We just need to have Fine Cotton around if there's any trouble. We can switch them back and forth.'

This type of chicanery appealed deeply to Gillespie's love of deception. In his mind, you could never have enough hocus-pocus. Now you see it, now you don't. A bit of the old legerdemain. The more the merrier.

He almost smiled, but not quite. 'What about the float? You can't fit 'em both in that thing of yours.'

'Way ahead of ya, John.'

'Yeah? Well, first time for everything.'

Haitana got on the phone to di Luzio, horse whisperer and transporter without peer. Christ, the condition Bold Personality was in when the silly prick had dropped him off. That was the start of all the trouble. Tommy had driven up all the way from Coffs Harbour, pulling the float and a thousand pounds of glassy-eyed, rapidly dehydrating horseflesh up the Princes Highway behind a clapped-out Toyota Corolla.

Tommy didn't know much about horses. The best thing was he didn't have a fuckin' clue what was going on, and that made him the perfect choice.

'Tommy. Waddya know?'

'Sittin' here awaiting further instructions, mate.'

'Get up to the Gertrude Street hire joint, and get me a double horse float for the day. I'll give you the cash when you get here.'

'Sure. Can do.'

'I need you to be here by 11. Don't fuck around.'

'I'm on my way now, H.'

'Oh, and Tommy . . .'

'Yes, H?'

'Don't bring that fuckin' Toyota Corolla.'

'Got me ute back. No sweat there. Sweet as.'

Haitana had it set. The Phantom was suspicious but he was on board. Fuckin' Bobby North, the Lord Fauntleroy of Brisbane, was shitting himself at the prospect of having a couple of thoroughbred racehorses wandering around in his yard, but as reluctant as he was had said very little. He knew he was in this up to his eye teeth.

Hayden took a deep breath and marched off. He felt like he could at least wade through the shit now instead of drowning in it. It wasn't great but it was better, and he felt he was in charge for a change.

What Haitana needed was a spruce-up. The three S's. A shit, a shave and a shower. In that order. He made his way to the bathroom via the kitchen and reached into the fridge for another beer. Fuck, they still weren't cold. Oh, well . . .

The money kept pouring in for Fine Cotton and the bookies stood to lose a fortune.

If any one of Fine Cotton's thousands of supporters, anyone who had a lash on the nine-year-old gelding on the basis of slightly dodgy mail from a track insider, had been driving that Saturday morning around the original Brisbane leafy-green suburb of

St Lucia, reeking of old money and National Party connections, they might have had cause to march back to the TAB and demand their money back.

There, on the front lawn of the expansive home owned by one of Brisbane's 'better' families, passers-by were being entertained by a gaggle of middle-aged men surrounding a wet, vaguely orange horse.

The men were feverishly mopping and sponging the horse down, leaving puddles of ochre at the horse's hooves to overflow and run across the lawn, over the retaining wall and into the storm-water drain on the street. The men stopped from time to time to admire their handiwork and guzzle their beers. To one side of all the commotion, another horse, of dark chocolate brown, gently nibbled at the lawns, stopping only to drop a couple of enormous, steaming turds near the jacaranda tree.

Proud homeowner Robert North marinated in profound anxiety. He'd consumed more beers that morning than he cared to count, but the alcohol had only taken the edge off his foreboding of doom and held off the desperate urge to run inside, lock the front door and bury himself deep under a doona.

As if captivated by a surreal table-tennis tournament, his eyes darted from the hosing down of the ringer to the street as cars drove by, slowing to watch mouth agape in incredulity at the lurid scene being played out on his lovely front lawn.

Not so lovely now. The grass was fucked. He'd already consigned thoughts of what was happening to his zealously clipped turf to oblivion.

His wife would never forgive him for the state of the front garden but that was the least of his worries. The orange horse had done it for him. The sight of the ringer standing in the stable that morning in a blaze of tangerine had etched itself deep into his subconscious and provided an ugly reminder of what he had got himself into.

It was no longer a lark, a bit of fun and happy thoughts of a nice chunk of change over a few beers. This was a criminal conspiracy and North was looking at a largish stretch in the slammer for his role in it.

Bobby couldn't go to jail. It'd be a feeding frenzy. One tattooed goon roughly gyrating his cock up his bleeding arse with North in a forced crouch, a Penthouse centrefold duct-taped to his back, while goon number two took wild swings at North's head with a can of tuna in a sock.

Oh, fuck.

He returned to watching the water show. His head hurt and he could hardly breathe. He didn't hear Gillespie emerge from the garage and sidle up next to him.

'No fuckin' worries, Bobby.'

'You think it'll be all right?'

'The ringer's coming up trumps, mate. Another beer?'

Gillespie chugged down his stubby and wandered off without waiting for North's reply.

Haitana, who'd been supervising the scrub-down from a safe distance, was wearing what he thought of as his Sunday best. The Del Monti suit, Pelaco shirt and cheap rayon tie. The whole ensemble would have cost less than North's shoes. These were Hayden's race-day clothes, fancy clobber that also did its duty as court attire when he got caught kite-flying – cop and crim vernacular for passing bad cheques.

Haitana may not have comprehended North's grim jailhouse fantasy but he understood the man's unease. Hayden winked at him and Bobby nodded back.

Finally, the hoses were turned off and Bold Personality stood before them dripping. The horrid cantaloupe hue was gone, leaving only a bay horse, its light brown coat turned dark from the countless litres of water that remained on it. Fine Cotton gently nibbled at the lawn in the background and, for a moment, North thought they looked like they could be twins.

All right, not identical twins but twins possibly. Fraternal, maybe. A bit.

North had deliberately overlooked the white socks on Fine Cotton's four fetlocks. Let's not get picky. At least the ringer doesn't look like it belongs in a freak show anymore.

Gillespie returned and pressed an open stubby into North's hand. 'You ever been to India, Bobby?'

'No. Why?'

'Well, get that India!'

Gillespie laughed and Haitana walked up to them, breaking into a rare smile. At least, North felt he could breathe again. He took a gulp and felt a little better.

'Waddya reckon?' Hayden asked.

'He looks cherry ripe, mate,' Gillespie answered.

'What about the socks?'

Haitana was loath to concede that he had forgotten to add the peroxide the night before. The application of the henna rinse had been a difficult task, made more onerous by the fact that he'd quaffed eight stubbies during the process. When it had come time to sponge Bold Personality's fetlocks down with hydrogen peroxide, he was heavily refreshed and beyond caring.

Examining Bold Personality now, he was glad of his drunken absentmindedness. An orange horse with bleached blond legs might have been a step too far. The hilarity that had met the sight

18

of Bold Personality's mandarin hue could have been notched up to the point where they'd still be rolling around in the stables laughing.

'Easy fixed,' Haitana replied and pointed to an aerosol spray can of Dulux white high gloss beside the float. 'Better let him dry off a bit first but.'

Haitana looked directly at Gillespie.

'We keep the blanket on him right up until the jump. As long as possible. If the stewards haven't jerried by then, we'll be sweet. They wouldn't have a fucking clue what it's supposed to look like.'

Gillespie nodded. Smiles all round. Even North felt the sudden urge to grin.

'OK. Let's get this show on the road,' Gillespie said.

The bonhomie was quickly shattered when Haitana swore out loud.

'Shit.'

It was loud enough to stir the neighbours, and North started to panic again.

'We haven't shod the fuckin' ringer yet,' Haitana explained. 'Shit. Fuck.'

Gillespie didn't seem overly concerned, but North could see disaster looming anew. Disgrace. Humiliation. Jail. Arse rape.

'What are we going to do?' North asked plaintively.

'It's all right, Bobby,' Haitana said. 'Don't fuckin' panic. Pop inside and get me a copy of the *Yellow Pages*. Quick as you can. We're cutting it a bit fine now.'

Bobby scuttled inside through the garage entrance and was quickly aware that Hayden was following in his wake.

'It's all right,' North said. 'I'll get it.'

'How am I supposed to ring the fuckin' farrier from outside, Bobby? Eh? The fuckin' bat phone?'

'Oh, sorry, mate. Yeah, I get it.'

Haitana tore through the phone book before scanning listings with his index finger.

'Teddy. He'll do the job. Good bloke too. Won't say a word.'

While North stood nervously, Haitana grabbed the phone and placed the call.

'Teddy, mate. I got a problem. Hope you can help. Got a horse needs some shoes. Quickish. And I mean yesterday.'

'What's the address here, Bobby?'

North gave him the street, street number and suburb, slowly so Haitana could repeat it to the farrier.

'You're a fuckin' champion, Teddy. I'll keep the beer on ice for you.'

Haitana handed the phone and the phone book to North and made his way back to the garage. For a moment, Bobby held the receiver in his hand and wondered stupidly if he should say something to Teddy at the other end of the line.

Haitana stopped and turned. 'Calm down, Bobby. He's gone. He's on his way. Ten minutes tops.'

Teddy arrived on time as promised and drove his van straight up the driveway. North's front garden looked like a used car yard for clapped-out bombs. Haitana's filthy Ford F100. Now there was Teddy's rusting van, which could have rolled off the assembly line during the Korean War. Only Gillespie's Jag gave the collection a bit of respectability.

Teddy got out of his truck with the casual air of a man untroubled by looming deadlines. You don't see many small farriers and Teddy fit the stereotype. He was 25 stone if he was an ounce.

A pair of footy shorts and singlet on. His massive gut wobbled free and at the back an impressive arse crack appeared between the two garments.

'Which one?' he asked Haitana.

'The wet one.'

Haitana handed Teddy a stubby. He squeezed the top off and drank the lot in a couple of deep gulps.

'Doesn't look like a pacer.'

'He's not, mate. He'll be going around at Eagle Farm in little over an hour.'

Teddy told Haitana he wanted another beer. It was in his hand in a trice and emptied down his throat almost as quickly.

'I've only got pacers' shoes.'

'Really?'

This was a problem. Shoes for horses in harness racing are heavier, helping the horse maintain its gait and still manoeuvre through the field. In thoroughbred racing, the plates are wafer thin, allowing for maximum bursts of speed.

Haitana knew there was no alternative.

'Bung 'em on, Teddy.'

Teddy was unused to moving quickly but once he'd necked his second stubby, he wandered over to Bold Personality, gently lifted its right rear leg at the hock, and with a couple of light cracks with a hammer, had the first shoe in. Within minutes the job was done.

Gillespie wedged a couple of $50 notes in Teddy's hand, before thrusting another XXXX the farrier's way.

'Terrific work, Teddy. You're a genius,' Haitana said. 'Not a word about this, mate. OK?'

Gillespie put his finger to his lips in emphasis.

'I couldn't give a flying fuck either way,' the farrier said over his shoulder, getting back into his truck. 'Best of luck to you.'

Teddy was only halfway down the driveway when Haitana stepped forward with the Dulux can. He blasted all four of Bold Personality's pasterns in a constant up-and-down motion, the atomised paint quickly gathering substance above Bold Personality's hooves. Haitana stopped and stood back to admire his handiwork, before returning to spray a bit more here and there on the horse's legs until he was satisfied.

He threw the can into the back seat of his truck and called for order.

'Let's get 'em in, guys. We are now officially running late.'

They scrambled the horses into the float and took off for their rendezvous with destiny at Eagle Farm. North jumped in with Gillespie, figuring The Phantom's eternal optimism was just what he needed.

The two vehicles travelled not quite in convoy but within sight of each other for the journey. They drove fast, aware that time was not their friend. North watched the float hooked onto Haitana's F100 and saw Bold Personality's head bob up and down with each corrugation of the road.

The trip would normally take 20 minutes, but with some creative interpretations of stop signs and red lights, they managed to make it in 15.

At last, something was going right.

Their cars were all waved through at the Eagle Farm car park. North got out and stretched his legs. Haitana was fiddling about with the back of the float, eager to get the ringer out and into the stables. The others stood there watching.

Zero hour was upon them. All things considered, they'd done well to make it this far. There was a sense of excitement among the group and even North felt a tiny surge of confidence.

That's when they heard it.

'Mr Hayden Haitana to the stewards' room. Mr Hayden Haitana to the stewards' room, please.'

And in that instant North knew they were fucked.

CHAPTER TWO
Piss buckets and plans

'If you fuck Mick, Mick'll fuck you back harder.'
— Bertie Kidd

THE BIGGEST RESERVOIR in south-east Queensland is the Hinze Dam. Given that it's named after the Hinze clan, whose vast acreage made up much of the territory submerged in order to create it, it is a fitting monument, almost a metaphor, for that family's most famous son, Russ Hinze, the state's titanically obese and shamelessly corrupt Minister for Racing in the 1980s.

Both man and dam are justly famous for their bulk, inertia and astonishing capacity for fluid retention.

For some time, a trickle of its output provided lukewarm refreshment for the residents of Brisbane's Boggo Road Gaol.

One can only wonder what inspired the urban planners of the nineteenth century to bestow the name 'Boggo' on the street in question, but it is not a nickname. You might imagine it to be a typical Aussie abbreviation, maybe of 'Bougainvillea Boulevard' or 'Begonia Avenue'.

But no, it has always, and officially, been known as Boggo Road, and given the nature of its most famous edifice, it seems on reflection that the good burghers of Brisbane had it right from the outset.

Since the day in 1863 that the iron gates of Boggo Road Gaol first swung open, for over a century they were to be slammed shut behind all manner of miscreants, from petty thieves and murderers to the likes of a young Gordon Brown, a socialist troublemaker who was a guest of the Governor there in the 1930s, before clambering up the greasy pole to become President of the Australian Senate a decade later.

Then again, political fortunes in Queensland have always been prone to wild oscillations.

All in all, the institution was not a very nice place, and nor was it intended to be. Forty-two prisoners were executed there, between

1883 and 1913, including Ellen Thompson, the only woman to hang in Queensland, in 1887. And while the rope has long been retired, the joint remained notorious until the end for cruel and degrading treatment.

Living conditions were unpleasant, even by 19th-century corrective services standards. In fact, they were downright disgraceful – plumbing in the cells consisted of a steel bucket which inmates would 'muck out' each morning – and the 1970s and '80s saw regular protests and violent riots by prisoners.

Much of it has since been demolished; what's left is a museum that offers ghost tours. The prison served not only as a house of correction, but of concoction, and for every crime punished behind its stone walls, at least as many were planned there.

Like most criminal endeavours, almost all of the ones that were eventually brought to fruition by the alumni of the Boggo Road Academy of Anti-Social Behaviour ended in the students being dragged back for lengthy periods of post-graduate study.

It has been ever thus – lock up scores of criminals in a stinking hellhole, treat them like shit, and inevitably many of them will while away their time dreaming of that one last caper, the brilliant sting that will come up trumps.

But criminal masterminds were not typical of the population of Boggo Road – just being there in the first place was reasonable evidence of serious skill deficiencies in the planning and execution of inspired evil.

While most of the involuntary residents of this establishment had given a lot of thought to the 'where it all went wrong' question, their reasoning, such as it was, centred on minor improvements to their original get-rich-quick schemes, rather than any radical intellectual departure. Paradigm shifts are not the long suits of such thinkers.

It seemed logical to them that, if they'd finally got caught after robbing six petrol stations at knifepoint in six months, well, that was only because they never got enough money each time, so they had to go back and do it again to get some more.

A risky business model. Even they could see that.

The obvious solution to many of them was to obtain a firearm, by fair means or foul, and rob a bank – hey, they've got *heaps* of money – and thus they would only have to do so once. One big show, then luxurious retirement. What could possibly go wrong?

Yep, the villains and morons of Boggo Road tended to stick to what they knew, even if they didn't know much about even that one small thing. Hence the iron gates were destined to become a revolving door for more than a few of them.

Pat Haitana knew nothing about armed robbery. Well, he knew a lot of violent thieves, but it wasn't his stock in trade, and not the reason he wound up in the place.

Gillespie had given counter-jumping a crack, but fell flat on his arse, both physically and metaphorically. The wallopers circled, guns pointed. They had him bang to rights. Remanded into custody, court, then Boggo Road. A circle not just vicious but tediously inevitable. He learnt then that stick-ups were a young man's game and never contemplated rushing into a bank or sticking a loaded gun under the nose of an antsy payroll clerk again.

Bugger that.

Gillespie discovered fraud was his *oeuvre*. Talking gullible people out of their hard-earned with hyperbolic tales of sure-fire, too-good-to-be-true-but-bloody-tempting business proposals was not just what he did, it's what he was. A congenital liar with no sense of right or wrong, he never showed the slightest remorse for the catastrophic damage he left in his wake, because he didn't have any. The very concept of guilt was alien to him.

For all his deceit, he was a man of conviction. After all, he had over 358 of them. The armed-robbery conviction stood in contrast to the felonies listed on his three-page-long rap sheet. Fraud, obtaining financial advantage by deception, making false utterances, counterfeiting, forgery.

He liked to think he had the perspicacity to be in exactly the right place and at precisely the right time to facilitate the separation of a fool and his money. Truth be told, he had contrived the circumstances of these divorces in ways so elaborate that it was only well after he'd whisked off with the cash and prizes that the fool in question experienced a joyless epiphany.

Many fools were too embarrassed to go to the police and admit their stupidity, while others threw themselves at the mercy of the Queensland Fraud Squad, hoping to have at least some of their money returned but knowing deep in their hearts it was already gone, invested in fast cars, loose women and slow racehorses.

While Gillespie was a good talker, he had the failing of occasionally talking too much, which was why he spent a solid percentage of his adult life behind bars. But that didn't stop him successfully deluding whoever was around at the time, including judges and parole officers, and this time around, in Boggo Road, he went to work on the most convenient target at hand, Pat Haitana.

Pat Haitana was a third-rate jockey from Coffs Harbour, New South Wales, who had been banged up for kite flying. Gillespie was of the same mould, but in a different league. He was a conman too, but not a simple trickster who'd surrender to temptation when he needed a quid and saw an easy mark.

By the time he started chatting with the amateurish Haitana, Gillespie was a very convincing fellow who would have made a legitimate fortune in the advertising game, but holding down a steady job, no matter how well paid, wasn't his style. Indeed, it would have been a genetic impossibility, because unlike most professional yarn-spinners, the bloke was a true sociopath.

The result of this meeting of minds was arguably the most preposterous, almost surreal, case of fraud ever perpetrated in the annals of Australian horseracing, or indeed of Australian crime.

For it was in the stinking cells and perilous exercise yard of Boggo Road Gaol that, in early 1984, the seeds were sown for what was to become infamous as the Fine Cotton fiasco.

History does not record it, but it's fair to assume that the time that elapsed between the invention of the first game, and the discovery of how to win said game by cheating, was probably less than 24 hours.

It may have taken millennia of evolution and experiment for prehistoric man to devise the game of dice, for instance, but no great leap of the imagination to work out that loading the things could give a nefarious fellow a crucial advantage.

Whether it be a game of chance or a contest of skill, every playing field can be rendered uneven, and the fewer people who know about it, the richer the rewards for those in the know.

Since the dawning of civilisation, rigging games and sports is older than agriculture. Only sex and violence predate it, and you'd be hard pressed to find any competitive recreation that has not been fiddled for fun and profit.

From the hammer throw to hurling, fencing to football, not a single contest is, or has ever been, immune. The second coin ever minted probably had two heads.

Scams come unstuck, of course. Many a man with a loaded die in his pocket has found himself exposed and wound up floating down the Tiber with his throat cut, just as the mighty Mississippi has carried its fair share of revealed and bullet-riddled riverboat hustlers with decks of marked cards in their boots out to sea.

There are risks, and the risks are starkest when the caper in question involves only the interplay between human beings and each other, and inanimate objects, like dice or cards, javelins or billiard balls.

But these hazards can be offset, and the odds weighted dramatically in the con artist's favour, by the introduction of a variable, reliable only for its inherent uncertainty.

A non-human, living element. A thing with a mind of its own, but a mind with no notions of rules, cheating or fair play. A powerful but erratic force of nature.

Something like, say, a horse.

We don't know much about the earliest horse races, but it's a fair bet that the deranged horsemen of Central Asia were chasing each other around the steppe for centuries before the sport became established in Europe. We do know that racing, with jockeys riding bareback, was popular in Greece and later in Rome, but in contrast to today, it played a poor second fiddle to what we now see at 'the trots'.

But all that modern trotting has in common with the chariot racing of Greece and Rome was horses, wheels and drivers. Chariot racing, especially when it reached its blood-soaked zenith in the Roman Empire, resembled warfare more than sport.

31

There is little evidence to suggest chariot races were subject to bribes or other forms of cheating. In any case, they were so anarchic, violent and horrifically dangerous that such sophistications as ring-ins, doping or the paying off of charioteers would have been overwhelmed by the sheer homicidal madness of the event itself.

Deaths and ghastly injuries were common at the Circus Maximus, Rome's hysterical prototype of Flemington or Royal Randwick, and consequently chariot racing was wildly popular, with some race days attracting massive crowds of over 200,000 bloodthirsty punters.

Safety was certainly not a priority. Roman drivers didn't hold the reins in their hands, but wrapped them round their waists, and so couldn't let go of them in a crash. Given that there were up to 24 races every race day (which, by the fourth century, took place on 66 days each year), there was no shortage of spectacular prangs. A fallen charioteer would be dragged around 'the circus' until he was killed or managed to free himself. In order to cut the reins in a crisis, they all carried a curved knife called a falx.

Betting did go on, of course, but punters hoping to affect the outcome were reduced to hurling lead balls studded with nails from the stands at horses and drivers they wanted to stymie.

Later, in the Byzantine Empire, there is one of the first recorded, albeit metaphysical, attempts to regulate the racing industry in the Ancient World. Justinian I's reformed legal code, the *Codex Justianus* of 534 AD, prohibited drivers from placing curses on their opponents.

After the final collapse of the Empire, equestrian contests were confined largely to the battlefield – for over a thousand years Europe was simply too impoverished and decrepit to afford such luxuries as hippodromes, professional jockeys and trainers, or anything else we would associate with a 'racing industry'.

We do know that Richard the Lionheart put up a purse of £40 for a three-mile race between knights at some point during the 12th century (whether or not they raced in full armour is not recorded). However, it wasn't until the reign of Charles II (1660–85), acknowledged by racing historians to be the 'father of the English turf', that racing as we would recognise it finally emerged from the gloom.

Charles had over 100 horses in his stables, which he established at Newmarket, and was the first fellow since Justinian to have a crack at formalising the business, with a flurry of royal edicts.

It was, ironically enough, not until the rules and regulations of horseracing were laboriously codified, then universally acknowledged over the next century, that nefarious activity was finally able to flourish.

Once the idea of fair play took hold – a concept that would have both baffled and amused the Romans – it opened an Aladdin's Cave of ill-gotten gain for the parasites of the turf to ease from the pockets of the unwary.

The gambler is the easiest of targets for the man on the make. For a start, they come ready-made with a gullibility born of a complete misunderstanding of the laws of probability. Add to that the inherent greed and laziness that are the hallmarks of the 'mug punter', and you have fruit ripe for the picking. Money doesn't grow on trees, it's true, but a fine harvest can be reaped from the fellow who reasons that 'someone always wins – there's no reason it can't be me'.

Better still, unlike most other forms of gambling, at the track there is the supreme seduction of the notion that one can be 'good at it', in a way that no-one can be good at roulette or buying lottery tickets. At the heart of this is that mighty variable that the Greeks and Romans knew about – the horse.

If a gambler will happily throw his money away at a game like roulette, where it is patently obvious that no matter how much you know about the layout of the wheel, the table and the weight of the ball, you are just as likely to lose as the bloke standing next to you, how much more likely is he to take a chance if he thinks he knows something that the bloke next to him doesn't? Information that can give him the winning edge?

A lot more likely, as it turns out. Just as boys and girls are told that if they study hard, they'll get ahead, millions of mugs around the globe spend hours poring over form guides, breeding histories and weather forecasts, in an attempt to maximise their chances.

And it is indeed true that some horses are better than others, and that you actually do have a better chance of winning if you back, say, Winx instead of, say, a nag named Gluepot. But where's the percentage in that?

If Winx wins as predicted, and you've invested $1000 on it, you might win $50. If Gluepot wins at 100/1, and you've invested 50 bucks on it, you'll wind up with five large in your pocket.

Now, old 'Gluey' Gluepot is not likely to salute the judges, which is why the odds on the beast winning are so long. Winx, in stark contrast, has never lost a race, so you stand a pretty good chance of making that $50 backing her, rather than blowing it on Gluey.

Psychologically, there is the nightmare scenario of Winx falling over at the first turn and breaking a leg. There goes Winx, along with your thousand bucks. But gee, she just keeps on winning. Gluey, on the other hand, has never won anything, and will almost certainly come second last or thereabouts, but at least you've only lost $50.

But what if, by some miracle, you could get 100/1, not on Gluepot, but Winx?

You won't. No-one will offer you odds like that. But if no-one except you and a select group of mates knew about a race where you *could* get Gluey odds on the champ, because no-one except you knew that Gluey was lazing away in a paddock somewhere as Winx arrived at the barrier wearing the number of the unloved and unfavoured, well, you'd never have to punt again in your life.

Throw away the form guides, mortgage the house, put the champagne on ice. This would be the closest thing to a certainty in the history of the track.

And while in reality you'd never be able to do it with Winx, on many occasions any number of Gluepots have been given the day off in order for much better horses to take their places and make very handsome profits for those brazen enough to pull it off. And it was precisely such a stunt that Gillespie was cooking up in Boggo Road back in 1984.

A ring-in.

A ring-in is the act of substituting a very fast horse for a hopelessly slow one, like Gluey, and investing heavily in its long odds, knowing that the animal actually running the race should be odds-on favourite. The art and craft of success in such an endeavour is making certain than nobody gets wind of it, not a soul; before, during or after the race in question.

The ring-in doesn't have to be a champion. It just has to be by far the best horse in the field. And given that races come in various categories according to the average strength of the horses competing, a good horse that consistently does well among fast company can, barring disaster, be confidently expected to run rings around a field of mediocre opposition.

The sport's handicappers, who decide what weight a horse must carry in a race, will also be deceived. The good horse will carry the weight of one poorly performed, allowing it to sprint to the line with little or no impediment.

In the confines of Boggo Road's sandstone and basalt walls, John Gillespie was hardly cooking up something new. The ring-in has a long and dishonourable history in racing, and while the scam can end catastrophically, over the years these swaps have made a lot of people a good deal of dough.

Inevitably, the only ones we know about are the ones that went wrong. Perhaps the most prolific substitute in Australian racing history was the 1930s galloper Erbie. Erbie was a very handy nag, with an impressive official record of 23 wins. But historians of the track reckon the gelding claimed at least another dozen wins under other names before being exposed in 1934.

Erbie's last recorded run (as Erbie, that is) was in Sydney in 1933, but he continued racing across several states under names including Duke Bombita and Chrybean. It all came undone when greed got the better of owner/trainer Charlie Prince at Murray Bridge, South Australia, where the less-than-impressive Redlock won easily after carrying one of the race's lightest weights into the Trial Stakes. Suspicions were raised as he was heavily backed despite recent ordinary form.

Charlie Prince personally pocketed more than £1000, very handy money in those days. A tip-off sent stewards after Prince, but they accepted his claim that all was above board, producing a 'receipt' for Redlock's purchase.

Racing writer Bert Wolfe was unconvinced. After seeing a photo of Redlock's finish, he chased evidence of a ring-in by attending the gelding's next race at Kadina, South Australia.

Wolfe asked to examine the horse after the race, which Redlock had won by 12 lengths, and, as he suspected, found that dye had been used to conceal Erbie's distinctive white blaze.

'I have no hesitation in asserting that the gelding which raced at Kadina on Saturday is our old friend, Erbie, in a new guise,' Wolfe wrote. 'I have watched him race and win on numerous occasions in Sydney and on provincial tracks within the metropolitan radius. I know his markings and characteristics.

'This time he hasn't a blaze down his face and his brands are different . . . but despite his new face, the gelding is Erbie.'

The chief steward was summoned and used petrol to remove the dye and reveal Erbie's blaze. The brands had also been clumsily tampered with for good measure. Erbie was impounded, having run his last race under any name, real or imagined. The real Redlock was eventually found where he'd been hidden, taking it easy in a paddock at Malmsbury, in central Victoria.

Prince was arrested and spent two years in jail for fraud, though his lifetime ban was later lifted.

Another substitution that ended in tears and jail time for the plotters came to light in May 1972, when a car salesman from the Melbourne suburb of Brighton, Vittorio 'Rick' Renzella, pulled off a $33,000 coup with a ring-in at a Victorian provincial track at Casterton. Renzella bought a mediocre bush galloper called Royal School, then purchased a far superior specimen with a string of city wins named Regal Vista.

Renzella had done his homework – the two horses had very similar markings and could easily have been mistaken one for the other, so he was able to switch them for the Casterton race without any problem. Well, except that Regal Vista had a brand on its left hind leg, which Royal School did not.

But Renzella had that covered. The registration papers he handed to the steward for Royal School before the race were fake, and Renzella had made sure that they mentioned the brand. This should have seen him well covered, but for one problem – there was a bloke in the crowd who wasn't buying it.

Veteran trainer Jim Cerchi declared after the race that he'd seen the real Royal School run before, and that the Royal School he was looking at that afternoon in Casterton wasn't him.

'This is a ring-in!' he announced to anyone who was listening, which turned out to be just about everybody there.

It also became clear that, in its previous four starts, the real Royal School had run last, third last, last and second last, so little wonder that it started at 40/1.

An inquiry led to Rick Renzella, jockey Stephen Wood and three others being charged with fraud, and Renzella being jailed. As well as being warned off tracks for life, Renzella got a two-year holiday at Her Majesty's pleasure into the bargain. Oddly, the stewards disqualified the plodder Royal School for life too, as if the horse had been in on the scam all along.

Where the old gelding ended up is unknown but if you were a dog owner in the late 1970s, it's a fair bet your pooch might have sampled what was left of Royal School out of a tin.

Bertie Kidd was doing a four-year stretch in Boggo Road. Kidd was a large, muscular man in his physical prime, with a shock of wavy brown hair he constantly flicked back before letting it bounce back onto his forehead.

At his induction at Boggo Road little more than a year earlier, Kidd glared at the prison barber, who knew immediately to sheath the razor and confine his work to giving the man a quick trim.

Kidd had known his fair share of impossibly stupid criminal conspiracies. He'd been involved in more than a few. At the time Gillespie and Haitana introduced themselves to him, he'd been banged up for a year for his role in 'The Great Plane Robbery' – an impressive, even august title for a heist that went horribly, comically wrong.

Back in 1982, a plane would leave Brisbane Airport every month loaded to the gunwales with cash from the Reserve Bank. The plane would be whisked around the backblocks of Queensland, leaving money in commercial bank vaults, here and there.

Kidd decided the money would be better in his pocket than anybody else's, and so, with a couple of accomplices, arranged for himself to be concealed in a crate and was heaved into the cargo hold right next to a million dollars of Reserve Bank loot. He was so close he could smell the printer's ink on the freshly minted $20 and $50 notes.

However, neither the plan nor the plane got off the ground after a leery security guard noticed the gloved hand of Bertie Kidd poking out through a hole in the crate.

Kidd lived by the aphorism, 'Never plead guilty.' One day soon it may well become his epitaph. But on this occasion, he was banged to rights. Arrested at gunpoint after the Queensland Police roughly disassembled the crate with a crowbar, without any apparent concern for Kidd's health and safety, he determined in this rare instance discretion to be the better part of valour and threw himself on the mercy of the judge.

With a list of priors that included armed robbery, counterfeiting and safe breaking, Kidd faced a judge who determined that the quality of mercy is, in fact, strained and sent him off for seven years with a minimum of four.

Kidd was a mad punter, almost to the point of recklessness but, like Gillespie, he preferred manipulating probabilities in his favour. He was a horse doper, dropping bombs into the alimentary canals of thoroughbred racehorses, either to speed them up or to slow them down, depending on who he had his money on.

He was a firm believer in the axiom that money won was infinitely superior to money earned, although how he came to this conclusion is unclear. Certainly not through direct experience, as Kidd, a £10 Pom who arrived in Australia at 14, had never done an honest day's work in his life. He was pathologically opposed to gainful employment, preferring not to grasp a share of the take from the company safe in wages, but to break into the premises at night, blow the safe open and take the lot.

Kidd was cooling his heels in Boggo Road, sharing a cell and a piss bucket with Graham Labe, a racetrack pimp, who enjoyed a brief sparkle of fame when he declared he had discovered a remarkable cure for equine arthritis. This shining moment was followed by a lifetime of ignominy when it was discovered his miracle cream was little more than a concoction of cetearyl alcohol, tea-tree oil and bees' wax.

Like Kidd, Labe was a doper although his motivation was somewhat different. He would lovingly massage a horse's banged-up fetlocks with his dodgy cream, but in order to make the unguent appear truly miraculous, he would slip the horse a tablet consisting of pure amphetamine and bask in personal glory when the horse not only saluted at the ledger but kept galloping at ferocious speed to the back straight, before the jockey could pull it up.

Kidd had heard of Gillespie and was immediately wary. He avoided criminal conspiracies for the most part, preferring the trust that can only be assured in a criminal enterprise of one person and one person only. However, in discussion with Labe, he thought his old mate 'Melbourne Mick' Sayers might be interested.

Sayers' debts had billowed out to become the stuff of turf legend. He owed over a million to George Freeman and the little man was not known for his patience or his generosity. Still, no matter how much shit Mick was in, he always seemed capable of scrambling the money together for another betting splurge.

Mick could fund the ring-in. Kidd would sit back and have a few bob on it with the prison bookie.

The other thing that bothered Kidd was Gillespie was always blowing his bags, claiming he had more pull in the Queensland government than Premier Joh Bjelke-Petersen himself. More ins with the wallopers than J. Edgar Hoover. He had the stewards onboard too, or so he reckoned.

Kidd knew Gillespie had had a crack at a ring-in back in 1982 when he slipped Apparent Heir in for Mannasong at Doomben. Mannasong went in from 66/1 to 5/2 in a betting plunge that everyone seemed to know about. That was bad enough but there was another, bigger problem that day.

The ringer, Apparent Heir, didn't run a drum and everyone did their dough. Mannasong's trainer was warned off racetracks for life but the slippery Gillespie evaded the clutches of the cops. That alone was noteworthy for a man with a lifetime of criminal behaviour like Kidd.

Maybe Gillespie had coughed on the trainer and had done a deal with the cops. Maybe he was as well connected as he said. Maybe he was full of shit. Who knows? Sociopaths in jail? Dime a dozen.

Now, with both men banged up in Boggo Road, Gillespie had been babbling to Kidd about another ring-in. And Gillespie was ingratiating himself with Pat Haitana, knowing that Pat's brother Hayden was a licensed trainer who ran a few horses out of Coffs Harbour. In Gillespie's mind, it was a sure-fire thing. Money for old rope. And lots of it.

Gillespie might have had a good lurk on his hands, but Kidd preferred to run his own race.

The miracle-cream man, Labe, thought likewise. Besides he'd only been in six months and prison did not agree with him. The thought of going back anytime soon was not in his plans.

Sharing a cell with a violent career criminal had its challenges. Sure, Kidd's reputation ensured Labe was off limits to the stand-over men and the jailhouse rapists, but he had a ferocious temper, and while prison may have been an occupational hazard for him, confinement often set Kidd off into violent rages.

After losing a bet on a St George v. South Sydney rugby league match where Kidd had blown the princely sum of a Violet Crumble bar and three cigarettes, he had dumped the piss bucket over Labe's head. Solids and liquids. It was hard to say which was worse but Labe often found himself weighing up the pros and cons.

Labe remembered that awful moment with a shudder. No more of that, thank you very much. If someone was going to put shit on him, the metaphorical was far better than the actual.

No. Kidd would tip Mick in, stand back and watch the fun.

Gillespie hadn't heard of Mick Sayers. What sort of man was he?

'Good bloke,' Kidd said, motioning to Pat Haitana to hand over a cigarette.

The banged-up jockey fumbled with his packet of smokes, handed Kidd one and struck a match. Kidd clutched the much smaller hand forcefully and pulled it towards him, lighting the cigarette, inhaling hard while maintaining his fierce grip. The match burnt down, sizzling the skin of Pat's thumb and index finger.

'Fuck! Jesus, Bertie.'

Haitana waved his blistering hand back and forth in the fetid air before sticking his index finger in his mouth. It was more to prevent him directing a stream of abuse at Kidd than to ease the pain. A first-degree burn to his fingers he could live with. A bashing from Bertie Kidd might not be so easy to get over.

Kidd watched Haitana suppress his anger and turned again to Gillespie.

'Terrific bloke to get on the piss with. Knows his horses too, though he never seems to back the right ones . . .'

'We can help him there,' Gillespie said.

Kidd glared at Gillespie, annoyed at the interruption.

'But if you fuck Mick, Mick'll fuck you back harder. And he'll keep fucking you until you love him. Then he'll put a couple of bullets in the back of your head.'

It was an odd threat, but Gillespie didn't stop to contemplate it. He was already thinking of fucking Mick and how he'd go about it. Even in the presence of a violent man uttering dark threats of rough sodomy and murder, the notion of consequence remained unfamiliar to him.

Gillespie understood two things. Firstly, that he could make a hell of a lot of money with a successful ring-in. Secondly, he knew enough about the history of the scam to be aware of the potential pitfalls, and where it could all go wrong unless it was done with great care, total secrecy and rigorous attention to detail.

Unfortunately for him, as he plotted his imminent triumph, he focused his mind only on the first thing.

Consequently, what followed was inevitable. But nobody could have predicted the magnitude of the disaster that awaited him, and everybody else who bought into their scheme – the most outrageous ring-in of them all.

CHAPTER THREE
The Joke

'When we find those responsible, they will face
the full force of the law.'
– Detective Chief Inspector Bert Holland,
Queensland Police Fraud Squad

Race Day: 18 August 1984. Eagle Farm Racecourse, Brisbane, Queensland. Midday.

THERE WERE QUEENSLAND coppers in the stands who had never been to the races before. Many would never go again, which, in hindsight, makes a lot of sense.

Those with a sharp eye could spot them wading their way through the crowded stands or gulping beers at the bars. The cheap suits and narrow ties of cops on duty or the beige cardigans with zippers, pale blue business shirts and brown trousers of those off the clock.

There were tall ones, and short ones, beer-gutted and slim. Plods of all sizes and shades bright and dim, the young and the youthful, the worn out and buggered, the abrupt, the corrupt and the alluringly rugged. They were there at the bars, pockets bursting with cash, or down at the ring having a lash. There were round ones and square ones who tried to fit in. In every pocket, race four, horse five to win.

The only Queensland walloper of note who was not present at Eagle Farm on Saturday, 18 August 1984 was the head honcho, the Chief Commissioner, Terry Lewis. But his absence was no sign that he was out of the loop or above the fray. Lewis wasn't just in the loop. He was its starting point and its finish line, the alpha and omega of the loop. Lewis made the loop and if the loop fell apart, he would make another one.

Terry was no Sherlock Holmes. He'd risen through the ranks like a bubble up a sewer pipe, but he had sufficient pub smarts to appreciate irony, and smiled at the joke that only he would ever know about when he sent his mum in his stead to Eagle Farm to get on Fine Cotton.

He also had enough pub smarts to know that when something dodgy was in the wind, it was best to be one step away from the action. Plausible deniability.

That morning, Terry had prodded his septuagenarian mother, Mona Lewis, into a cab with precise instructions to the driver to drop her at the Member's Entrance at Eagle Farm racecourse. He went back inside and spruced himself up a bit. A shit and a shave.

'You're looking good, Terry,' the bathroom mirror assured him as he glided the razor across his chin. 'You're looking great.'

He wasn't a member of the Brisbane Race Club. Terry Lewis didn't have to be a member of anything. Except, of course, holding the number one member's badge in the Queensland Police Service. That opened every door in the state that he might be inclined to walk through.

That included the Brisbane Race Club, though he didn't much care for horseracing. Mug's game. But Terry was no mug, and he knew it. He confirmed it looking in the mirror when he shaved every morning.

In any case, membership of a turf club would have looked unseemly on his 'Who's Who' entry. He'd been badgering Joh for a knighthood for years. The premier handed them out like Christmas cards to the faithful, but Lewis was still waiting for his.

What did he have to do to get it done and shut the missus up? She wouldn't let up about it, wanted to see her husband donged on the shoulder with a sword held by the Queen, dressed in her finery at Buckingham Palace.

Not the Queen. *Her* finery.

The woman's outfit alone was going to cost him a small fortune. Commissioner Lewis made a mental note to have his bagman,

Jack Herbert, kick up some extra cash when Joh finally gave him the nod. Travelling expenses, or some such rubbish. Premier Bjelke-Petersen would get around to it, eventually – he'd knighted some very suspect blokes. Men that made Terry look almost angelic. Men that he should have arrested years ago and dragged before the courts.

But this was Queensland. Life didn't work that way here. And hey – Terry had done all right.

That was because he was a survivor and knew when to look the other way. He avoided the company of other coppers in public. Any crook with even a passing eye for detail would have spotted them a mile off. Polyester suits. Bad haircuts. Dead giveaways.

Everyone, or at least everyone who mattered all the way from the Tweed River to Cooktown, knew who Terry Lewis was. So, wisely, the Chief Commissioner decided to stay at home.

Old mother Lewis made her way into the betting ring. For her age she showed no sign of frailty. She maintained a fierce expression as she strode through the throng. It was her stern visage rather than her age or gender that made the crowd part and allow her through.

Sidling up to rails bookmaker John Sinclair, she opened her handbag and took 20 crisp $50 notes out. She knew what to do. She'd been punting on the bookies for her son for years.

'A thousand to win, Mr Sinclair. Race four, number five. Fine Cotton.'

Sinclair had already taken hundreds of bets on Fine Cotton and he stood to take not just a bath but a kerosene delousing. He grimaced briefly at the thought of the state of his bookie bag at the end of the day, but he knew better than to appear displeased with the mother of the Chief Commissioner of Queensland Police.

'Of course, Mona,' he said and pointed to his penciller to scribble down the bet. A thousand to $5000. He took the money gently from Mona's hand. 'Pleasure to do business with you as always.'

Mona Lewis smiled, placing the betting ticket in the inside pouch of her handbag and carefully zipping it up.

'Good day, Mr Sinclair.'

She turned and walked away and the mob at the ring parted again to allow her exit.

Bert Holland, the head of the fraud squad, had a cigarette hanging from his gob at a table as usual. He was not bent in the way Lewis was, not incorrigibly, not beyond the pale. He'd found his niche in the force, charging shit-kickers passing dud cheques. He was good at that stuff. But confronted by any swindle with even a hint of sophistication about it, he was miserably out of his depth.

Holland directed his junior to shove off to the bar and buy him a drink. The usual. A pony of XXXX. The young detective meandered away, leaving Holland to make the company of two of Queensland's most dangerous cops, Tony Murphy and Glen Hallahan.

Murphy was now one of Lewis's assistant commissioners. He didn't feel insulted by being described as 'cunning as a shithouse rat', and in fact would have run rings around most shithouse rats when push came to shove. Always one step away from the mud and the blood. He'd successfully navigated his way through the political labyrinth of the QPS. Stayed out of view, copped a sling on the quiet, climbed the ladder.

Murphy was a ghastly vision, something you'd get from a fly-specked looking-glass in a Fortitude Valley pub shithouse. But Murphy was affable enough and easy to handle.

Glen Hallahan, on the other hand, was bad news. Dressed up like a pimp as usual, the detective sergeant had the morals of a virus. Garish pink tie, loud blue shirt – Christ, he even *looked* like a virus. Not that Holland had ever seen one. Most people haven't. But if a pathologist offered you a peek through his microscope, telling you that he'd isolated a particularly deadly, flesh-eating virus, you wouldn't be surprised to catch a glimpse of a microscopic Glen Hallahan staring back at you.

In the bleak vernacular of the Queensland cops, Hallahan was known as 'The Magician'. He made people disappear. Only they didn't turn up again later with the drum roll. A brothel owner here, a hooker with a big mouth there. Gone. Vanished.

He was the sort of magician who cut the pretty girl in half, but never showed you her smiling and dancing afterwards. He'd be too busy lumbering her body parts into a wood-chipper. Don't forget the turpentine or the bloody thing would seize up, shudder to a halt trying to grind through a femur. He and a sidekick had performed that act, or one pretty close to it, to a very restricted audience of nobody but the girl in question.

Later, Hallahan and a bent copper from the breaking squad in New South Wales, Fred Krahe, had knocked off the brothel madam Shirley Brifman. Hallahan held her down while Krahe stuck a tube down her throat, forcing a bunch of pills into her gut.

After this show, the starlet did turn up. The next day. Dead. Suicide. The coroner could hardly say otherwise.

Holland knew all the stories, but never asked Hallahan about them. That was a one-way ticket to being an accessory after the fact. Don't ask, don't tell. That was the policy. It was enough that Hallahan knew his place.

Holland wouldn't get in a car with Hallahan alone. Oh, not that he was afraid of him, and he outranked him, of course. He was just being sensible. In this caper it paid to be cautious.

While Holland took the first sip of his lager, the young fraud squad detective asked who was getting on Fine Cotton. The others had chipped in their own cash, even Murphy. He'd ripped a hundred out of his wallet.

The only bet Holland liked was a sure thing. And the sycophants in the force had sworn blind that Fine Cotton was it. Fifty down for $250 back. A bit of spending money. A small drink.

Every copper at Eagle Farm was on it. Fine Cotton on the nose. No place bets. No quinellas or exotics. On the nose. Fine Cotton wasn't going to make up the numbers. It was going to win and win easily.

Ever the pessimist, Holland mused that if the horse didn't win, he could always ask the young detective for his money back. Or maybe he'd let him off the hook. A pineapple here or there. Who gives a shit? The kid might come in handy one day.

Back at the Lewis residence, Terry was still looking at himself in the mirror. The biggest money problem Terry Lewis had wasn't a lazy flutter at the track going belly-up. It was hiding all his dough – from the press, the tax office, and, above all, his wife.

'Melbourne Mick' Sayers was sitting at the breakfast bar of his Bronte home, in Sydney's cash-drenched eastern suburbs. The sun poured in from a vast window looking over the beach. It would have brought a welcome warmth to most houses in Bronte that morning – a cheerful antidote to a chilly winter's day. But here it was ignored, fated to die pointlessly amidst the stinking cloud of Mick's cigarette smoke rising lazily towards the ceiling.

The radio whispered horseracing tips and other allegedly useful information in the background. It was like elevator music for Mick. Only fools got their mail from the radio. Mick made his own.

He was pretty good at it, to hear him tell it. Some people listened to him tell it too. But most didn't listen for long. Sensibly, at least for the sake of his ego, Mick never bothered to check his tips against the ones on the radio. Not late on Saturday night, when all bets were off.

Not ever, really.

Marian Ware walked into the kitchen, dressed in a short silk robe that barely covered her arse. As she pottered around in the kitchen, Sayers' eyes followed her movements. As female arses went, he had to concede that Marian's was pretty good. He'd had intimate dealings with a lot worse.

He briefly considered jumping the bench and enjoying a brief respite with his tarty partner. She was good fun when you got her going.

Marian went the grope first. She turned to the bench and grabbed Mick's Viscount pack, plucked one out and lit it up.

'Hey!'

'I'm out. Told you that.'

'All right. Yeah. Look, make us a coffee, will ya?'

Marian meandered her lazy, blousy way through the formica and chipboard cupboards and filled the jug.

The house looked pretty fancy, but like a lot of men she knew, it was actually cheap and tacky when you looked closely. Big, sure. Impressive from a distance? Yeah. But the finish? The detail, the feel of the place? Tacky. Sloppy. No style.

Speaking of which, Mick Sayers, wagering wizard of the turf as he was, the prince of probabilities, flipped through the form guide and tapped a pen on the countertop. Marian had seen this all before. She raised her eyebrows, looked to the ceiling and sighed, as she poured the hot water onto the coarse grains of instant coffee. She had the brains not to say anything. Mick was about to make a big mistake, she could see. Another one. But now was not the time to warn him.

It was never a good time to warn Mick Sayers about anything.

He overheard the tipsters' offerings for the Melbourne and Sydney meetings. Normally he wouldn't pay any attention. He knew most of these clowns personally. Like pockets on a singlet, the lot of 'em. By the end of the day, almost all of 'em would have the arse out of their strides. Come Sunday they'd be on the phones, hitting up the shylocks to bail them out.

Marian slid the steaming cup across the kitchen bench. White and two. Mick turned his ear to the radio, waiting for the final tip of the day from racing commentator Mal Meikle.

'And if you're having a bet in Brisbane, race four, number five. Fine Cotton. Watch for market moves, but it's a good each-way chance at odds.'

'Oh, for fuck's sake!'

'What?'

'Fine Cotton. This arsehole has just named it in his best bets for the day. Every man and their fuckin' dog is on it.'

This was getting out of hand. Who'd shot their mouth off? That fuckin' prick Gillespie? Mick knew that bastard would always try to run his own race. But not even Gillespie could be that stupid. Not today. Not with this.

'Can you get please get ready? We need to be there early.'

Marian held her tongue, but it took willpower. She could smell disaster already. But that meant someone was going to get hurt, and this time she was going to make sure it wasn't Marian Ware. She sighed, turned and sauntered off to the bathroom.

Who? Who'd blown the lid off it? The only person he'd told was Freeman. Mick grabbed the phone. He knew the number off by heart.

The call sounded Sayers' alarm eight times downstairs at George Freeman's Yowie Bay mansion. Eventually the phone was picked up. He heard a long raspy wheeze and knew it was George, an asthmatic who smoked like a chimney. It was creepy, the sounds he made. It was like talking to a pervert who was having one off the wrist down the other end of the line. Well, George was a pervert in many ways, so maybe he was doing exactly that.

'Speak.'

'G'day, George. It's Mick.'

'Morning, mate. Big day today.'

'Yeah, it is. But there's a lot of noise out there, George. Too fuckin' much.'

'What are you worried about? You got on early.'

'Yeah. But you? You havin' a big lash at it?' He had to ask. There was a long pause.

'No, Mick. Maybe a small investment, on your say so. I'll think about it. This is your go.'

'Fuckin' Meikle just tipped it on the radio!'

'M&M? He wouldn't know if a tram was up him.'

'Yeah, but he's on point today, isn't he?'

'Every dog has his day, Mick. Even that dog.'

'It can't be just him. He couldn't tip Fine Cotton by looking at any form guide in the country. Who would? Someone up high has mouthed off.'

'I hope you're not suggesting I'd be involved in any of that, Mick.'

The menace in George's voice gave Mick pause. He'd heard this tone before, and it rarely bode well.

'No, course not. It's just that . . .'

'Mick, let me remind you. You're into me for just under a million. A million in cash. Not a few grand here and there. Real money. I've been very patient. And I'm not known for my patience. But I've been patient because you told me you were going to get well. Today.'

'It'll be good, George. Fuck, you know I could retire if Fine Cotton stayed at 20s, but . . . Anyway, don't worry. You'll be sorted.'

'I'm not worried, Mick. I never worry. It's not good for me health.'

'Righto, George.'

'I'll see you soon, son.'

Mick put the phone down slowly, carefully, as if it might bite him if he made it angry. 'Health.' The way George had said the word was ominous.

And as for the 'See you soon' – that was fucking terrifying.

Freeman put his phone down with a clunk. Like Mick's girl-friend Marian, he was still in his dressing gown. Not that that was odd. He often spent the whole day draped in a pair of Speedos and his trademark towelling robe.

And why not? He wasn't in a hurry to do anything, didn't need to go anywhere. Being in a hurry wasn't George's style. He might take a dip in the pool later on. Maybe.

He reached for the phone again, dialled a number and peered out through the door to the pool. It did look inviting. George had a rule when he called anybody. More than eight rings and he put the phone down. Life was too short. Answering machines? Fuck them for a box of chocolates.

There were only five electronic blurts before it was picked up.

'You know what to do?' Freeman asked. 'Right. Happy travels.'

It was time for a dip.

It was a bumper day at Eagle Farm, and the Queensland Turf Club committeemen were engaged in an orgy of self-congratulation. The movers and shakers of Queensland thoroughbred horseracing were collectively patting themselves on the back. As their eyes shifted from left to right across the stands below, the smiles grew wider.

Surely this was a record crowd! And in August, with the smattering of Group One races held in Queensland run and won months ago. They'd never seen anything like it, and they loved what they saw. Well done, everyone. Hats off!

They mingled at the table where the caterer had left the fare prepared according to specific instructions, issued in writing by QTC chairman Clarrie Roberts. Finger sandwiches (no egg), party pies and piles of sausage rolls. Little saveloys on sticks. Lots of them. Plenty of tomato sauce.

The spread just oozed class, he said to himself. Well done, everyone. Hats off . . .

Well, not quite, not at all. It looked like a gargantuan rendering of a fat kid's 10th birthday party feast, but it was exactly what the chairman wanted, so who was the caterer to argue? Clarrie Roberts could have asked for a dozen lobsters thermidor, lashings of Peking duck and finished it off with bombe Alaska, and it would have been there.

But his taste leaned more to the elemental. He liked to eat his food from a little ceramic plate or, even better, straight off a stick. And those saveloys looked the goods!

Clarrie had been running Queensland racing since its halcyon days in the 1950s, but today's meeting was especially satisfying. He figured his marketing techniques were finally bearing fruit. It wasn't just the big attendance. Quality not quantity was one of his favourite dictums.

Why, some of Queensland's finest people were in attendance. Members of the judiciary, heavy hitters from the National Party. The Members' Stand and betting rings were full to burst with fat fellows wearing white shoes, the unmistakable fashion statement of the brash Queensland up and comer.

Clarrie was roused from his reverie by a polite knock on the door. It was John Mort 'The Butterfly' Green. The Butterfly was the biggest punter on Queensland's tracks. He didn't have a wad of cash at his disposal the size of the big Sydney punters, but it was big enough.

The Butterfly was an affable bloke, who had a deep understanding of Queensland racing and, more importantly, a profound understanding that it was as bent as a Dwarf Cavendish. He'd taken the bookies to the cleaners with some valuable inside mail and sometimes old-fashioned racetrack gossip. A good man, in Clarrie's book.

'Come on in, Jack! Tremendous to see you.'

Clarrie extended his hand and Jack shook it with feigned warmth, his QTC membership badge jerking and gyrating from his middle suitcoat button, as they both tried to work out how to diplomatically bring this tectonic clasping of hands to a halt.

Clarrie ended it by pulling away and using his right hand to wave at the cornucopia of trashy snacks. 'Party pie, Jack?'

'No, thank you.'

The two men walked to the windows and surveyed the scene below.

'It's a beautiful day, Clarrie.'

'A beautiful day, yes. A great day for Queensland racing. We haven't seen these crowds since Bernborough won the Doomben Ten Thousand.'

'You go back a lot further than me, Clarrie,' The Butterfly conceded. 'But you've got a big mob in today. The bookies' bags are heavy with cash and the turnstiles are still clicking over. You deserve all the credit.'

'Thank you, and I mean that. We're all good racing people here, and I know you have the best interests of Queensland racing at heart.'

The Butterfly had heard this sickening spiel more times than he cared to think about. This fatuous old turd – oozing vicarious pride in things he'd had virtually nothing to do with, dragging unwary people who may be of use into a sugary orgy of mutual congratulation and back-slappery.

He took a deep breath and looked the beaming bozo in the eye. 'I've got a nice little surprise for you, Clarrie.'

'Oh?'

The Butterfly handed the QTC chairman a yellow betting ticket. Clarrie looked down and almost choked up one of the 15 saveloys he'd scarfed in the last half an hour.

Four thousand six hundred dollars to win $36,800. Fine Cotton to win at 8/1.

'Fine Cotton, eh?' Clarrie said, determined not to appear flabbergasted by the absurd sum of money involved. 'There's been a bit of talk about it. Big mover in the markets, I hear.'

'Well, the punters know a good thing when they see one, Clarrie.'

'That they do, Jack. They do indeed. This isn't out of your pocket, is it?'

'Erm, no. It's an anonymous bet, from a very good friend of Queensland racing.'

'Well, is it indeed? This will go a long way towards the seeding money for the new stand, Jack.'

'A noble thought. But it's good for whatever you want to do with it, Clarrie.'

'Provided it wins, Jack.'

'Oh, I wouldn't be too surprised if it saluted at the leger, Clarrie.'

'Well, this day just got a whole lot better. Grab yourself a saveloy, Jack!'

Down in the mounting yards, jockey Gus Philpot was waiting for his ride. He'd donned the black-and-red silks and was raring to go. The 17-year-old was happy to take any ride going, and when it came to a Saturday meet in Brisbane, he'd leapt at the chance. He needed the experience. He wanted to get ahead, like every other apprentice jockey.

Apprentices were expected to say little more than 'Yes, sir, no, sir, three bags full, sir', and as gormless as young Gus was, he knew that much at least. Don't complain. Work insane hours for 20 per cent of the square root of fuck all and keep your spirits up by dreaming of riding the winner of the Melbourne Cup one day.

So, he was pleasantly surprised to get the call from the trainer just after midday. Did he want the ride on Fine Cotton in the fourth? You bet he did.

Gus Philpot examined the contenders for race four, the Second Division Commerce Novice Handicap. It was a field of 12 starters, all try-hards and battlers. Some had eked the occasional win, stuck their noses in front at just the right time. It was a perfect race for a jockey making his way in the caper, a test of his skill to get the best out of his ride.

Apprentice jockey Philpot didn't have time to have a good look at his ride's form or breeding. None in fact, but by the time he'd stripped and got into his silks, the horse was nowhere to be seen. He reckoned the trainer would cop a spray and probably a fine from the stewards.

That wasn't Gus Philpot's worry. He had two rides scheduled for the rest of the meeting, and getting a ride in the fourth made it a good day.

He hadn't heard of Fine Cotton, but thought he must have seen him around the traps somewhere. Maybe Bundamba. A nine-year-old miler. He was almost as old as Philpot. That suited him fine. The old geldings were usually pretty easy to handle. Any bad habits they might have had were long gone. Still, it'd be nice if the horse and its trainer turned up sometime soon.

Hayden Haitana was still in the car park. Walking back and forth, trying to figure out a plan, sweating out the last couple of stubbies he'd consumed at North's place. He looked into the double float and there was Fine Cotton with Bold Personality. Like chalk and cheese.

This was a jail sentence just waiting to be handed down. He could sense that his life could well fall to pieces, right here, today, probably within the hour. The foreboding was becoming a certainty. But what could he do about it now?

John Gillespie emerged from the stands and strode down to Haitana and the horse float. 'Good to go, mate. Everything's in place.'

'This isn't going to work, John. We'll all be locked up before the last race.'

'The committee's onboard, Hayden. The cops are with us. Nothing can go wrong.'

'Fine Cotton can win this on its own. Just give me a couple of minutes with it.'

'We've already been through this, Hayden.'

Gillespie put his hand on Haitana's slumped shoulder. 'I know you love that bloody horse, but the ringer has to run.'

'I'll give it a bomb. It'll get out of the jump like shit out of a shanghai and won't let up. Trust me, John. Fine Cotton can win this.'

Gillespie tightened his grip on Haitana's shoulder. A little squeeze. A little reminder. This was his show.

'The fuckin' ringer runs, Hayden. Cop it sweet, here and now, and don't fuck this up.'

Haitana exhaled and looked again at Bold Personality. Looked down at its hooves. The white paint wasn't setting. Instead it continued to smear itself into the paint that was already running, dripping onto the floor of the float. There was paint everywhere. Sticky, wet paint. This was a disaster.

Gillespie rammed his point home. 'Our friend in Sydney is going to be very unhappy if the ringer doesn't run, mate. When he gets unhappy, he gets upset. And when he gets upset, people get murdered. I don't want to be one of those people, and I don't want you to be one of those people. Don't forget what happened to Georgie Brown, sunshine.'

Haitana had not forgotten what had happened to Georgie Brown. He approached Fine Cotton, and the old racehorse nuzzled him affectionately. The trainer reached into his pocket and pulled out a Steam Roller, a peppermint lolly. Fine Cotton's favourite. The horse gobbled it off the flat of his outstretched hand.

Haitana went to his other pocket and produced a white capsule, the size of a .38 calibre bullet. Fine Cotton's bomb. Pure amphetamine. The horse licked it up off the trainer's hand.

'Fuck's sake, Hayden! What the hell do you think you're doing?'

'We need a plan B.'

'Leave that fucking horse in the float. The ringer runs. I'm getting tired of repeating myself here.'

A couple of stray punters walked past the float on their way to the stands. Gillespie smiled at them and nodded.

He lowered his voice. 'Hayden. Listen to me. Get the ringer out, leave the rug on it and get it up to the stewards for inspection. We're running out of time. I've got to get on. Bill fuckin' Naoum's turned up. He's sitting in the Members' Stand.'

'Aw, Jesus. He'll clock Bold Personality from a mile away.'

'That's why I've got to get on. Run a little interference. A little distraction. A bit of the old sleight of hand. Leave Bill Naoum with me. The only thing he's going to see of the race is through the bottom of a schooner glass.'

'Fuck's sake.'

'Don't fuck around, Hayden. Stick to the plan.'

With that unambiguous advice, The Phantom was on his way back to the Members' Stand.

Haitana sighed. He needed a beer. Badly – his throat felt like sandpaper.

All right. Get this done. Get Bold Personality up to the stables and let the stewards give it the once over. He gave the bay gelding a pat on the neck and grabbed its bridle. The ringer threw its head back in a brief moment of protest. Bold Personality didn't want to leave the safety of the float.

'Come on.'

The horse edged forward. Fine Cotton made a move to follow, but Haitana turned his body and nudged the older brown gelding with his shoulder. He noticed Fine Cotton's eyes had already begun to dilate.

The bomb was kicking in. Fine Cotton was in for a hard day and a long night. He'd have to work it out in the float somehow. Jesus, Haitana thought, Fine Cotton was going to kick the shit out of that float. Panel-beat it from the inside. He briefly fretted that he might lose his rental bond when he took the float back tomorrow, all buckled and banged up.

What the fuck was he thinking? The bond on the float? The least of his worries now.

The stewards were after him. That was his first port of call. What did they want? Had they really been rumbled?

Haitana trotted into the stands, quickening his pace as he drew closer to the stewards' room. He was sweating profusely. He felt the heat on his face – always red from the grog – had ratcheted up a shade to scarlet with the heat and the stress. He slowed to a walk, stopped and took a breath before he entered, eager not to look careworn or troubled. Or guilty. When he got in the sparsely furnished room, there were no wallopers inside waiting to pounce. No fierce faces demanding answers, only a junior racing official sitting at a card table, looking bored.

'Hayden Haitana,' Haitana said, extending his hand.

The young track official ignored the offering.

'You're late.'

'Yeah, I hit a bit of traffic on the way over.'

'No, you're late. If you're going to announce your ride, it'd be nice if you let us know,' the young steward said, thrusting an envelope into Haitana's hand. 'On time.'

Haitana stammered his apologies, turned and left. He'd announced Philpot as the rider late. He'd been fined $10.

He rushed back to the car park. If that was the worst thing that happened to him today, he'd be the luckiest man in Australia. Hayden Haitana was now seriously addled. A beer would be good . . .

The trainer closed the gate on the float, leaving Fine Cotton to deal with the onset of amphetamine psychosis all on his own. Hayden pulled Bold Personality's bridle and the horse trotted along behind him slowly, head bowed.

The ringer had been through hell, an equine ordeal that was the worst possible preparation for the race. For any race. A good three or four classes above the rest of the field, Bold Personality would be a lay-down misère to win in normal circumstances. But these were not normal circumstances.

The last 24 hours must have been the worst of Bold Personality's life. Pulled to and fro by idiots and drunken morons, barely surviving the drive up to Brisbane. Subjected to all manner of indignities once he had arrived, including the full dye treatment. Then a chilly hour under the hose to wash it all off. The poor bloody thing didn't even have a decent pair of racing plates on.

Haitana wondered if Bold Personality still had it in him to win. The horse had endured so much strife in the lead-up, so who knows, it might not want to come out of the barrier. Just stand there. Ignore the jockey. Take the rest of the day off. The last thing Bold Personality needed was a 1500 metre dash.

He somehow shifted the baffled beast into the stable and let him rest up, the blanket still on him as the heat of the day rose, the white paint congealing roughly on his hooves.

Haitana was late. He'd been running late all day. He guessed the steward had already been past, looked into the stable and found it empty. There was another fine. Bugger that. The Phantom could pay it.

But the QTC steward had not been through to see the field for the Second Division Commerce Novice Handicap. Bob Hess, life member of the QTC and veteran of the stewards' room, tended to approach his duties in a more casual manner. This was Queensland racing, and it required a different approach to the nit-pickers at the big meets down south.

He strolled along down the stables chatting amiably with the trainers and strappers, intermittently lighting his pipe and huffing huge palls of smoke in his wake. Hess reckoned he could spot a crook horse with nothing more than a glance.

As he got to stable 12, he saw Haitana leaning out and smiling at him. Hess had seen Haitana around the traps over the years. Good horseman. He'd had a few problems with the law over the years, but he was a decent bloke.

'Hayden. Good to see you. Fine Cotton, is it? Any problems?'

Hess peered in. Bold Personality was still wearing its rug and as the heat of the day increased had started sweating. Any more than a quick glance at the horse would have shown the white paint dripping onto the horse's hooves. But thoroughness was not Hess's go, and the tell-tale drips of white paint were allowed to go through to the keeper.

'No. All good. He's raring to go.' Haitana turned and looked at Bold Personality, whose head was bowed. He looked crook or buggered or both, even to the untrained eye. It was obvious.

'Righto then. Good luck.'

That was the full extent of the steward's inspection at Eagle Farm. Bold Personality as Fine Cotton had been cleared for take-off.

Haitana looked at his watch. Ten minutes to race time. OK. Time to get the ringer into the yard.

He grabbed Bold Personality's bridle. Bold Personality demurred again before clattering slowly away to the mounting yard. When the man and his horse arrived, the other horses had already commenced their parade before the punters, jockeys on board. Gus Philpot was the only jockey there without a ride, anxiously strolling back and forth with his persuader in his hand.

'Sorry, pal. I've been looking for you in the jockey's room.'

Philpot was relieved. He'd thought Fine Cotton might have been a late scratching. Pulled out at the last moment. Philpot admired the bay gelding, noting its smooth athletic gait as it sauntered towards him.

'You going to saddle him up, Mr Haitana?'

'Yeah, sure. He's a funny bugger. Doesn't like the saddle on him too early. He doesn't like crowds much either, so we keep the blanket over him. It seems to keep him calm. We'll wait till the last minute.'

With a flourish, Haitana at last removed the sweat-sodden blanket and quickly saddled Bold Personality up with the number five saddlecloth. There was a crowd watching, checking the appearance of the field before placing last-minute bets. The horse responsible for the biggest betting plunge in Australian history drew a few comments from the crowd.

'Is that the horse?' one punter asked his mate. 'Can't see what all the fuss is about.'

Philpot climbed aboard and slowly trotted around the mounting yard, slipping into the 12-horse field. While he did a slow lap, he noticed the other jockeys staring at Fine Cotton. When he returned their gaze, they looked up at him. One jockey smiled. Two more winked at Philpot. Another gave him the thumbs-up signal.

This sort of camaraderie was unusual in the racing industry. Unusual? It was straight-out weird, and left Philpot baffled and smiling awkwardly in response. Oh well, no point in worrying about it now.

'Any instructions, Mr Haitana?'

'Just get him out of the blocks. He'll do the rest.'

Philpot nodded and joined the field meandering down the home straight towards the barriers. He gave Fine Cotton a gentle nudge with his knees and it broke into a gallop on command. It had seemed a bit off in the mounting yard but now, on the track, Philpot could feel the power of the horse beneath him and thought, hey, we might have a real chance here.

The track hands didn't need to offer Fine Cotton any persuasion into the number two gate. Philpot eased the horse into the barrier and gave his ride a gentle stroke on his neck.

The gates flew open, but Fine Cotton missed the start. Stood there in the barrier like a rock, ignoring the jockey's increasingly desperate urgings. He was four lengths behind the field when he finally jumped out.

Mr Haitana was not going to be happy.

CHAPTER FOUR
The Team

'You can deal with a bad man, but you can't do
business with a mad man.'
— Len McPherson

GEORGE DAVID FREEMAN was the Pope of Sydney; that is, if the Pope lounged around a swimming pool in a pair of Speedos and chain-smoked.

Everybody knew it. Freeman had judges, politicians and cops in his back pocket. He didn't need to bribe them. A race tip over the phone was all that was required. Everyone was sweet.

George's friends in the seats of power would get the call. No pleasantries. No chitchat. Just a simple, one-sentence message.

'Sydney race four, number seven.'

Everyone would jump on it and, true enough, the number seven would salute at the ledger. Easy money. Who wouldn't want to be friends with George?

George wasn't a punting genius, a man scribbling down some tortured betting algorithm based on a complex mathematical model combining racing form and delicate arbitrage betting. He would rig the races, pay the riders, the trainers and sometimes race officials to determine the outcome long before the horses jumped out of the barriers.

There wasn't a race meet anywhere in Australia on any given day that Freeman didn't have his hands on. His particular favourite scam was in harness racing. The trots.

In an eight-race field, George would have every rider paid off. George would place a $50 wager on the winner on behalf of all of the riders. Let's say the chosen horse was the number five and it was 8/1. The riders knew they had to discreetly back off on their own rides and allow the five to win. When it did, every rider won $400. Easy money. Those riders who fretted over ethical concerns, or the more consequential worry that if the scam was rumbled they faced being cast out of the sport for life, were warned, gently at first and then more forcefully, that disloyalty to George Freeman was a health hazard. Nobody said no to George Freeman.

'The Little Man', as he was sometimes called (out of his earshot), had a taste for violence.

In 1977 Michael Hurley was a young up-and-comer in the crime scene. Two decades later he would go on to become one of Sydney's biggest drug traffickers, but back then he was just doing his apprenticeship. He got on pretty well with Freeman, and when he asked for Lena Muller's hand in marriage, George stepped up to sign the marriage certificate as a witness.

Almost as a rite of passage, Hurley got pinched for hijacking a delivery of 5000 watches and was sentenced to four years in prison. He asked George to keep an eye on Lena. George certainly did. With Hurley banged up at Long Bay, George was banging her three times a week. After six months of frenzied fornication, George grew tired of cuckolding Hurley and set Lena up to work in a brothel.

Unsurprisingly, Hurley was not at all pleased to discover George had put his wife on the game, but when he was released from jail, the young crook decided retribution would not be a smart career move.

Lena's stepfather, career criminal Jackie Muller, thought otherwise and determined Freeman should pay a hefty price. On ANZAC Day 1979, Jackie lay in wait for George in the front yard of Freeman's Yowie Bay home, armed with .22 pistol. When George returned home after a big day on the punt, Jackie stepped up and shot him in the face.

George went down. Jackie took off.

Alas, Jackie Muller wasn't the sharpest tool in the shed. He'd used a virtual pea gun when something bigger and uglier was called for. The .22 round struck Freeman in the neck and twisted its way upward to lodge underneath his cheekbone, narrowly missing his eye.

Jackie Muller had missed. That meant he was a dead man walking.

The last time he did walk was down the driveway of his Bronte home. He'd spent the six weeks since the shooting on his toes, barely leaving home and peering out through the curtains at any suspicious noise or anything else that appeared untoward. On that winter evening, he'd spotted a car parked out the front, engine running, and decided to investigate.

George had put the word out to his foot soldiers. 'You find him, and I'll pop him.'

George didn't use a .22. He went well armed with a .38.

Jackie was hit in the chest three times. It was his turn to go down and George made sure he wasn't going to get back up. He stood over Muller's bleeding body and put two more into his head.

It wasn't George's first, nor would it be his last. The first had been five years earlier when George and Stan 'The Man' Smith shot dead the psychopathic hoon, John Stewart Regan. Freeman had been along as cover, glad-handing Regan like they were old mates. Stan did the heavy lifting that time, emerging from his hiding spot in a shopfront window on Chapel Street, Marrickville to put three rounds into Regan. With Regan mortally wounded, George stepped in. It had all been planned. One in, all in. George did the coup de grâce.

When word got around that Regan was dead, Long Bay Gaol erupted in cheers. Regan was feared and despised in equal measure. Elsewhere, including among the cops, there was a profound sense of relief that Regan had been dispatched. The homicide investigation went by the numbers. There was no real desire to catch Regan's killers.

The Pope of Sydney's power was not unfettered. He ruled Sydney as part of a gangster triumvirate: Len 'Mr Big' McPherson, George Freeman and Stan 'The Man' Smith. The father, the son and the Holy Ghost. Collectively, and with their foot soldiers assembled around them, they were known as The Team and they ruled Sydney for 30 years.

Stan Smith was a hood from Balmain who overcame his sudden, violent impulses to become one of the most successful criminals Australia has seen. He started out as McPherson's sidekick, handing out beatings and threats. In his early days, he got so used to bashing the working girls who worked in McPherson's brothels that Len would follow in his wake, handing out cash and apologies to the stunned, bleeding prostitutes.

In his middle years, Stan calmed down to become a cunning and shrewd operator. He'd had some trouble in the courts as a kid, but after that his only pinch was a small marijuana blue in Victoria in 1971. He finally showed up to do his six months in the clink in 1980. He was involved in at least 15 murders and 25 shooting incidents in Sydney, yet he didn't spend a day in a New South Wales prison as an adult.

He was The Team's go-to assassin, a hit man without peer, and the one The Team turned to when any difficult characters had to be dealt with.

Smith had turned to drug trafficking in the mid-1970s. McPherson and Freeman didn't want a bar of it and stayed well away. They knew their political and judicial connections would run a mile if there was a hint of involvement in drugs, but Smith was insistent this was where the future of organised crime lay.

At the Woodward Royal Commission he gave evidence saying he hated drugs. His eldest son had become addicted to heroin and Smith had put the kid through rehab more times than he could count. Finally and sadly, Smith's son died, as so many heroin users do, by lethal overdose.

When Smith found out, he grieved only briefly and then set about revenge. He hunted down the dealer who had supplied his son with heroin. He organised to meet the dealer in a park on Sydney's upper north shore. When the dealer arrived and got out of his car, Smith ran him down in his and then ran over the fallen body four times. Unlike his gangland murders that always concluded at the barrel of a gun, Smith took his time and made the man suffer. This was personal.

His son's tragic death didn't stop Smith from trafficking drugs. Smith reconciled it in his own mind by claiming he was only involved in marijuana smuggling. He received shipments of weed and hashish from the Philippines and Thailand, and operated plantations in the Sunshine Coast hinterland in Queensland. The dope was driven down to Sydney using vans with the names of a well-known freight company etched onto them.

The shipments rarely got pinched. Even when Smith was under surveillance, the cops were never able to get enough on him to charge him. They'd see a shadowy figure suddenly appear in their camera lenses sporting a baseball cap and sunglasses, only to disappear just as quickly.

What sort of man commits murder on his wedding day? That sort of man would be Len McPherson.

In 1964, a roughhouse pimp, Robert 'Pretty Boy' Walker, had the nerve to challenge The Team's prostitution business in the

Cross. Stan Smith paid Walker a visit to warn him off and got shot for his trouble. Stan wore some shotgun pellets in his right thigh and left arm and took off. A doctor pulled them out with a pair of tweezers at St Vincent's Hospital and bandaged him up. The doc urged Stan to spend a night or two in hospital just to make sure the wounds didn't get infected, but Stan was having none of that.

Revenge was now Stan's business, and he planned to go about it swiftly and brutally. The trouble was the Pretty Boy had gone to ground. The Team put the feelers out but Walker was nowhere to be seen.

Meanwhile Len was getting ready to marry for the second time. Let's just say the first marriage, to Balmain girl Dawn Joy, didn't work out. Len was staying out all hours and rooting anything that moved. When she blew up, Len reacted in typical fashion, tying her left leg to a tree and her right leg to the towbar of his car and trying to pull her apart.

He gave her such a fearful hiding the coppers had to get involved. Ray 'Machine Gun' Kelly was head of the breaking squad at the time. He played marriage counsellor and forced Len to guarantee Dawn's safe passage out of the state. She was more than happy with the divorce settlement. She didn't get the house or a cent of Len's dough, but she did get out alive.

Three years later, wedding bells were pealing for Len and his new belle, Marlene Gilligan. She was 20 years his junior and genuinely in love with the bloke, who even at just 42 years of age had a face like a bull elephant's scrotum.

Len's best man was Stan Smith. As the two men fiddled with their tuxedos and struggled with their bowties and cummerbunds, the word came through. Pretty Boy Walker had been spotted holed up in a Randwick motel.

Len and Stan resisted the urge to jump in a car right away and go see Pretty Boy with the shooters. Len couldn't leave Marlene weeping at the altar. So, the two men took off to the Darling Street Anglican Church with Marlene's wedding ring bouncing about in Stan's pocket.

Len got through the 'I dos' and sealed his vows with a big kiss, to the applause of the 100 or so guests. The wedding party went outside for the photos while the guests took off to the reception at Balmain Town Hall and got on the drink. It was only then that Len gave Marlene a peck on the cheek and told her he had some business to attend to.

'Don't worry,' he told the blushing bride. 'I'll be back in an hour.'

In the end he was gone a couple of hours. Enough time for him and Stan to change clothes and cars at a house in Kingsford, grab Len's much beloved sten gun and head over to Randwick.

When they arrived at the motel, Walker was nowhere to be seen. They found his room, but he'd taken off. Len and Stan jumped back in the car and drove around Randwick. It wasn't long before they spotted Walker strolling down towards a nearby pub. Stan pulled up alongside Walker while Len pulled the sten gun out.

'Hey, Bobby boy,' the bridegroom said. 'This is for you.'

Len let rip with a burst of fire. Walker was hit more than 20 times. The Pretty Boy was dead before he hit the ground. Len and Stan made it back to the reception just in time for the speeches.

No-one who was there would say Len was gone for any length of time. They'd seen him at the church and there he was at the reception, sipping champagne with his new bride. It was the perfect alibi. That's why, more than 50 years later, the police file on the murder of Robert 'Pretty Boy' Walker sits gathering dust in the 'too hard' basket.

Truth be told, it's not the entire reason Walker's murder remains unsolved. McPherson was a 'fizz gig', a police informer who had strategically given up his rivals to curry favour with cops. Machine Gun Kelly was his contact for the most part throughout the '60s. It was an ideal situation. McPherson had protection from police interference and was allowed to go on with business – standover rackets, prostitution, hijackings from the Balmain docks and illegal gaming.

McPherson, who by the age of 50 was a gargantuan blob of grossly obese, menacing flesh, may have been a violent thug, but he was a shrewd and conniving one. He hated police, distrusting the bent ones especially, however he was able to manipulate them to look the other way while he climbed the ladder.

Effectively given the green light by a grateful constabulary, McPherson and Smith built up their empire by dealing with threats in much the same way as they did with Walker. But there was still something missing and McPherson knew the real key to riches in Sydney's organised crime networks came from illegal gambling.

One day at the Royal Oak Hotel in Double Bay, McPherson buttonholed George Freeman. Len only spoke at one volume, a coarse bellow, laced with expletives that startled anyone within a 30-metre radius.

'You're always gettin' fuckin' pinched for shopliftin' blues, George. Be like Agent 86. Get fuckin' smart. You're good with the horses. Come along with us and we'll have some real fuckin' fun.'

George had grown weary of the occupational hazards of the professional thief. He didn't need to be asked twice. He nodded and shook Len's big hand. He was on The Team.

True to form, McPherson's invitation wasn't a matter of charity for a mate. He knew Freeman's success with the horses could give them all a credible explanation as to why they had so much money, so much undeclared income. If they were ever pulled up, the answer was easy. George had tipped them into a big winner.

The Team thrived with Freeman's gambling nous. They bank-rolled illegal casinos, established an army of SP bookmakers and skimmed off the profits on the pokies in the licensed clubs. They made fortunes.

Whenever a rival came along to have a crack at their empire, they did so knowing at some point they would come across a grim-faced Stan Smith staring back at them over the barrel of a gun.

Other crooks understood this. They learned to play with The Team, not against them. There hadn't been a serious challenge to the triumvirate since George and Stan had air-conditioned Johnny Regan.

But by 1984 the world was changing. A global heroin epidemic had taken hold in Australia. Smith might have been happy to move marijuana around, but his son's premature death with a needle stuck in his arm had made Stan leery about delving into the supply of harder drugs. McPherson and Freeman hated drugs, and heroin especially.

Other crime groups were emerging who didn't share The Team's ethical concerns. Danny Chubb, the merchant seaman with the face of a ferret and the general demeanour to match, was bringing heroin and guns into the country on the ships he worked on. He had no distribution network so he turned to a group of emerging criminals led by Barry McCann, a racetrack pimp The Team had at first ignored, but when they discovered he was running illegal casinos in Sydney, they packed him off to Wollongong. He could operate there without getting in The Team's way.

McCann's heroin supply networks had cashed him up. With all the money rolling in, he'd assembled an army of goons and gunmen eager to do his bidding. He'd determined that when he came back to Sydney, he wouldn't be beholden to The Team. Never mind The Pope, Barry McCann wanted to be the King of Sydney.

Add a raft of Melbourne criminals who'd drifted up the Hume Highway looking for trouble to this potentially explosive mix and The Team had every reason to be on their toes.

Mick Sayers had arrived in Sydney quietly and without a fuss in 1980. Sayers, a De La Salle College boy from a good Melbourne family, had done time for armed robbery. His family had been left stunned when the armed robbery squad had kicked down the doors of their Caulfield home and ordered them all on the ground face down. The cops handcuffed Mick and took him away. He was just 22 years old.

He had no priors, or at least nothing of any note that would make his mother and father conclude he was a gun-toting counter jumper, but he was remanded in custody and a jury found him guilty. He got eight years and spent every one of them adding to his criminal connections.

He was a good man on the punt and took up bookmaking in jail. He wasn't always popular with his fellow inmates, but he had a likable way about him and if anyone got into him for too much money, he was patient and generous with time. Some solution could always be found that was not too onerous for the jailhouse punter.

For a brief period in 1978, while in Pentridge's B Division, Sayers shared a cell with Christopher Dale Flannery. He, too, was doing time for armed robbery. Flannery was a good style of bloke. He'd had a legitimate job for a while working in the menswear section of David Jones at their Perth store. The managers thought so highly of him, they decided to promote him to a buying role.

That meant Flannery would be travelling back east on buying expeditions on the company coin. The only problem was that he had an outstanding warrant for his arrest for armed robbery in Victoria. Flannery declined the promotion, resigned his job and turned up the next day to rob the payroll.

He fled to Sydney and was arrested by none other than Roger Rogerson, then a detective inspector with the Armed Robbery squad. Rogerson described the arrest as the most violent of his career as a New South Wales police officer. This was saying something given that Rogerson had already shot and killed two men in the line of duty, and three years later would shoot dead another, Warren Lanfranchi.

Rogerson bundled Flannery back off to Victoria into the waiting arms of the Victoria Police force.

While both men languished in jail, Flannery made an admission that would lead to him becoming a notorious figure in the Sydney crime scene and ultimately lead to his premature death. 'I'm not very good at robbing banks, Mick. I think I'll kill people for a living.'

When Flannery was released, he put the hit man's shingle out. Rentakill. It was both his business and his nickname. For $50,000 he'd kill anybody. Pretty soon Flannery's business was booming.

Unlike the flamboyant Flannery, Mick Sayers eased quietly out of jail. There was nothing in Melbourne for him anymore. Always keen on a punt he took off for Sydney. His first thought was to set himself up as an SP there, but he quickly became aware of the labyrinthine nature of arrangements for anyone moving in on the established networks. There were people to pay off here, there and everywhere and George Freeman ran the lot. So he decided to get on the other side of the ledger and punt for a living.

Unfortunately, his jailhouse luck began to elude him on the outside and pretty soon he was in to George Freeman for a large sum. Sayers started bankrolling his losses by buying heroin from McCann. McCann extended credit for 72 hours, which allowed Sayers to buy the gear, jump on it with baby formula and sell it on at a profit. McCann got paid first because Sayers knew he was a violent bastard who would rather shoot than negotiate. As far as creditors were concerned, Freeman was next cab off the rank.

Before Mick Sayers knew it, he had a line of credit with Freeman for a million dollars. Sayers became known as the biggest punter in Sydney both to the rails bookies at the tracks and the SPs around town. He had a few big wins but they were invariably followed by some catastrophic losses. One step forward, three back.

Freeman had no idea about Sayers' heroin transactions and Mick planned to keep it that way. He didn't tell anybody, not even his girlfriend Marian Ware. If he got pinched with a kilo of smack, he'd go away for a long time.

He didn't know it then. He couldn't be expected to understand the intricate politics at play in the Sydney underworld. He just tried to run his own race but in doing so he put himself on the high wire, traversing two criminal organisations that would soon be at war.

Worse was to follow when Flannery made his way to Sydney. Flannery didn't have much choice about the trip. He was driven up by Victoria Police in handcuffs, handed over to the NSW Homicide squad and charged with the murder of a standover man named Ray Locksley. Locksley's body had been found in Menai in Sydney's south-west, with free air-conditioning. Two in the back of the head.

It's not often a bloke on a murder blue gets bail but Flannery managed it. It was Roger Rogerson to the rescue. Once he was released, The Dodger started showing Flannery around town, introducing him to all the best people.

Rogerson introduced 'Rentakill' to Len McPherson. Afterwards, The Big Man said he thought the dapper Flannery was 'a fuckin' real estate agent'.

Next thing, Flannery was appointed George's bodyguard. Fuck's sake, Mick thought, I wonder if they know what they've got on their hands?

Mick felt uneasy about it all. There was a shit storm looming. He could feel it. McCann was spoiling for a fight. Freeman and his mob considered themselves unstoppable. And now there was a homicidal psychopath running around offering to kill somebody, anybody, for 50 large.

Mick just needed one big payday and he'd be shot of the joint once and for all. Grab Marian, jet off and spend the rest of his life poolside on a banana lounge.

That wasn't too much to ask for, was it?

CHAPTER FIVE
Beautiful one day, perfect the next

'Joh delivered wealth and freedom to Queenslanders.'
— Bob Katter

It DIDN'T SEEM to matter how many politicians, cops, public servants or murderous thugs were exposed, investigated, prosecuted and incarcerated in the 1980s. Even at the time, as the crumbling facade of what passed for law and order north of the Tweed River was collapsing in a flaming ruin, in plain view and for all to see, it was a refrain you could hear from Cunnamulla to Carpentaria.

'Joh did a lot of good things for Queensland.'

You can still hear it said to this day. This is because Queenslanders are far and away the most gullible inhabitants of the Australian continent, a phenomenon born of a cultural delusion underpinning the preconceptions of just about everyone born between Caloundra and Cape York, and from Bundaberg to Birdsville.

In essence, Queenslanders have, since before federation, been brought up to consider themselves hard done by. Not only robbed blind and sold litters of pups by the federal government and other shady characters from south of the 29th parallel, but worse. Disrespected, unappreciated, mocked and ignored.

And, by virtue of a perverse logic that shapes the thinking of self-ostracised subgroups around the world, they somehow conflate their certainty into a heartfelt sense they are more genuinely Australian than anyone else in the nation with disgruntled separatist leanings, and so see southern Australia as a snake pit of conspiracy and deceit.

In Premier Joh Bjelke-Petersen's day in Brisbane, at any time one would see hoardings surrounding vast construction sites, proclaiming that the hideous developments rising from the debris within would provide 'Jobs for Two Thousand Queenslanders!'

There has never been, and never will be, a Sydney builder insisting that completion of his or her imminent edifice will result in gainful employment for 'Two Thousand New South Welshmen!'

And while it's true that every state other than New South Wales has its post-colonial ration of shoulder chips to carry about, none comes close to bearing the cross of abiding mistrust and wounded pride that underlies the Queensland psyche. This arrogant defensiveness manifests itself on sporting fields, in Rotary clubs, surf carnivals and public bars far and wide, but it has had its fullest flowering in the blood-drenched coliseum that is Queensland state politics.

It could be, and indeed is, argued that the electoral process in Queensland has become a shade more sophisticated in recent times. Some date the origins of this gradual transformation back to Brisbane's Expo 88, when the good burghers of the town finally had to deal realistically not only with Canberra, but cashed-up foreigners. Worldly, wealthy ones, and in large numbers.

Yet it was a far more revealing late-'80s exposition that displayed Queensland's political culture for what it was. The Fitzgerald Inquiry into Possible Illegal Activities and Associated Police Misconduct just down the road blew Expo out of the water for sheer entertainment value alone. It revealed what happens when self-made men want to make a hell of a lot more, and hop on board the bandwagon of Queensland's secessionist psychosis.

'Joh did a lot of good for Queensland,' because he said so, loud and often, right to the bitter end, and enough people believed him to make it almost indisputable. And back then, that was a lot of people. And although he's been disgraced, derided and dead for many moons, some people still believe it.

Joh could only have become a force to be reckoned with in Queensland. As it turns out, the man who was to personify the Queensland identity for decades was himself a ring-in. Johannes Bjelke-Petersen was born on Friday the 13th of January 1911 in the town of Dannevirke in New Zealand's North Island. The area had been settled in the 1870s by immigrants from Scandinavia and named after an ancient Viking fortress. The place burned to the ground when the pub caught fire in 1917.

But by then Joh's dad, Carl, a Lutheran pastor, had pulled up stumps and moved his family to Queensland, where they established a farm, 'Bethany', near the town of Kingaroy. It remained the Bjelke-Petersen manor for decades. Joh was eventually buried there in 2005.

The family was not well off. Carl was a sickly chap, and young Joh didn't have a great run health-wise either, coming down with polio as a kid, leaving him with a limp for the rest of his life. He left school at 14 to work on the farm, and by rights that should have been his lot.

But whatever else you make of the man, Joh Bjelke-Petersen wasn't afraid of hard work, and, despite the country bumpkin airs he was to later adopt as his public persona, was no fool. Impressed by muscle machinery from an early age, as soon as he could scrape the money together he bought himself a bulldozer, and then a second one. Realising that by stretching a heavy chain between the two, he and a mate could drive through virgin bush and flatten everything trapped between the dozers in a trice, he was soon doing a roaring trade in land clearing.

From then on, Joh was not one to let anything, or anyone, stand in his way. He planted peanuts, bought more heavy equipment, got his pilot's licence and went into the aerial crop-spraying caper. By the time of his 30th birthday, the Kingaroy Kid was a prosperous farmer and businessman.

In 1947, at the age of 36, he was elected as the Country Party member for the state seat of Nanango (later renamed Barambah, before reverting to Nanango, its current name). Perhaps in acknowledgement that the abbreviated form was causing distress to womenfolk, the Country Party decided to rebrand itself as the National Party in 1974.

In the 1980s Brisbane was rather unfairly derided as 'the biggest country town in Australia', but it's true that any cosmopolitan aspirations the population had were thwarted by a ruling class better suited to running remote rural shires than a state capital. This was no accident and was largely due to the most inequitable voting system to emerge in a western democracy outside of South Africa's apartheid.

Until 1949, Queensland had a 'one person, one vote, one value' electoral regime. The key words here, when thinking of what was to come, are 'one value'. Joh became the National Party member for Barambah until death, or until he'd had a gutful of it – whichever came first – based largely on a whopping gerrymander that gave the denizens of Barambah one vote, and approximately four values compared to the humble voters in Brisbane.

In the days before electoral boundaries were based on census data and determined by the Australian Electoral Commission, governments of the day had the power to declare not only the boundaries of the various electorates, but the number of voters in each one.

Each electorate had equal value, as in, one electorate elected one member of parliament, but if your electorate had a much bigger population than the one across the river, your vote was worth much less than the opinion of the bloke on the opposite bank.

The tactical redistribution of Queensland electorates for less than idealistic purposes began not, as later developments would suggest, with Joh's Country/National crowd, but with the Labor Party.

Back in 1949 Labor's electoral base sat largely in rural areas, so they decreed that electorates would be populated in inverse proportion to their proximity to Brisbane, ostensibly so that the long-suffering inhabitants of the bush would be compensated for their wretched lives by getting some decent roads, rail and refrigeration.

The ALP redrew the map, and by the time of the 1956 election, the results of their cartographic efforts were evident. The Brisbane suburban seat of Mount Gravatt had a voter enrolment of 26,307, while remote Charters Towers, west of Townsville, had all of 4367. In effect, a bloke at the public bar at the White Horse pub in Charters Towers had six votes to the one sucking suds at the Mansfield Hotel in Mount Gravatt. Labor romped home.

The by now well-ensconced MP for Nanango was outraged at this state of affairs, asserting in high dudgeon that 'the majority will be ruled by the minority', but as noted, Joh was no fool, and the opportunities that such manipulation presented were certainly not lost on him.

When Labor split under the weight of factional disputes, which extended from the Stalinist Left to the religious Right, and imploded in Queensland in 1957 forcing another state election after only a year, the Country Party took hold of many of these rural seats. Over time, by rolling out the maps and going to work with ruler and compass, they cemented in stone a very cosy arrangement indeed.

Labor, fighting as two separate parties, was annihilated in the '57 election.

Eleven years later Joh became premier and by the time of his 1972 victory the Country Party won just 20 per cent of the vote and claimed 26 seats, with their coalition partners, the Liberals, receiving 22.1 per cent for 21 seats, while Labor's massive 46.7 per cent garnered them only 33 seats in the House. The Country Party would remain in charge (as senior coalition partner with the Liberals) for 32 years. This, of course, was plenty of time for a serious rot to set in.

For a fellow who, in his teens, had spent the Sabbath teaching Sunday school to the wide-eyed kids of Kingaroy, the mature Bjelke-Petersen had a rather shaky grasp of the difference between right and wrong. That's not to say that he didn't have strong views on the subject, mind you. Protesting in the streets against Springbok rugby tours and inadequate education funding was wrong and had to be suppressed with the full force of the law, and far beyond the law if need be.

On the other hand, making fortunes from preferential share deals, as he was to do more than once, seemed utterly right. He regarded conflicts of interest as mere speed humps to gathering a vast personal wealth. Most famously, he determined to divest himself of a substantial pile of Comalco shares he'd picked up for a song before they started trading and doubled in value in 24 hours by simply handing them over to his wife, Flo. In Joh's mind it was simply good business sense.

Several members of Joh's cabinet felt much the same and didn't bother themselves overly with the minutiae of oversight, due process and transparency. Those who had any qualms kept their traps shut, took their pay cheques and concentrated on cutting ribbons, attending fetes and handing out bravery awards at their local surf lifesaving clubs.

Those who took Joh's 'Don't you worry about that' approach to high office literally did very well for themselves, and in this regard perhaps the most notorious of his various lieutenants was Russ Hinze.

Baby Russ burst into the world, fat and squealing, on 19 June 1919 in Oxenford on the Gold Coast, a neck of the woods that has produced and seduced more shameless spivs than just about anywhere else in Australia. Of course, in the days after World War I it had about as much in common with today's Gold Coast as Humpty Doo does now, and Russ started his working life cutting cane, before following his old man into dairy farming.

He made a decent fist of it, becoming chairman of the local dairy cooperative before being elected to the Albert Shire Council in the early 1950s, an outfit which he chaired in the '60s until being elected to parliament in 1966 as the Country Party member for South Coast.

He spent eight years as a backbencher, and in 1971 was part of a cabal plotting the ousting of Joh from the premiership. When it came to a vote, it was a tie, which Joh broke in the party room by voting for himself. But this act of treachery clearly didn't faze him. Perhaps he saw in Hinze a kindred spirit, or possibly Joh felt safer having Russ in the tent pissing out than copping a golden shower from some vast distance. Either way, before long Russ had stumbled into Joh's cabinet, where he was to stay until the ghastly end, firstly as Minister for Roads and Local Government, then Minster for Racing, and for a time as Minister for Police. In the early 1980s he held all three portfolios at once, so the gargantuan figure inevitably became known as the 'Minister for Everything'.

Russ learned a lot from Joh when it came to the fine art of dismissing criticism with a grunt and ducking and weaving curly questions, but unlike his boss's point-blank refusal to acknowledge any dodgy dealing as being problematic, he would brazenly contend that the alleged problem was in fact a solution.

When asked once whether it was fit and proper that he was the owner of several racehorses while also being the Minister for Racing, he shrugged it off by declaring that 'It isn't a conflict of interests, it's a convergence of interests.'

Conflict of interest or not, he certainly had his ear to the ground when it came to the punt. British TV interviewer Michael Parkinson once spent a remarkable day at the races with Mr Hinze, at the Magic Millions on the Gold Coast.

Years later, Parkinson remembered Big Russ as a fine fellow and great company, and his expansive host asking if he'd made any selections for wagering purposes. 'He then proceeded to go through the race book and marked five horses for the day. They all duly won, and I can tell you that it was a pleasure to meet a government minister who was truly on top of his portfolio.'

He was also the Minister for Roads (which, given his vast bulk, inevitably led to him being known as the Colossus of Roads), and he took a similarly laissez faire approach to this portfolio. He notoriously decreed that the dirt road leading to his rural property be paved and saw no need for subtlety when he issued the command. He didn't bother pretending that this work was for the benefit of the district – the road was paved only as far as his front gate, and there the bitumen ended. Further flung neighbours were to eat his dust for years afterwards.

Another tale, when first told, seemed a little far-fetched even for Russ, but he corroborated it himself on television years later. He'd been pulled over for speeding by a traffic cop on Brisbane's outskirts sometime in the early 1980s, and was in the process of being booked when he reached into the glovebox of his car and pulled out a map of Queensland. Slowly getting out of the vehicle – Russ never moved in a hurry – he stood beside the police officer and spread the map out on the car's bonnet.

The young cop stared at the large human in front of him. Clearly unaware of the grave risk his career as a police officer was under, he pressed on. 'What are you doing?'

Russ turned and looked the young cop in the eye before returning to the map and sliding an index finger along the border between Queensland and the Northern Territory.

'I'm just wonderin' what God forsaken shithole I'm going to transfer you to, son.'

The story, which did the rounds for years, was widely considered an apocryphal caricature of the man, until he was eventually asked about it on TV. Not only did he confirm the veracity of the report, he shrugged it off with 'Well, you'd think he'd have enough bloody brains to know his own minister, wouldn'ya?'

Some political scientists might see Joh's Queensland as a theocracy, with Joh as the high priest. Overtly, the old Lutheran streak of austerity, hard work and a profound distaste for the sins of the flesh and of moral weakness pervaded National Party politics in Queensland.

Joh and the Nationals introduced new laws with longer jail terms for any streetwalker trying to earn a quid or an SP bookie who would take a punter's bets. Queensland's jails filled to the brim shortly after Joh became premier and remained so until he left.

It was all for show, a piece of law-and-order deception which met with the approval of the broad National Party constituency who fretted about crime but rarely experienced it. The evils they read about from down south in those dens of iniquity in Sydney and Melbourne had no place in Queensland. They believed Joh would keep those wolves from their door. Good Christian folk need never have their gentle sensitivities provoked or challenged.

While there is much to chuckle about when looking back at the shenanigans of the Queensland ruling class of the time, the ugly fact remains that by the time Bold Personality was dripping wet paint and hair dye all over the mounting yard of Eagle Farm, Queensland had become, for all intents and purposes, a police state.

So fixated had Joh and his cabinet become on the maintenance of law and order, and protecting the populace from the twin evils of socialism and free speech, that they effectively gave the police force free rein to do whatever was necessary to keep the state of Queensland wholesome and family-friendly.

The inevitable result was that senior police, or at least a fair number of them, took this as carte blanche to do 'whatever was necessary' across the board, especially in relation to real crimes, like armed robbery, rape, murder – the things that are the day-to-day concerns of police forces everywhere.

The difference in Queensland at the time was that the cops were accountable to no-one except themselves. This didn't bother Joh. The way he saw it, the cops' job was to thwart villains. So long as Mr and Mrs National Voter felt safe in their beds at night, he didn't much care how the wallopers went about their work.

The fact that this work included standover tactics, protection rackets, the milking of illegal brothels and putting the hard word on SP bookies was neither here nor there, and in any case easily denied. And indeed, after years of denial and zero consequences, the arrangement settled into a cosy status quo of two Queenslands – the 'beautiful one day, perfect the next' Sunshine State, and the sleazy, violent Moonlight State graphically exposed in the *Four Corners* program of that name, and by relentless investigation by the *Courier-Mail*'s Phil Dickie.

In 1988, Joh was in the witness box at the Fitzgerald Royal Commission. Counsel assisting the commission, Michael Forde, sought answers from the Queensland Premier. What did Joh understand by the doctrine of the separation of powers in the Westminster system?

'The Westminster system? The stock?' Joh babbled in reply.

'The doctrine of the separation of powers under the Westminster system?' counsel repeated.

'No, I don't quite know what you're driving at. The document?'

'No, I'll say it again. What do you understand by the doctrine of the separation of powers under the Westminster system?'

'I don't know which doctrine you refer to.'

'There is only one doctrine of the separation of powers.'

'I believe in it very strongly, and despite what you may say, I believe that we do have a great responsibility to the people who elect us to government. And that's to maintain their freedom and their rights, and I did that, sought to do it always.'

'I'm sure you're trying to be responsive to the question, but the question related to the doctrine of the separation of powers or the principles,' Forde added patiently.

Joh's brow furrowed, and he squirmed in his seat. 'Between the government and the . . . is it?'

'No, you tell me what you understand.'

'Well, the separation of the doctrine that you refer to, in relation to where the government stands, and the rest of the community stands, or where the rest of the instruments of government stand. Is that what . . .?'

'No.'

'Well, you tell me. And I'll tell you whether you're right or not. Don't you know?'

Joh hadn't the faintest idea about the doctrine of separation of powers in the Westminster system. He regarded this high tenet of a free and fair democracy a pointless detail; so pointless, in fact, that after 20 years as premier, he hadn't bothered to make its acquaintance, in theory let alone practice.

The bluster and bullshit that had served Joh so well for two decades wasn't cutting it anymore. Humiliated, he completed his evidence. Having perjured himself on at least three occasions, he was finally exposed as a crook, a shonk and a devious simpleton.

As he waded through the media throng outside the court, roughly ignoring the increasingly urgent questions of reporters, one bystander enjoyed a brief flirtation with fame when he asked Joh if he was aware of criminal proceedings going on in one of the adjoining courtrooms, where one of Joh's ministers, Don Lane, was staring down the barrel of a long stretch in prison.

Joh looked towards the heckler, perhaps expecting a compliment or at least some expression of sympathy from a fellow Queenslander. He got none.

'You're fuckin' next,' the bystander shouted, and the mob burst out laughing.

Alas, Joh was not quite next to stand in the dock, but it did come in 1991 when he was tried for perjury. Happily for Joh, the jury was unable to reach a unanimous verdict, due in large part to the presence of a former member of the Young Nationals on the panel. Joh walked and a retrial was considered a step too far for someone of his advanced years.

Democracy in Queensland had been defenestrated, and left a bloody, amorphous blob on the footpath 14 storeys below.

In reality, Joh's notion of government was a study in Machiavellian practicalities. The cabinet tacitly acknowledged that those who came from down south, or indeed from other points of the globe, to bask in the Queensland sun would need more than a choice of banana lounges pool side. What tourists wanted was a drink, a bet and a root.

The grim realisation from good Christian men that humanity was fixated on a reckless pursuit of the illicit must have left them shaken, but only momentarily. There was a solution and it was a simple one. The cops would run it. They already controlled liquor licensing, so they could stand over brothels and turn a blind eye to the illegal casinos, provided the criminal entrepreneurs weighed in at the end of the day. Meanwhile, the politicians, with Joh and Big Russ at the helm, would pretend none of these sordid businesses existed.

As it turned out, the wages of sin would pay handsomely. In the dark parlance of the cops, the black money bonanza became known as 'The Joke', a complex network of bribery and pay-offs to cops to look the other way. Any police officer who showed any investigative zeal and abiding sense of justice was quickly transferred to the boondocks, where they would cast an eye across thousands of hectares of western Queensland nothingness and contemplate where it all went wrong.

In time The Joke would produce another shadowy moniker, 'The Rat Pack', a reference to a quartet of cops who sat at the pointy end of The Joke and enjoyed the lion's share of the largesse. The source of the appellation is unclear, but it paid due reverence to the talents of the Vegas cabaret stars, as if Dean Martin, Sammy Davis Junior, Peter Lawford and Frank Sinatra had secretly run a pyramid marketing scheme.

The Queensland Rat Pack showed no particular musical ability and even less for the bright lights of stardom, that is if we don't count the oddly well-luminated entrance to 142 Wickham Street, Fortitude Valley – the casino run by Geraldo Bellino, which anyone in the Bjelke-Petersen government from Joh down would swear blind didn't exist.

Jack Herbert was the bag man kicking bribe money from Bellino and a hundred other pimps and bludgers up to the bosses – Assistant Commissioner Tony Murphy, Detective Sergeant Glen Hallahan, and the boss of bosses, Chief Commissioner Terry Lewis. Herbert eschewed the traditional method of conveyance – cash in a brown paper bag, preferring the more distinctive gold-coloured manila envelope fit to burst with the bounty of extortion and bribery.

The Rat Pack would find these envelopes in the strangest of places. Sometimes in their lockers, or in drawers in their offices they had believed were locked shut, or sometimes sitting in the glovebox of their cars. One time, Lewis returned home to find an envelope in his sock drawer. Herbert may have moved in mysterious ways, but the money arrived on time, every time.

By 1984, the pot had grown larger on two counts. The bribes were getting bigger by the year. Herbert was a master at extortion and had worked his way through every criminal racket going, spreading the net wider and wider. Murphy and Hallahan had moved in to comfortable retirements. Lewis remained in the top job. He was the last man standing and his cut was bigger than ever before.

Terence Lewis was in his eighth year as Chief Commissioner of the QPS. He had so much power at his fingertips, he was able to elbow troublesome police ministers out of the way. On Lewis's recommendations, Joh replaced them almost as often as he changed his underpants. Even Hinze, who Joh thought might be a good fit, was given his marching orders as Police Minister in 1982. Lewis had found the big man a little too hands-on for his liking, and in one of his private meetings with the Premier demanded the Minister for Everything become the Minister for Almost Everything. Joh obliged.

National Party powerbroker Sir Edward Lyons was parachuted in to chair the Queensland TAB. He doled out agency licences to ex-cops looking to put their feet up after careers on the take, giving them cash businesses and the opportunity to launder a little black money on the sly. The National Party ran the tote, the cops ran the bookies and the punters could get fucked.

Joh handed out knighthoods in the manner of a feudal lord, so much so that even shifty property developers, who quietly planned to cut out the sun from the white sand beaches of the Gold Coast, could demand the public refer to them in the honorific.

Almost any National Party apparatchik with a law degree was handed a judge's wig and gown. Thus, the nexus between the legislative, executive and judicial branches of government drew tighter.

The Queensland Police Service served itself and its political masters only. In time it became little more than a paramilitary wing of the National Party. The moral turpitude sank deep into the morale of the cops. Even the good ones found the normal business of police work had become a bothersome chore.

Police officers from other states seconded to duty in Queensland would leave mouths agape, hurrying back home to tell tales of astonishing investigative ineptitude to their colleagues, who shook their heads in disbelief.

One federal cop who'd been attached to the Queensland Armed Robbery Squad was on the hunt for a gang of armed robbers who'd been sticking up banks and payrolls down the east coast of Australia for years. The counter-jumpers in question directed their attention and loaded their guns for another heist, a hefty cash payroll from Royal Brisbane Hospital.

The masked bandits had done their thing, scaring the hell out of payroll clerks, barking orders and waving sawn-off shotguns about. They gathered the cash and made their way out of the hospital grounds on foot. The wallopers had got wind of the stick-up and, under the watchful eye of their federal colleague, set up a cordon around the area.

When the gang raced to their stolen getaway car, they saw two police officers waiting for them, gormlessly checking the vehicle out, peering in through the windows. This was only a minor setback as the leader of the gang stuck his shotgun under the chin of one of the officers, purloined his sidearm and then helped himself to the cop's unmarked car nearby.

When the federal copper got to the scene, he discovered the abandoned getaway car contained a few pieces of crucial evidence, including a copy of a *Soldiers of Fortune* magazine with a price sticker revealing not just its cost but its place of purchase – a newsagent in Noosa Heads.

The federal copper had it in mind to drive straight up to the Sunshine Coast with a couple of members of the squad in tow in the hope that a shopkeeper might identify the gang. Normal police detective work, one might think.

But the armed robbery squad was having none of that. The fact that one of their own was a firearm short, and that firearm was now in the hands of a dangerous and violent man, caused only minor concern. They'd get around to it. In the fullness of time. All things being equal. Instead, the squad decided to pull up stumps for the day and head to the pub for the remainder of the afternoon to drown their sorrows, adding this episode to a long list of the ones that got away.

Reluctant at first, the fed joined in and ended up horrifically drunk. It would be another seven years and numerous armed hold-ups later before the gang and its leader were finally arrested. It should come as no surprise to learn the villains were placed in handcuffs in another jurisdiction by police detectives not known for their willingness to walk off the job.

In Queensland policing, corruption in high places had bred inertia elsewhere. Even wallopers who'd never had to countenance taking a backhander knew how The Joke worked. When it came to serious villainy, the QPS was just going through the motions. In a systemically corrupt environment, what was the point of putting yourself on the line? Why do the hard yards? What was the point of anything?

In Joh's Queensland, detractors were ushered quietly out the door, driven to the Tweed, told to get out and keep on walking. Those who promised to spill the beans simply disappeared or were found face down with a belly full of barbiturates.

So, if you were considering pulling off a blatant, hare-brained race ring-in anywhere in Australia, where would you do it?

There really is no other place. Career fraudster John Gillespie, an expert at identifying marks and with a keen sense of recognising vulnerabilities, knew it had to be Queensland. Where else but Queensland could you find the Minister for Racing, the Police Commissioner, the stewards and the cops all on the take? Where else but Queensland could you find a brace of racing authorities who were more likely to get on your horse than get on with their work?

Put it this way, when asked about his role, if any, in the Fine Cotton affair on television years later, one Russell James Hinze,

Queensland's Minister for Racing in 1984, simply shrugged and said, 'By the time I got wind of it, the thing was paying 6/4, so I didn't bother.'

That was at least one that got away, to hear Russ tell it. Maybe, just maybe, he really didn't throw money at the painted pony after all, and if so, all the better for him as, like everybody else, he would never have been able to collect.

CHAPTER SIX
One jail to another

'Someone's gonna get knocked over this.'
– John Gillespie

Brisbane, March 1984

TO THE CRIMINAL ear, there is no sweeter note struck by any orchestra on earth than the 'clank!' of a prison door being slammed shut. Provided, of course, that the listener is hearing it from outside the concert hall.

Gillespie heard the happy onomatopoeic clatter as he walked through the gates of Boggo Road a free man. He had plans. Big plans. He had some cash hidden away in a bank account he kept under a false name. He could kickstart the whole thing and make himself a fortune. He had Mick Sayers' phone number and a trainer in Hayden Haitana he would have do his dirty work.

His first port of call was the George Hotel in Brisbane where he sank six beers, one after the other. The barmaid stood at the jump, deeply impressed, and kept pulling the XXXX while Gillespie guzzled away. Not one of those six middies hit the sides and his thirst remained unquenched. It was only on his seventh beer that he took a sip and a look around.

He eyed the barmaid and gave her a smile. He could do with a root. Being banged up with Pat Haitana was not exactly conducive to a healthy male libido. In Boggo Road, he'd sometimes knock the top off it late at night over a couple of young sheilas that leered at him from a dog-eared copy of *Penthouse* while Pat snored in the top bunk.

Vive l'amour.

Gillespie wondered briefly what the barmaid's life savings might amount to. Four-fifths of fuck all, probably.

He was wasting time. His dick would have to stay in his pants. There were buttons to be pushed, marks to be conned, money to be made. He had a job to do. A mix of business and pleasure anyway.

One of the numerous terms and conditions of Gillespie's parole was that he was not permitted to cross state borders without obtaining permission from the wallopers. Fuck that, he thought. He'd served his time.

Gillespie hit up one of his old mates in the used-car caper and got himself an old rust bucket for a couple of hundred, cash in hand. The vehicle was registered in the name of Lee Falk, in homage to the cartoon Phantom's creator; the residential address, 449 Vulture Street, Woolloongabba, the location of the cricket ground and accompanying greyhound track that bore the abbreviated form of the Brisbane suburb's name. If the cops came sniffing around, they'd have to get past Greg Chappell and Allan Border first.

Gillespie had a keen eye for cars and he knew this old HZ Holden would do the job. It wasn't pretty. Point A to B. That was all he needed. If he played his cards right, in six months he'd be driving around in a Roller.

He filled the old car full of petrol and took off out of Brisbane. He wound the window down and fiddled with the dials on the radio. The racing station popped up with a gravel-voiced tipster offering his guide to the day's races. Gillespie listened for long enough to get the track conditions before turning the dial of the radio again.

A clash of electric guitars and screaming vocals immediately reverberated in the car. Gillespie recognised the tune but not well enough to name the song. Years later he'd learn it was an AC/DC track, 'Riff Raff', and he'd come to regard it as something of a personal anthem. He hadn't the faintest idea what the song was about, but he imagined it was biographical, a rags-to-riches story about him and a two-fingered salute to all the pricks who'd tried to tell him he was the shit under their shoes.

He couldn't sing along: Bon Scott sang fast and hard and Gillespie couldn't keep up. For now, it was loud, and loud was good. He shot down the Pacific Highway, his foot growing heavier on the accelerator as the Young brothers, Angus and Malcolm, went to town.

Gillespie looked into the rear-view mirror at the Brisbane cityscape disappearing on the horizon. He'd be back soon enough, and when he got there he'd tear the place apart.

He just wished more people would call him The Phantom.

The Northern Rivers' city of Grafton, bisected by the Clarence River, is home to 20,000 people. It remains one of the few regional spots yet to suffer the indignity of being by-passed by the new Pacific Highway, although it is coming and with it one imagines a fairly significant loss to the city's income and reputation.

Today humble tourists might consult the internet guide, Trip Advisor, and find things to do in town. Truth be told, there isn't much. A park, an art gallery and a performing arts theatre pock mark the takeaways, bakeries and the pubs spruiking their counter lunches. Standard country fare. The beach at Yamba is an hour's drive away.

In 1984, there were only two reasons one might travel to Grafton, to go to the races or to go to jail. Back then HM Grafton Gaol was a relic of Australia's 19th-century prison system. It was a place of institutionalised evil. Grafton was reserved for the worst of the worst, prisoners deemed by corrective services authorities as 'intractable'.

Behind its grim brick walls, inmates who the system had yet to break would undergo the reception biff, referred to in bleak humour as 'The Jacaranda Festival', a nod to the trees that lined the entrance to the jail and offered up their stark purple blooms in spring, a colour not dissimilar to an equally vivid shade of purple that bursts through human tissue after a bashing.

The intractables would stand in line and be set upon by prison officers with batons. Bashed, smashed and bloodied, they'd be hurled into their cells semi-conscious or sometimes semi-comatose. Welcome to Grafton.

This rough introduction would be the first of many beatings. If a prisoner died, and many did, no-one seemed to care much, and the fatality would be casually explained away as another unfortunate trip and fall accident. Oopsy-daisy.

Locals would drive past its walls daily, going from one place in town to another, from south to north across the bridge. They rarely looked at the slammer and barely gave what went on behind its walls a moment's thought.

It was only at night, lying in their beds, that Grafton's residents might have had cause to reflect they shared their town not only with the most violent prisoners in the state but also that many of those shanghaied to Grafton Gaol had shown a particular talent for escaping lawful custody.

If they thought about it for long enough, they would shift uneasily under the blankets knowing that anyone who scaled the walls of Grafton might well be inclined to extract a terrible revenge on society in general, and Grafton's residents were nice and handy.

Career criminal and peerless escapologist Darcy Dugan had been a resident at Grafton for almost a decade of the 35 years in total he spent as a guest of Her Majesty. He'd escaped so often from Long Bay Correctional Centre in Sydney that prison guards there had almost become accustomed to peering into his cell and finding only a note Dugan had left. 'Gone to Gowings' was his trademark mockery, a colloquial phrase referring to the gentlemen's tailors in the Sydney CBD as a metaphor for a departure in haste.

But even Dugan found it impossible to escape from Grafton Gaol. The only inmate who did was Ray Denning in 1981. Denning had bashed a guard, Will Farber, half to death at Parramatta Gaol with a claw hammer while attempting to escape. Farber suffered a severe brain injury but remained alive for more than a year before he died from his injuries.

Denning evaded a murder charge as a result but was handed an extended sentence for the attempted escape and the bashing of Farber. A year later, he fled custody from Maitland Gaol with a group of criminals. After being recaptured two days later, Denning was pronounced intractable and sent to Grafton.

News of the bashing of Farber preceded him, and Denning's Jacaranda Festival was worse than most. He suffered a bashing at Grafton almost every day and the increasing severity of each thump of the baton convinced the other inmates that Denning had to get out or he would be beaten to death.

The plot to escape from what was supposed to be an escape-proof prison was a fairly simple one. Denning was hidden in a crate of combustible waste and he remained hidden until the crate was taken outside to the prison's incinerator. Once outside the walls, Denning emerged and took off. He remained on the run for 18 months before being recaptured in Sydney, using his time at large to press for prison reform.

Denning took to the media. He was a regular on Sydney's 2JJ while on the lam and famously plastered a letter of demand to close Grafton Gaol onto the front door of NSW Police headquarters in Sydney, along with his grimy handprint to convince the wallopers of his authorship.

Under public pressure, the gaol was shut down as a home for New South Wales' intractables in 1991.

Hayden drove across the Grafton Bridge with his brother alongside him on the way to the track. The town was only vaguely familiar to Hayden and he took a wrong turn, perhaps drawn by the street name, Hoof Street, which took them on an uneasy drive past Grafton Gaol. The easy conversation between the two brothers came to a sudden pause as Hayden's old F100 rolled past the brown brick edifice.

They'd both been in the clink. Boggo Road was a shithole, an ugly hub of arse rape and reckless violence, but Grafton was something else. Both men shuddered involuntarily. There but for the grace of God. They remained in silence until Hayden spotted a left-hand turn, took it and sped off.

Hayden and Pat Haitana had not seen each other since Pat had got out of jail in February. They'd embraced awkwardly minutes earlier on the platform at Grafton Station, smiled at each other and walked off to the car park.

Pat had been doing track work at Eagle Farm and Doomben, making a few dollars getting up at sparrow's fart and riding anything that was going. A couple of trainers looked after him and gave him rides.

He was desperate to get a ride at a city meet, or in the country – anywhere – but like Gillespie, he was still on parole. Unlike Gillespie, Pat Haitana took the conditions of his parole seriously. He had no plans to return to Boggo Road anytime soon.

He was still living in a halfway house at Wooloowin in Brisbane's east. He didn't have to stay there anymore but it was cheap and just a stroll down the road to the track. He'd asked his parole officer if it was okay to travel down to Grafton and was assured that it was.

The only caveat was that he had to avoid the company of other criminals. That was not going to be easy, given his brother's antecedents and harder still considering the man they were going to meet, John Gillespie, was on world-record pace with his rap sheet.

'What's this bloke's name?' Hayden asked.

'Gillespie. John Gillespie. They call him The Phantom. But he ain't no crime fightin' hero.'

'What was he in for?'

'Armed rob, mate.'

'I don't want to have anything to do with guns, Pat.'

'No, no. He's not a gunnie. The armed rob was a one off. Y'know, wrong place, wrong time. The silly prick tripped over outside the bank, the cash fell out of the bag and was swirlin' around in the wind. People came from everywhere, helping themselves. The cops only got a 10th of it back.'

They both laughed at the thought of it.

'No, he's a horseman,' Pat said. 'Buys and sells 'em, mate. Good punter. Makes things happen.'

'Oh, well,' Hayden replied. 'It couldn't hurt to hear him out.'

By the time they got to the track, Gillespie was already at the bar. He marched up to the two brothers and introduced himself. He shook hands with Pat without taking his eyes off Hayden.

He peeled his hand out of Pat's and stuck it straight out to Hayden, so close it bounced off his belly. 'John Gillespie, mate. They call me The Phantom.'

Hayden burbled out a greeting, a clumsy portmanteau of Gillespie's name and nickname. 'Phantomjohn.'

'Come and meet Wendy, Hayden. She's a top sheila and she'll back you up in a stink.'

Hayden knew the blonde-haired Wendy Smith. She was a part-time trainer like Hayden. Had a property in Coffs, not far from his own. He'd seen her around the traps.

Gillespie got a round in and the quartet held the easy conversation one sees with any racing folk at any racetrack, discussing their fancies on the eight-race card.

Wendy and Hayden both liked horse four, race five, Winter Burn. Smith shared a little gossip on the horse that further convinced him it was the bet of the day.

'Freshened up then beaten favourite last start, but goes well second up. It'll go close today,' Smith said.

'I told ya, Hayden. She's a good 'un,' Gillespie said, placing his arm over Smith's shoulder.

Smith downed her glass of Coke and pecked Gillespie on the cheek. 'I'm going to have a look around. You boys going to still be here in half an hour?'

Gillespie rolled his eyes. It was the only bar at the track. Where else would they be? 'Yeah, darlin'. We'll be here.'

She turned and left, her blonde curls bouncing gently on her shoulders with each step. Gillespie's eyes stared at her backside as she made her way out of the bar. 'Bloody good sort,' he said to himself before turning back to catch the eye of his former cellmate, Pat Haitana.

Gillespie took a swig from his beer and got down to business. He spoke quickly and softly to Hayden, ignoring Pat, who felt obliged to look away and turn his attention to the television in the corner.

'I haven't told your brother, but I've got a little lurk running. You wouldn't have any moral qualms about joining in with me, would ya?'

Hayden shook his head.

'Wendy will look after the ringer. You look after the plodder. They'll be identical. I'll make sure of that. You race the plodder, give it a few starts and make sure it runs in the back of the field. Run the odds down before we run it in Brisbane. I'll have the stewards and the cops sweet. Nothin' like a hot tip to keep them out of our way.'

Hayden was nodding throughout. It all seemed reasonable. It was hardly a new idea, but the fact Gillespie had the stewards on board was a bonus. Like any racing man, Hayden understood the bent nature of the sport in Queensland.

'Mick Sayers – you know him?' Gillespie asked Hayden.

'Never heard of him.'

'Mick's puttin' up the cash. It's his go. He's a serious bloke, you know what I mean?'

Again, Gillespie intimated that there were things he expected Haitana should know and seemed disappointed that he did not.

In time, Haitana would learn this was Gillespie's manner. Gillespie would control the conversation by ending almost every sentence he uttered with a question that could not be answered any other way than in the negative. It was his way of establishing power, what Gillespie called climbing the mountain of no's until he got the no he wanted.

'Put it this way, mate. He's not the sort of bloke you'd want to stand between and a bucket of money. You wouldn't want to be that poor bastard, would ya?'

Haitana shook his head again.

'You'll be on Mick's payroll. Twenty grand cash on completion. Win, lose or falls over and dies at the 400, you get paid. You're not the sort of bloke who'd turn down an opportunity like that, are ya, mate?'

Haitana had to say no. Ironically it would be the last time he ever said no to John Gillespie. They shook hands again and Gillespie got another round in.

Winter Burn won the fifth in a canter paying 4/1. They all had a win. Smith walked back from the betting ring with what turned out to be $500 in 50s and 20s, which she fanned out extravagantly. She folded the wad and placed it in her pocket before grabbing at Gillespie's arse and giving it a good squeeze.

Gillespie turned and looked at her, feigning outrage before giving the broadest of smiles. Looked like he was going to get a root after all.

The following month, Gillespie purchased a sprinter named Dashing Soltaire for $10,000. The dark chocolate brown five-year-old had Group Two wins in Sydney and Melbourne. He had the horse transported to Wendy Smith's modest stables in Coffs Harbour.

She was delighted that Gillespie had given her charge of the horse. It may not have been the best she had trained, but it was close.

'It needs a spell before we race it,' Gillespie told her, spitting out words at a ferocious pace and brooking no interruption. 'Set it up in that big paddock of yours and let it rest up. Come May, get it back in track work, get it fit. We'll let it loose in Brisbane in August. You get it cherry ripe and it could win us the Doomben Ten Thousand.'

Smith knew the five-year-old would be hard pressed to win the 1200 metre weight-for-age Group One sprint, but she was accustomed to Gillespie's excited hyperbole. Dashing Soltaire was a good horse and preparing it for Queensland winter carnival would be both a pleasure and a challenge to her training skills. She thought she could get it to salute at the ledger a couple of times at least.

She had no idea that Dashing Soltaire was Gillespie's ringer which, of course, was just the way Gillespie wanted it. She earnestly went about her task, tending to the horse for months, resting it up, controlling its food intake before saddling it up and letting it gallop and feel its muscles stretch.

She rode it herself at the track. Dawn starts had never bothered her. Afterwards she would take the horse down to the beach and let it wade through the surf before Dashing Soltaire would wander back to the shore. She'd drop the reins and the horse would collapse and roll and rollick in the sand, a gritty, grainy self-administered shiatsu.

A month later it was fit to race. When she let it unwind on the hard Coffs Harbour track, it ran 1200 metres in a minute, 15 seconds. A professional jockey on its back would shave at least another five seconds off that time.

Gillespie had set up house in Murwillumbah in a rental property out of town. He'd drive down to Coffs Harbour a couple of times a month to have a look at Dashing Soltaire and bounce around on a mattress with the trainer.

In one post-coital moment in July, Smith offered what she hoped would please Gillespie. 'It's ready,' she said. 'It's time to give our boy a run.'

'Not yet,' Gillespie said, pulling his trousers on. 'The connections want to hold it back.'

'What connections? You're the bloody connections.'

Gillespie looked around the room and found his polo shirt where he'd left it in a crumpled heap at the foot of the bed. He pulled it over his head and fiddled with the buttons before deciding not to button up. He was about to do a runner.

'I'm just a partner. Equal share with another bloke and he wants to hold it back. We live in a democracy, you know.'

A minute later and he was out the door.

Two weeks after Gillespie had bought Dashing Soltaire, he came across a horse that was the perfect match. At first he thought there must be some shortcoming, some ghastly marking, some awful imperfection. He circled the horse, time and time again, scrutinising the horse at almost a cellular level.

The horse's owners, a middle-aged couple, imagined the man was something of a connoisseur of horse flesh, an equine savant, such were the rigours of his examination.

They had enjoyed watching their horse get around a few country meets with little luck and no success. It had become their hobby, and this was their hobby horse. But they had finally grown tired of the early starts, the long drives to racetracks and the even longer drives home, lighter in the pocket and never a trophy to show for it. The gelding was old now, too old for racing. They had to put him on the market.

'He's eight years old now. Past his best. We've retired him.'

'Oh, I'm not going to race him,' the man said still circling the horse, eyes going back and forth, up and down. 'I just want him for the missus. She loves riding around the farm. We lost her old mare last month. Colic. She was heartbroken. This bloke could make a very nice birthday present.'

'He's a lovely horse. Beautiful nature.'

'Tell you what. I'll give you a grand, right now.'

The owners couldn't believe their luck. A good price and a good home for their beloved.

'There's just one proviso. Can you get him down to Coffs Harbour in the next week or so?'

The owners certainly could and gladly accepted the man's cheque.

'Thank you, erm, Mr Falk,' the husband said glancing at the name on the cheque.

'My pleasure. I'll scribble down the address.'

The man the owners believed to be Mr Falk made his way back to his HZ Holden. It was not the car of a wealthy landowner, but he seemed nice, and knowing their horse was off to live out the rest of his days on a farm was everything they could have hoped for.

'What did you say his name was?'

'Fine Cotton,' the wife replied.

'Fine Cotton. I like that. The missus is going to be rapt.'

A week later, after Mr Falk's cheque was banked, the couple drove off to Coffs Harbour with Fine Cotton bouncing around in the float behind them. They delivered the horse to a Mr Hayden Haitana, who Mr Falk had said was going to stable it until Mr Falk's wife's birthday.

Mr Haitana lived in a decrepit house, his backyard a cemetery for old banged-up cars and clapped-out tractors. He smelled vaguely of beer and more conspicuously of cigarettes, but the couple noted his stables were clean. More importantly, he obviously had a way with horses.

They saw this when they pulled down the back of the float and eased the animal out. Mr Haitana approached Fine Cotton and stroked the neck of the horse, and the dark chocolate brown gelding nuzzled Haitana's beery shirt. Haitana murmured sweet nothings into Fine Cotton's ear.

It was love at first sight.

Fine Cotton's retirement from racing was short-lived. The eight-year-old was back racing in July. Haitana got it fit, fitter than it had ever been, so fit in fact that by the time it had its comeback race, it was exhausted and finished last.

This was exactly what Gillespie had demanded.

The punters had given Fine Cotton a wide berth. In a field of has-beens and never-would-bes, he started in the betting markets at 25/1 and dropped out to 33s by the time the mediocre field jumped.

Hayden had been on board ever since he'd clasped Gillespie's hand at Grafton. His brother was not. Pat had decided to give the ring-in and Gillespie a big swerve. After their win on Winter Burn, the brothers got on the piss, ate pizza and babbled drunkenly, a wild mix of childhood anecdotes, scrubbed up to exclude the more painful memories of a drunken, violent father and their extravagant dreams and fantasies of Cox Plate rides and Derby wins.

The next morning the two brothers were nursing economy-size hangovers. Pat took the opportunity to declare his hand and deal himself out. 'Mate, I can't do this. I have to keep out of trouble. I want to ride again. Boggo Road – I'm never going to go back there again.'

Hayden understood. He drove his brother back to the station early that morning. He was on his own.

Gillespie had a talent for making Hayden think the trainer was out there all on his own, heavily exposed, taking all the risk. The Sydney gangster, the serious bloke, Sayers, was mentioned time and time again.

Gillespie would mutter darkly, painting ugly pictures of Sayers' homicidal instincts and abiding love of inflicting pain. The nightmarish threats only grew when Gillespie added another bogeyman into the mix, Sayers' mate Chris Flannery.

'Ever heard of Chris Flannery, mate? Rentakill, they call him. He's a real piece of work. He'd clip you just for practice.'

Haitana might have suspected Gillespie was revving him up, except for one thing.

Back in April, the Wollongong-based trainer George Brown had been found incinerated in his car at the top of Bulli Pass. He'd been tortured, his legs and arms broken. A gallon or so of petrol had been tipped over his car. Haitana didn't know if the poor bloke had died before the flames engulfed him. He only hoped the bastards that knocked him had done the right thing and put him out of his misery before the fire took hold.

It was the big story around racing up and down the east coast, and even though Haitana was head down, arse up training Fine Cotton to within an inch of its life, he'd heard the gossip.

The story went that Brown, an honest type, had fallen in with some Sydney heavies who'd put it on him to pull a ring-in. Brown was tempted initially. Or was subject to crude and violent forms of persuasion.

His ex-wife, Rose, later told investigators that in late March he'd been offered 'big money' to ring-in one of his horses at a Brisbane meeting, but that he wouldn't say who, or what meeting. The horse to be switched was named Risley, and the meeting was the one held at Doomben just two days before what was left of George was found incinerated in Bulli.

The parallels with Fine Cotton are striking. Risley had pretty ordinary lead-up form, to say the least, having placed last in its two previous runs, in Wollongong and Canberra. But when it jumped at Doomben, it was at the unlikely odds of 12/1, shortening to 8/1, and interestingly, as low as 4/1 in the Illawarra. Risley ran true to form, or to give him his due, slightly better. He came second last.

The ring-in hadn't happened. George Brown had baulked at the last minute.

So who tortured him to death and set him alight two days after his horse strolled lazily across the Doomben finish line? It's hard not to assume it was the nameless fellows he'd mentioned to his wife, the blokes who'd told him to put a decent racehorse in Risley's colours, only to discover that he'd not 'done as he was told'.

They weren't after money by this point. That was long lost. History. Why the brutality, the ghastly, relentless torture they put him through? Well, it certainly put the frighteners on anyone else who might get an offer that they would otherwise have refused. So they turned him into the contents of one of Haitana's overflowing ashtrays.

Sayers, or the other prick, Rentakill, didn't get a mention in the racetrack chatter but it was no stretch of Haitana's imagination to put the two murderous gangsters at the scene: Sayers going to work on George Brown with a cricket bat while the other bloke lit a match.

Whenever Haitana had an argument with Gillespie, the con artist would end it with a swift brutal reply. 'Don't forget Georgie Brown, mate.'

Come late July, Haitana and Gillespie were arguing almost constantly. Gillespie was always wanting more out of Fine Cotton, another run here, another there. As of 1 August – the birthday for all horses in the southern hemisphere – Fine Cotton officially turned nine years of age.

It had had six starts in the previous 18 days. It hadn't run a drum, but the harsh business of racing would eventually take its toll.

'People will think I'm a fuckin' slave-master, Phant,' Haitana said. 'It's not right, mate.'

'Get him in at Bundamba next week. We're almost there.'

'What comes after Bundamba? What's next? There's always something.'

'Don't forget Georgie Brown, sunshine.'

'Listen, you tell your fuckin' gangster mate, I don't give a fuck what happens, we can't keep racing the old horse like this. It'll keel over and die in the straight.'

'Come on, mate. Give us one more.'

Gillespie had been in contact with Mick Sayers, although not quite as often as he'd led Hayden to believe.

In fact, by the time Fine Cotton jumped at Bundamba, he'd only spoken to Sayers once over the telephone. It was the early evening, not too late when Sayers would answer tired and irritable, nor too early when he thought Mick might still be out and about. He plonked a couple of coins into the public phone and dialled the number from The Courthouse pub in Murwillumbah.

Gillespie had practised his spiel on the drive to the pub. He had to sound commanding. In charge.

The phone rang three times before it picked up. A gruff voice answered. 'Yeah.'

'Aw, g'day, is that Michael – Mick Sayers?'

'Who's this?'

'Yeah, g'day Mick. My name's Pat Haitana. I did a stretch up here in Brisbane. Bertie Kidd and I got on like a house on fire. He told me you might be interested in a thing we got going here. You and him bein' good mates.'

'Bertie runs his own race and I run mine.'

'Oh yeah. Good man in a blue, I know. But he told me to get hold of you and tip you in.'

'Tip me in to what?'

'We got a little switcheroo going at Eagle Farm next week. We're running it in an improvers and maiden's race. Fine Cotton will win.'

'Never heard of it.'

'That's the beauty of it, Mick. We're ringin'-in Dashing Soltaire for Fine Cotton. You should see the two of them together. Peas in a pod.'

Mick had heard of Dashing Soltaire. He'd backed it each way in the Epsom Handicap two years ago at Royal Randwick. It ran second at long odds. Mick had a good day on the back of Dashing Soltaire's late run through the pack. Not great, but better than break even. Dashing Soltaire might even have won it had the fuckin' dwarf on its back given it a bit of curry before the turn.

'When's this?'

'Next Saturday at Eagle Farm. I'll give you a bell with the details a couple of days beforehand.'

'I can read a form guide.'

'Do you want me to –'

'You ring me three days before the race. You say yes or no. We don't need to have a conversation, right. Yes or no.'

'Righto. Will do.'

'And if it's yes, you have a thousand on it for Bertie.'

'No worries, Mick. I was thinkin' of doin' that already.'

'Don't think about it. Just fuckin' do it.'

Gillespie had more to say and was about to say it when he heard the click and the line go dead. The public phone spat back 40 cents. He trousered the two coins and went to buy a beer.

For a bloke who wasn't legally permitted to leave the state of Queensland, John Gillespie sure moved around a lot. He was forever clambering in and out of his HZ Holden dashing between parts of eastern Australia. He crossed the border between New South Wales and Queensland routinely and with the easy air of a libertarian unconcerned about the apparatus of the state.

On one occasion he travelled up to Brisbane and put some money down on a ramshackle house with a small stable in the city's western suburbs, about a half an hour's drive from Eagle Farm. He always hated spending his own money. Not that it was in any legal sense his. It was merely the well-concealed receipts of a long-ago successful scam, where he'd breezily taken some long-forgotten mark to the cleaners. Nevertheless, he regarded it as his and his alone. Parting with it caused him discomfort, almost tangible physical pain. But it had to be done.

On another journey, he drove south to Coffs Harbour to monitor Dashing Soltaire's preparation and engage in sexual congress with Wendy. Two birds, one stone. He'd driven out to the racecourse and watched her gallop Dashing Soltaire around the track at blazing speed.

While Gillespie watched, noted horseman and trainer Bill Naoum waddled past with one of his four-legged fancies in tow. Naoum was a former jockey who, like many who'd viewed retirement as emancipation from a daily diet of a Salada biscuit and two hours in a sauna trying to make weight, had spent a considerable time since with the nose bag on. Naoum was almost as wide as he was long.

He had noticed Gillespie admiring his horse, a bay gelding still sweating from the rigours of trackwork. 'You looking to buy?' he asked.

'You looking to sell?'

'Could be. For the right price. Group Two winner at Randwick last autumn. Fit as a fiddle.'

'What's its name?'

'Bold Personality,' Naoum replied with pride.

'I'll give you five large for it.'

'I'd want at least 15.'

'Too rich for my blood, mate,' Gillespie said. He knew at once that he could get the trainer down to 10 with a little bit of haggling and Gillespie was better at haggling than most. But why bother? He didn't need the horse. Besides, Bold Personality looked all wrong.

Being on parole held no restraints and why would it? Gillespie had never laid on a couch, pouring his heart out to a psychiatrist. Even if he had, he wouldn't have understood the diagnosis. He'd be flat out spelling 'sociopath'. But anyone who had spent any time with Gillespie and could thumb their way through *The Diagnostic and Statistical Manual of Mental Disorders* would have found he ticked, if not all the boxes, then a large majority of them.

Psychopath or sociopath? Even the shrinks are uncertain. The street-corner psychoanalysts sometimes claim the only difference between a psychopath and a sociopath is the sociopath has a more expensive shrink. Gillespie could have been one or the other. Maybe both.

Either way, his con artistry came easily to him. Having no capacity for remorse for any of his ghastly crimes meant he could rob people blind until at last the penny dropped, and victims headed off to the cops to tell bizarre, incredulous tales of financial loss. By then Gillespie had moved on to a new group and new piles of money to help himself to.

Having not a skerrick of empathy meant he could casually manipulate people to do his bidding and, by sheer force of his personality, they'd bend over backwards to accommodate his complex schemes in ways that would later bring heavy doses of victim's shame.

He was, in fact, the perfect person to organise a ring-in. A man who would happily leave a scene of carnage in his wake and drive off into the sunset with a boot load of cash.

Gillespie knew his relationship with Wendy Smith would soon come to an end. He'd had some fun with the horsey blonde, and with his deft skills he'd managed to pry open her legs and her heart. She'd got Dashing Soltaire cherry ripe too, just as he'd planned.

She loved Gillespie and told him so more than once. He murmured similar sentiments to her and was pleased to see it had the desired effect. Another root. Another spot of trampolining on her clapped-out mattress.

Love was for the weak, commitment a trap. Once he'd emptied her bank account and fire-sold every other asset she owned, what were they going to do then? Live happily ever after?

He didn't even bother to knock on her door. He pulled up outside her house with a horse float attached to his old bomb and strode out to the stables. Clocking Dashing Soltaire in the adjoining paddock, he grabbed the horse by the bridle and firmly led him out.

He knew Wendy was there but hoped she was taking a nap. Getting up at sparrow's fart every morning made it almost a necessity for racing folk. Not having to see her was a bonus. He would give her the bad news over the phone.

He'd just walked the horse in to the float and was fiddling with the gate when he realised Smith was not napping, or if she had been the clatter of hooves had roused her and she was angry.

'What the hell are you doing?'

It was time to bring the hammer down. 'You fucked this up, girl,' he shouted back at her. 'The connections are very unhappy.'

'You're the fucking connections,' she shouted back.

'And I'm very fucking unhappy.'

Smith stood on the porch, hands on hips. She wondered if she should get after Gillespie, start a fight and leave him sufficiently dazed for long enough to get her horse back. She felt angry enough to do it, but she knew she couldn't win that contest. Instead she turned and marched back inside.

Having secured the gate, Gillespie poked around in his pocket looking for his car keys. 'I suppose a root's out of the question?'

The only answer he got was a resounding crack as Smith's front door slammed.

He drove Dashing Soltaire across town to Haitana's joint and pulled Dashing Soltaire out of the float. Haitana was out the back in the stables fussing over Fine Cotton.

When Haitana saw Gillespie delicately guiding Dashing Soltaire, his jaw dropped. Gillespie had told him he'd find a Fine Cotton lookalike but this was something else. 'Jesus. The spitting image. Fuckin' twins,' he said.

Gillespie beamed. Haitana grabbed Dashing Soltaire by the bit and eased him into the stable next to Fine Cotton, so they could see for themselves the unmistakable beauty of it at close quarters.

The only problem was Dashing Soltaire didn't like the confinement of the stables and brayed in complaint, leaping up every so often to make clear his dissatisfaction. Gillespie didn't understand what was going on and thought darkly that the two geldings might be so much alike there'd be a blue.

God. No injuries, please.

But Haitana knew exactly what to do and led Dashing Soltaire out. No longer confined by the four timber walls of the stable, Dashing Soltaire quickly calmed down. By the time Hayden got him into the paddock, the horse was a picture of bucolic tranquillity.

Haitana wandered back to the stables smiling and reached into his old battered esky. 'Stubby, mate?'

'Is the Pope a kiddie fiddler?'

They downed three each while admiring Fine Cotton in the stables and then turning their gaze to Dashing Soltaire grazing peacefully in the paddock.

Ten days to go and things were starting to fall into place.

Fuckin' Bundamba. It wasn't just the extra half an hour added to the drive up from Coffs Harbour that irritated Haitana. He was fretting about Fine Cotton all the way up. It had run too often. Racing people were starting to talk about it. And here he was giving it another start.

Haitana didn't have much of a reputation in the caper but he was not regarded as being cruel to his horses. Besides, Fine Cotton was special. He saw a fair bit of himself in the nine-year-old. They'd both been around the traps a long time. They're weren't especially talented or well equipped for the caper and the pointy end of racing; Group One starts at the big Sydney and Melbourne meets were beyond their modest abilities.

Hayden had got the old nag ready. Gave him a solid run around the track in the morning just to tire him out, and then the try-hard pair, man and beast, headed off to fuckin' Bundamba.

Gillespie had a way of making Haitana feel the ring-in was just a delicate conspiracy of two with the violent gunman, Sayers, making up a tight little criminal triumvirate. Hayden was surprised when he got to Bundamba to see Gillespie standing around with a small gathering of men who seemed to be in on the ring-in, or had, to coin a phrase that would soon come into vogue, prior knowledge.

There was Bobby North, who introduced himself to everyone as Robert but could scarcely hide his disappointment when he was referred to in the diminutive by everyone that shook his hand, Haitana included.

And finally, Gillespie introduced a bloke whose name was Mal, but, according to Gillespie, preferred the moniker 'The Lizard'.

The nickname made perfect sense to Haitana. The tall, gaunt figure with grey thinning hair smoked constantly, and even though the cigarette smoke would waft past his nose and dance around his face, his eyes remained astonishingly devoid of irritation. He seemed only to blink every four or five minutes, slowly once, then a second time, before resuming a hard stare. He grunted when Haitana shook his hand and said nothing more. Clearly, The Lizard was no conversationalist.

It transpired that Mal was not called The Lizard due to any particular reptilian characteristics, but the name was hard won due to his major activity when not engaged in horse-race fixing, smuggling native wildlife to other parts of the globe. Some of this black fare, drugged up, secreted in crates, headed for the United States where the big money was, were actual lizards, while others were snakes, turtles and birds.

During the first race, Gillespie regaled the small group with a tale of The Lizard's greatest haul, a breeding pair of palm cocka-toos. The Lizard had snared them himself in the far north, bound them up and shipped them off to a buyer in Miami who forked out a quarter of a million US for the rare, prized birds.

The Lizard offered a glimmer of a smile as yet another cigarette dangled from his gob. He blinked once and then a second time before resuming his cold glare at Haitana.

Not one of them had had any money on Fine Cotton in the Race Two Improvers and Maidens handicap over 1200 metres. They were not there to see the nine-year-old win. They were there to see Fine Cotton run last in its final run before the ring-in. The bookies offered 20/1 on Fine Cotton but by the time it jumped in the second race, it had blown out to 33/1.

Haitana had seen to it, even if it had made him uneasy. Fine Cotton had been trained and run to the point of equine exhaustion. There was no way it would end up in the prizemoney.

And so, with Gillespie full of contrived bonhomie and crook anecdotes, the five men watched in horror as Fine Cotton rounded the turn in front, two lengths ahead of the field. Gillespie fell into a grim silence. The Lizard showed the only emotion he would for the afternoon and possibly ever, raising his eyebrows slightly in a show of utter shock.

Bobby North raised his eyes skywards in prayer. Hayden Haitana could not look. His beloved Fine Cotton was going to have a win but at the worst possible time. In that moment he could only think of Georgie Brown, his mangled, smouldering, amputated corpse, and assumed that Brown's fate would soon be his when the gangsters caught up with him.

Fine Cotton saluting at the ledger at Bundamba would be a catastrophe and almost certainly bring premature death at the hand of angry, bloodthirsty men given to casual shows of mayhem and violence.

In that dark moment Haitana thought he could actually smell

petrol fumes. He turned around trying to map out an escape route and just as he figured the quickest path to the car park, Fine Cotton slowed to an exhausted dawdle at the 200 and was rounded up by all but two of the undistinguished field.

It finished 10th. Thank God.

It was still light when Haitana got home. He eased the tired Fine Cotton out of the float, gently walked him around to the stable and eased his nose bag on. Fine Cotton deserved a decent feed after all this.

He looked out towards the paddock and immediately felt something was wrong. The fence was buckled and bent, the barbed wire on top ripped apart. At first, he thought Dashing Soltaire had done a runner but in the growing gloom he could make the horse out, breathing heavily and in distress.

He approached the horse quietly, not wanting to send it into a galloping panic but Dashing Soltaire remained still. Haitana saw the blood, quite a lot of it, oozing down the horse's left flank and onto a growing puddle at his hooves.

There was a four-inch gash on Dashing Soltaire's shoulder. It would need at least 12 stitches. That was the easy part. It couldn't run. It wouldn't be able to for weeks. Even the dozy Queensland racing officials would jerry. There was no way it would pass even a casual veterinary inspection.

The ringer had to be scratched. The Phantom was going to be upset.

Haitana dressed the wound as best as he could with what little he had. He ran to the bathroom and grabbed a haemorrhoid cream he'd used on his own arse with various levels of success and slathered it all over the cut. Almost immediately the bleeding stopped.

He then called Gillespie and gave him the bad news. The Phantom summoned Haitana to the Currumbin Pub, a four-hour drive away on the Gold Coast.

'Mate, I'm fuckin' shot. I've had a long day.'

'Poor choice of words, mate. We need to work this out tonight. We need a Plan B.'

When Haitana got there and sat down, the group was morose. Gillespie barely said a word. They drank beer in silence, a murmur and a nod to the bar only when it came time for Hayden's shout.

After Haitana put the beers on the table, Gillespie got up from his bar stool and made his way to the phone in the corner. He left the four men staring into their beers.

Haitana had put his hand up. It was his fault. There was no point denying it. The Lizard seemed especially fierce but did not utter a word. North didn't seem quite so bothered. Perhaps like Haitana, he was relieved the ring-in could now no longer take place. They could have made a fortune, but just as easily the whole thing could have gone tits up and they'd all end up in jail.

Oh well, Haitana thought, another time. He might even ask Gillespie if he could keep Fine Cotton, give him a long spell and hit Sydney with him in the summer.

No-one was watching Gillespie. Had they kept a close eye on him, they would have noticed he'd only dialled four numbers.

When Haitana did look up, he noticed Gillespie in animated conversation. Whatever was being discussed was being hotly debated. From that distance he could not have known Gillespie was engaged in a shouting match with the talking clock.

The argument over, Gillespie returned the phone gently to its cradle, exhaled and walked back to the table ashen-faced. Haitana looked hopefully at Gillespie. Maybe it was all over. Pull up stumps and move on. Live to fight another day.

It was love at first sight. Hayden Haitana and Fine Cotton. (NEWS LTD/NEWSPIX)

Hayden Haitana in enforced retirement in 2003. Banned from racetracks for 27 years, he used to sneak in every now and then. If anyone noticed, they didn't seem to mind. (MARK BRAKE/NEWSPIX)

One half con artist, the other half bullshit artist, John Gillespie is a man of conviction. He has over 350 of them. (NEWS LTD/NEWSPIX)

Bobby North at home in 1986, free forever from thoughts of cans of tuna in socks, with *Penthouse* centrefolds taped to his back. (NEWS LTD/NEWSPIX)

A nation holds its breath. Bold Personality as Fine Cotton hits the line a short half-head in front of Harbour Gold. The conspirators' joy would last only a few minutes. (NEWS LTD/NEWSPIX)

Never one to let a punt go begging, 'Melbourne Mick' Sayers enjoys a day at the dishlickers.
(FAIRFAX SYNDICATION)

Criminal royalty. From left: peerless escapologist Darcy Dugan; 'The Big Man', Len McPherson – his face like a bull elephant's scrotum; and the Pope of Sydney, George Freeman. (NEWS LTD/NEWSPIX)

The architects of 'The Joke', Queensland Premier Joh Bjelke-Petersen and Commissioner of the Queensland Police Service, Terence Lewis. Utterly corrupt, and so unsubtle about it that eventually something had to give. It just took a while to happen. (STUART RILEY/NEWSPIX)

Former Assistant Commissioner of Queensland Police and 'Rat Pack' member, Tony Murphy. He never felt insulted by being described as 'cunning as a shithouse rat'. When push came to shove, Murphy would have run rings around most shithouse rats.
(NEWS LTD/NEWSPIX)

Nicknamed 'The Magician', Detective Sergeant Glen Hallahan made people disappear. Only they didn't turn up again later with a drum roll and a flourish.
(BARRY PASCOE/NEWSPIX)

The well-irrigated man of the cloth, Catholic priest Father Edward O'Dwyer. Gone to God in 2016. On this mortal coil, however, he was branded 'undesirable' and warned off racetracks for life.
(NEWS LTD/NEWSPIX)

From the penthouse to the doghouse. The Waterhouses, father Bill and son Robbie, face the music at AJC headquarters. It did not go well.
(IAN MAINSBRIDGE/NEWSPIX)

A man justly famous for his bulk, inertia and astonishing capacity for fluid retention, the Minister for Everything, Russ Hinze, seen here (centre) judging a beer-belly competition on the Gold Coast. He came third.
(PAUL RILEY/NEWSPIX)

The dapper hitman Chris 'Rentakill' Flannery thought he was an endangered species. He's now extinct. (NEWS LTD/NEWSPIX)

'The Team' catches up with Barry McCann, seen here under a white sheet in the deepest repose. He had been shot 25 times in the face. (FAIRFAX SYNDICATION/ SUMNER)

He who laughs last laughs loudest. Fine Cotton in 1998.
(NEWS LTD/NEWSPIX)

'Mick's spewin',' Gillespie said. He looked down at the table clutching his beer, pondering the situation and running all the angles in his mind, before turning his gaze to Haitana.

'Someone's going to get knocked over this.'

CHAPTER SEVEN
Plan B

'He'll come up trumps in the morning.'
– John Gillespie

CURRUMBIN, AT THE southern tip of the Gold Coast, has been a tourist trap since 1947, when the lorikeet-infested bird sanctuary first opened its gates to the wandering classes.

But right now, not far down the road from the feathered frenzy of cheeps and chirps, the Currumbin pub looked more like a human menagerie, a grim abode for humanity's misshapen and bedraggled. The rugged, the buggered and the shit out of luck.

The table at the pub had fallen into a long, dismal silence. What sounds there were came from the distance, the clink of glasses at the bar and the echo from the jukebox in the Ladies Lounge, playing light pop songs they didn't know or like. The only sounds at the table were the faint rustle of cigarette packets, the click of disposable lighters and the exaggerated heaving of great, ghastly plumes of smoke into the fetid air around them.

What they needed was time. With more time they would have more beer. They all understood the equation and one by one they emptied their glasses into their gullets and headed to the bar in the strictly observed unwritten roster of the shout.

It would be foolish to apply the standards of the general population to this group of men. Perhaps it is us who have it wrong. The public health nay-sayers who blight our television screens in our lounge rooms and the billboards on our roads with terrifying messages of death and personal disintegration incrementally have turned our minds. There is a general consensus that consuming more alcohol, rather than less or indeed none at all, is not a recipe for good decision making.

But the hectoring from men and women in white lab coats had had no discernible clinical effect on the Fine Cotton conspirators. Facing the prospect of imminent violent death or, at best, incarceration and public disgrace, they knew more beer was good.

Less beer would never be enough, and no beer was an unthinkable tragedy, a disastrous state of affairs that led to pain, desperation and a grim, white-knuckle ride back to the awfulness of reality.

Gillespie and Haitana especially were men given to rousing early in the morning and enjoying the breakfast of champions. It didn't particularly matter which of the major brewers' logos appeared on the bottles. They had their favourite sips of choice but were not inclined to be choosy. It just had to be beer. Preferably refrigerated although this, too, was optional.

Gillespie referred to beer consumed at an early hour as a 'Lachlan Macquarie' – an early settler. Shaking off the jitters and consigning anxiety to the distance.

Gillespie looked at his watch and laughed. 'Hey, look at the time. Ten past 10.'

'Eh?' grunted Bobby. 'Yeah, so what?'

'You seen those ads for fancy watches? The ones in magazines and in the papers? The watches always have the time telling you that it's 10 minutes after 10. Always.'

Hayden looked at his watch. It was indeed 10 past 10, but that made sense. That was what the time was.

'Yeah? Really? I've never noticed that. You sure?'

'Sure I'm sure. A bloke in a hock shop in Sydney pointed it out to me, when I was off-loading a few fake Cartiers. All the ones in his window display were set to 10 past 10 too. It's a marketing thing.'

'What the fuck makes 10 past 10 such a good time, though?' Haitana wanted to know. 'What makes it better than any other time?'

'The pawnbroker reckoned it's the time people are at their sharpest. Executives make their big decisions mid-morning. That's when they're in their most important meetings, moving and shaking. It's power time, he told me. Some watch sales guy told him that it's the same all over the world.'

'Power time, eh?'

'That's right,' Gillespie beamed. 'Time to make the right call. And here we are, beers in hand, at 10 past 10. We're on a roll and on the money. We're going to make this thing go like . . . clockwork!'

The table groaned, but their spirits were rising. Time for another round. And sure enough, the chemical magic that occurs when alcohol seeps into the human bloodstream in sufficient quantity to alter mood and outlook had begun.

No-one wanted to get knocked, least of all Haitana who, after his sixth beer, reverted from sullen and disagreeable to his most generous, helpful self.

He had a Plan B. Let Fine Cotton run. He'd spell it for a few days. Give it a run around The Gap, get it to the track, give it a 'bomb' and let it rip. He'd shown enough at Bundamba, Haitana argued, and with 300 grams of almost pure amphetamine coursing through its veins it would run out of sight.

Gillespie was having none of it. 'I've got the stewards on board but they're not going to stay that way if they see our jockey pulling the handbrake on a cranked-up nag on the back straight, before finally letting it go at the 400.'

More silence. Gillespie plonked his empty middy down in front of North. 'Your hook.'

North grappled at a handful of empties, his dirty fingers pressed against the inside of their glasses, and headed to the bar.

'Billy Naoum's got a horse. I took a look at it last month. Sprint specialist. Group Two winner in Sydney. Bold Personality.'

Haitana knew the horse well enough. 'It's a bay.'

'What are ya, a fuckin' horse racist? Who gives a fuck?'

'Phant, it's the wrong fuckin' colour. Fine Cotton is almost black. Bold Personality is brown . . .' Haitana said, looking around the bar for something that resembled the horse's hue but finding nothing. 'Like a . . . fuckin' Hereford bull.'

'We can fix that. Leave it with me.'

'Your gangster mate is going to shoot us all.'

'He doesn't have to know. He only wants a winner and Bold Personality will win.'

The Lizard nodded in agreement. He opened his mouth and the others turned to him, expecting him to utter words of such gravity and consequence that their consternation and doubt would be immediately swept aside. Instead, he merely plugged another cigarette into his mouth and burped.

Bobby North listened to the exchange from the bar, but dared not think further. He, too, did not want to get knocked but thought it might be better than a stint in jail.

He was making his way back to the table juggling five glasses and dripping beer on the sticky red carpet in the public bar.

The beer flowed and with it a rough optimism emerged. Haitana and Gillespie had argued but Gillespie won the battle of wits, if not logic, as Gillespie always did.

Haitana slept in his car in the car park. Just a couple of hours to shake off the drunkenness and sharpen his reflexes. He was still mightily pissed and had the wallopers pulled him over with a breathalyser at any stage on the Pacific Highway, he would have blown the thing up.

He weighed up the prospect and hoped he would get pulled over. He imagined a scene where the cops stopped him in his tracks, lights and sirens flashing. They wouldn't have to stick a tube in his mouth and ask him to blow.

By the time the wallopers had got their kit together, he would have stumbled out of his car and into the back seat of theirs. 'Take me to your leader.'

It was one way out of this shambles.

Gillespie had made it all up as he went along. He wanted Fine Cotton transported to Brisbane and stabled in the rented house at The Gap on the Friday night before the race. Haitana would take care of that.

He'd have Tommy di Luzio to get down to Coffs Harbour where Bold Personality was being stabled, pay by cheque and bring the horse up on a float the same day.

Haitana had offered to do the deal with Naoum but Gillespie shook his head. It was too risky. The less Naoum knew, the better. Gillespie would fob him off with some story over the phone. The last thing they needed was Naoum thinking they were going to race Bold Personality straightaway.

It made sense to Haitana and he was quietly pleased with the arrangements. He would take care of his beloved Fine Cotton and get him up to Brisbane in good nick. He grabbed a couple of bombs, two white tablets the size of bathroom plugs, and pocketed them. They might just come in handy.

Di Luzio had agreed to do the driving. He always agreed with Gillespie. He only ever said no to The Phantom when The Phantom expected to hear a reply in the negative. At all other times, di Luzio nodded his head. Yes, John. Sure, John. Whatever you say, mate.

Subservience came with some problems. In order to keep his master pleased, di Luzio suppressed any tales that might cause consternation. Thus di Luzio remained stoically disinclined to impart any piece of information that might attract Gillespie's ire and set him off on a rambling torrent of abuse.

Some things were best left unsaid, di Luzio thought, and in this case that thing was that di Luzio's ute was in the shop for mechanical repairs. The only car he had at his disposal was a canary yellow Toyota Corolla E30, an automobile banged together with precision Japanese engineering, albeit in 1974.

The Corolla had a towbar fitted and this gave di Luzio a surge of confidence. If the Japanese manufacturers deigned to have a towbar welded to the chassis, clearly they thought the vehicle was up for a little equine transportation.

He hired a float on the Gold Coast and hooked it up, paid the bloke with the cash Gillespie had given him for expenses. The bloke in the tiny little office looked at the Corolla and frowned. 'You don't want to be pullin' any weight with that, mate.'

Di Luzio knew the car would get from Brisbane to Coffs Harbour and back again with the float, but he'd begun to quietly acknowledge some doubts about its capacity to pull a float and a thousand pounds of racehorse.

He'd also been told not to look at the cheque but he failed Gillespie on this score. The temptation was too much and he yanked it out of his pocket and took a peek while he drove down the Pacific Highway. A little sneaky look wouldn't hurt. His eyes were drawn to the amount – $12,000 – the biggest cheque di Luzio had ever seen. He didn't notice that the cheque was signed by Lee Falk.

The boss had given him an important job. Best get on with it. No mistakes. The Corolla ploughed on all the way to Coffs Harbour without a problem.

When Naoum clocked the old Corolla, he frowned. 'This all you got?' the veteran jockey asked di Luzio.

'I'm swapping her over in town,' di Luzio lied.

The Corolla lurched and heaved under the extra weight. When di Luzio was out of sight of Naoum's stables, he pulled over.

He noticed the horse was jittery. So he did what one ignorant to the needs of horses might do. He grabbed a thick rug hanging off the side of the float and placed it over the horse. This seemed to calm Bold Personality down.

Pleased with his work, di Luzio climbed back into the Corolla and chugged off. Half an hour into the drive, both he and the Corolla were getting warm. He stripped off his sweatshirt and immediately felt better for it.

Another half-hour later, di Luzio noticed the temperature gauge spike ominously into the red. He turned the heater on in the car, desperately trying to suck some of the heat off the engine.

Ten minutes later, and with the heater pumping on full and with all the windows wound down, di Luzio burst into a sweat. He didn't know it but Bold Personality, swaddled in a blanket on a hot, humid spring day, had started sweating too.

Di Luzio and Haitana, who had been enthusiastically tending to Fine Cotton at his stables in Coffs Harbour, left the town at around the same time. Hayden pulled into Gillespie's rented house around midday. The Phantom was there to greet him and once Haitana had got Fine Cotton into the stables with a drink and a feed, he and Gillespie ripped the top off a couple of stubbies.

They sat out on the porch, drinking and eyeing the road for the arrival of di Luzio, who surely couldn't be far away. As it turned out, they waited four hours and had consumed half-a-dozen stubbies each by the time di Luzio's canary Corolla lurched into view.

Di Luzio had made the trip with the little car erupting in a mist of steam from the radiator approximately every 50 kilometres. He had to pull over each time, wait and then pour a few litres of water into the radiator and start all over again. By the time he arrived at The Gap, Bold Personality, still sporting its winter rug, was badly dehydrated and on the verge of collapse.

Haitana yanked the gate of the float down and stripped the horse of the thick blanket. 'You fuckin' idiot,' he said, glaring at di Luzio. 'Another hour of that and it'd be fuckin' dead.'

Haitana dragged a hose out and washed the horse down but Bold Personality remained listless. The horse urinated, a short shot of deep orange piss, and Hayden knew there was only one thing for it.

A vet would refer to the process as nasal intubation, a hose placed through the horse's nostril and pressed down into the oesophagus and then into the stomach. The gut would be flooded with water and the horse quickly rehydrated. It was a process that required great care to ensure the hose did not enter the lung. Even a small amount of water into the lung would kill a horse stone dead in minutes.

Haitana called it flushing. He'd done it before several times and hadn't killed a horse yet. Given the nature of their shenanigans, there was no possibility of a vet attending. He'd have to do it again.

They only had a garden hose and a smear of Vaseline. Still distressed, Bold Personality put up with the discomfort as about a metre of green hose was pushed up its nose. Its stomach was filled with water and almost immediately it became more animated.

Haitana knew it would get tricky from here and he carefully slid the hose out. He was almost there when Bold Personality pulled its head back and the end of the hose caught on tissue on its nasal cavity, ripping it and causing a bleeding attack.

Bleeding and thoroughbreds are always a messy business. Any horse that bleeds at the track from the mouth or nose faces a mandatory 12-month suspension. It is designed to allow the horse to rest and, more obviously, racing authorities don't like the idea of horses bleeding to death on the track.

'Fuck, Tommy,' Gillespie growled as he watched the blood flow from Bold Personality's left nostril. 'I reckon you've done all the fuckin' helping you possibly could today.'

Di Luzio was crestfallen.

'I'll hang around, Phant. You know me. I'm a willing hand.'

'No. Fuck off. I'm very fuckin' disappointed in you.'

Head bowed, di Luzio fumbled with the keys to the Corolla.

'Now-ish, Tommy. Don't make me get even angrier.'

Di Luzio's dripping shirt only added to the forlorn image. He looked at Haitana for comfort, but Hayden was busy trying to calm the wounded horse.

With a sniff, di Luzio turned and slowly made his way back to the Corolla. He opened the door and turned to look at the grim scene. He had let the boss down. He climbed into the car and took off.

'He can't even fuck off properly,' Gillespie said, as much to himself as to Haitana.

Bold Personality was bleeding heavily. Technically it could not race but Gillespie would race it anyway.

It was Haitana's job to stop the bleeding. The best way, he thought, was to do what he did when he had a blood nose himself. Put the head back and eventually the bleeding would stop.

Bold Personality didn't appreciate Haitana's attempt at equine first aid. The bay gelding bucked and shook as Haitana pulled his head back, tying a rope to the bridle and pulling upwards, drawing the horse's neck up until at last the rope could be lashed to the stable roof.

And so, already having a desperately bad day, Bold Personality now had his head strapped to the rafters at an 80-degree angle and would remain there until the bleeding stopped. It took an hour before that happened and he was released from bondage, but his indignities had only just begun.

Bold Personality was in a deeply distressed state as, to varying degrees, were the two blokes standing around him. Hayden Haitana was thoroughly drenched, as was the horse, but in Bold Personality's case the irrigation was both internal and external. John Gillespie had managed to escape the water torture that had taken place in that stable of horrors, declining all requests for assistance on the basis that he had a crucial errand to run.

He looked at the dripping duo – one equine, one human – and actually began to laugh, a rare sound to hear cackling from the mouth of The Phantom, and consequently rather menacing to boot. But even this cold-hearted criminal could see the funny side of what he was looking at.

They were running against the clock, they were going to commit a major fraud the next day in front of thousands of witnesses, and they had the wrong horse for the job.

They were committed, but desperate. Their mission was pure folly, but they couldn't turn back, and the consequences of failure simply didn't bear thinking about.

But this was pure Laurel and Hardy, Gillespie thought as he gazed upon their works. 'Haitana has to be Laurel and I'm Hardy,' he realised in a flashback to his childhood watching the silent slap-stick movies on TV. True, it wasn't exactly a flattering metaphor, but it was a truly ridiculous tableau that fate had laid out before him.

Haitana, on the other hand, was searching his soul. 'I can't believe we're doing this,' he said, to himself as much as those within earshot.

He raised his voice and declared, 'I've never been cruel to a horse. I've been firm, yeah, showed 'em who's boss, you've gotta do that, but this is deadset fuckin' ordinary what we're doing to this animal.'

'Listen to me,' said Gillespie. 'I know this isn't a whole lot of fun, but the worst is over, OK? The horse is here, you've got him watered, even though he didn't much care for how it was done, but it fuckin' had to be done, and now it is. Done.'

'He's bleeding from the nose, mate!' Haitana wailed. 'This is no good, I tell ya.'

The Phantom raised his eyes to the heavens, then turned them on the remorseful trainer. 'It'll pass, Hayden. If I stuck three metres of garden hose down your hooter you'd probably shed some red yourself. Look, we've got a horse that can run, and he's on the mend. Now we only have one problem to deal with.'

Haitana had taken his ruined shirt off and was wringing it out as best he could, sighing as he noticed flecks of Bold Personality's blood on the collar. He turned to Gillespie. 'The way I see it,' he said, his words dripping with helpless exasperation and barely suppressed fury, 'our "one problem" is that this nag looks fuckin' nothing like Fine fuckin' Cotton!'

'Precisely. Well done,' Gillespie replied, in the patient tone a teacher might use to congratulate a dim-witted child who has just added two and two to get four. 'So, we have to do something about that, don't we? That's why I'm going shopping now to purchase some hair dye, which will transform Bold Personality into Fine Cotton, so that we can all make a lot of money tomorrow, OK?'

The Phantom waved and walked to his car, calling over his shoulder pointlessly, 'Just look after the horse, will ya? I'll be back in an hour or so.'

Haitana watched as Gillespie slammed the driver's door of his old Holden and headed for the front gate in a cloud of red dust.

Gillespie had tried to create the impression that he knew what he was doing, that everything was hunky-dory, and he'd made a reasonable job of it, as usual. He knew how convincing he could be, but he was having trouble convincing himself. He knew nothing about dyes, hair colouring, or cosmetics of any description. He'd worn a disguise once or twice, but usually it consisted of a hat pulled low, a high collar and some jet-black wrap-around shades.

The way he saw it, chemicals were women's work, or at least the ones you smeared all over yourself to make a good impression certainly were. The last goop he'd used for the sake of keeping up appearances was a tube of Colgate.

But he'd seen the ads for something called Clairol, which girls sick of the view in their mirrors used to transform themselves from blondes to brunettes to God knows what else, and he knew that women were fussy about that sort of thing, so the stuff probably did the business all right. Anyway, he didn't have any other ideas.

Fifteen minutes later he was in the nearest shopping centre. He drove around for a little while, identifying five chemist's shops, all within walking distance. He seemed to be in luck with the neighbourhood; the locals here were a sickly bunch, by the look of it.

He parked in the main street and strode into the first one – a Soul Pattinson's that looked like it had opened for business some decades before Gallipoli – and, out of habit, went straight to the prescriptions counter at the back. John Gillespie only ever went into a pharmacy to purchase mind-altering substances that were available with a (usually forged) prescription.

'I'd like some hair dye for my wife,' he announced to an elderly bespectacled fellow in a white lab coat. 'I'll need a fair bit of it too.'

'I don't know anything about cosmetics,' the ancient apothecary replied in a disdainful tone. 'Not my department.'

'Alice!' he called over Gillespie's shoulder. 'Would you please help this gentleman with some, ah, ladies' business?'

The chemist chuckled to himself, then turned and wandered through a rear door into his private pharmacopoeia, as the half dozen customers in the shop, all women, stared at the newcomer.

'Thanks a lot,' he muttered over the counter as Alice approached him.

'How can I help you?' the beaming young lady asked.

Gillespie explained that he and his wife were planning a long trip, and that she wanted him to pick up as much hair dye as he could before they hit the road. 'Clairol, I think she said,' Gillespie offered.

'Well, there's a lot of different ones, in all sorts of colours,' Alice told him. 'Which one does she use?'

'Er, well, it's a sort of reddish, browny colour, I guess,' he shrugged, doing his best to look like a confused husband and finding it easy, because he really had no idea what he was talking about.

'Let me show you,' she said, with a helpful smile. 'You should be able to tell from the pictures on the bottles.'

She led him to a dozen shelves packed floor to ceiling with hair products, and for the gazillionth time in his life thanked whatever God there might be that he'd been born male.

'Thanks,' he said, looking at her tidy rear end as she waddled off to serve a hunched-over old lady with what looked like terminal rheumatism. 'I'm sure I'll be OK from here.'

'Pretty little thing,' he observed to himself, before turning his attention to the vast range of hair colourings. The next time he saw her was when he fronted up at the cash register, carrying six large packets of Miss Clairol Brown Shade No.4, which was 'guaranteed to work in minutes, and last and last'.

'Gee, that's an awful lot, you know,' Alice pointed out. 'How long are you and your wife going away for?'

'Oh, we're going away for a long time,' he said, and as he handed over the cash – more cash than he'd been expecting – a cold shiver ran through him. He'd only ever used the words 'going away for a long time' in a far less romantic context.

Two hours and four more pharmacies later, having stopped at a hardware shop to buy buckets, scrubbing brushes, rubber gloves and sponges, John 'The Phantom' Gillespie had hooked the gate behind him and driven his vehicle the last 100 metres to the ramshackle house.

He heard voices from the back and walked round to see Bobby North had arrived. The real estate agent was sitting with Haitana on a pair of decrepit wicker chairs.

On the other side of an old barbed-wire fence, in a tiny paddock, stood Bold Personality. He didn't look like he was having much fun, but at least the beast wasn't hysterical and half dead, which was how he'd looked when Gillespie had set off on his tour of the tints.

'Give us a hand with the stuff, will ya?' he said. But his heart wasn't in it. Not just yet. 'Oh, fuck it. Gimme a beer first. It was bloody horrible out there. The only person I met who made any sense was the hardware bloke. Fuck me, I thought I was a good con artist – I should have got into cosmetics. What a crock of shit. You tell a woman you can make her beautiful, and suddenly all her money's in your pocket . . .'

They sat and discussed the eternal mysteries of the female mind for a little while, and then a little longer, with The Phantom expressing the view that deep analysis was a complete waste of time and that women existed for one purpose only. Tired of the subject, Haitana got to his feet with intent and resolve, swaying only slightly, and telling his companions that now was the hour.

'Let's get to work. We've got to turn that tortured animal over there into Fine Cotton, and we've got about 12 hours left to do it.'

They did indeed go to work. Bold Personality was hitched to a fencepost, buckets were two-thirds filled with water and topped up with Miss Clairol Brown Shade No.4. The men put on their rubber gloves, took hold of their sponges and, after Hayden had calmed the beast, which had recoiled at the sight of yet another hose, sprayed him all over and began the transformation, from ear to tail.

Every five or 10 minutes, they'd stop and reach into the massive esky that Bobby had hauled down from the kitchen and partake of refreshment, for it was hard work, what with the horse refusing to stay still, each of them taking turns to fall on their arses in mud, horse shit and Clairol, laughing like demented witches over a cauldron.

For the first time there was a real sense of camaraderie, of a shared purpose. This was no longer a risky gamble, a disaster waiting to happen. Beer after beer, sponge after sponge, they became, at least for now, a team.

Their laughter, swearing and screaming rang across the country-side, and the filthier they got, the louder they became, reaching a crescendo when Bobby thrust his sponge between the horse's eyes and roared, 'Dye, ya bastard!'

Eventually, they walked, staggered and crawled back into the house. In the setting sun they'd inspected their handiwork, and had decided that all in all, it wasn't half bad. The horse actually looked a chocolaty brown colour, sort of. In any case, it sure looked a damn side more like Fine Cotton than it had when di Luzio had turned up with it.

'Hey, isn't that right, Bobby? Don't you reckon, Hayden? Abso-fucken-lutely!' Gillespie said. 'You think it looks good now. He'll come up trumps in the morning.'

The three drunken colourists closed the back door of the house behind them. Bobby North joined them an hour later. He clocked Bold Personality and he had to admit it looked pretty damned good.

And while all this was going on, the mysterious forces of organic chemistry went to work. Miss Clairol Brown Shade No.4 had been rigorously tested in salons and laboratories around the world, and the results always looked just like they appeared on the bottle. A hundred per cent guaranteed.

Oh yeah, this stuff worked as advertised. It worked just fine.

On human hair.

CHAPTER EIGHT
And they're racing . . .

'That's it. We're fucked.'
— Bobby North

THE VOICE OF Queensland racing, Wayne Wilson, cleared his throat, peered through his binoculars and got set to call the fourth race on the card. His voice was a spectacular combination of staccato inflection and crackling dissonance, as if each word had been dragged across an emery board before tumbling out of his mouth – which was odd, because his larynx had been reduced to inert grey sinew by the Rothmans cigarettes he sucked down at almost every waking moment. His calls were barely coherent, a jumble of incomplete sentences that would not have made sense anywhere else but over the speakers at a racetrack or broadcast on radio.

'Red light flashing. Racing. Cabaret Kingdom jumped out. Lord Radiant and Team Princess, Harbour Gold get away. Fine Cotton missed the start . . .'

Apprentice jockey Gus Philpot stared helplessly ahead. Perched high in the saddle, between the ears of his stationary steed, he could see the backsides of 11 racehorses sprinting into the distance.

The horse Philpot knew as Fine Cotton was, of course, the horse that only a few select folks knew to be Bold Personality, but whatever its name and breeding it may as well have been the stuffed remains of Phar Lap at that awful moment in the Eagle Farm starting gates – good looking, sure, but going nowhere.

In bars, cars, clubs and pubs across Australia, punters beyond counting were struck dumb. Stunned silence reigned. It was as if the Ode had been called, commemorating the tragic fate of their fallen dreams. Oh, dear God. It was over before it had even begun.

It was only a moment, but for the two brains sharing the gate at the time, it seemed an eternity. Philpot, eager and ambitious, was staring at humiliation and a trainer's fury, as well as the fast-receding pack ahead of him.

The beast beneath him – Bold Cotton, Fine Personality, call it what you will – was recovering from the worst 48 hours of his six years of life. He'd been hauled by an idiot cross-country in a float that felt like a furnace, overcooked, under-nourished, flushed with hoses and dyed with chemicals by other idiots, sprayed with more hoses, painted, wrapped in blankets till he was drowning in his own sweat, and now thousands upon thousands of idiots had risked a motza on him winning a race in another beast's livery.

He understood none of this. After all, he was a horse. But he was not a happy horse – that much he did understand. After staring mindlessly at the open gate in front of him, for the three short seconds that felt like three months to his jockey, a spasm of panic shot through his very being, and a desperate urge to escape, to somehow get out of this nightmare, suddenly translated into frenzied action. With a snort, a shake of the head and a rush of equine adrenaline, the dazed animal came to life.

With a rearing lurch, 'Fine Cotton' finally went to work, and Philpot's sigh of relief was echoed around the nation as he and his ride were propelled from the barrier into racing immortality. Punters from Petersham to the Pilbara stared as if hypnotised at their transistor radios in public bars. Bookies in betting rings from Warwick Farm to Whyalla held their collective breath.

It was on.

Just before Bold Personality was shanghaied into the mounting yard, Gillespie set off to place his bets. He looked around and saw no-one he knew. He had to move quickly. He had to get on and get back to Naoum. Gillespie's bonce was required as cover. He'd emptied his bank account and had been carrying the wad in his jacket all day.

'Race four. Number two. Twelve thousand each way. Cabaret Kingdom.'

TABs around the country run on a parimutuel system adjusting the odds depending on how much money has been bet on which horse. The bookies adjust their prices only after taking a bet.

Gillespie understood this. He didn't have time to go to the bookies but he knew the pile he'd just placed on Cabaret Kingdom would unsettle the markets. OK, he'd take a hit but big deal.

By the time he got to the bar and fixed his head directly between Naoum's line of sight and the television, he watched the tote screens blink and fizzle. Number two, Cabaret Kingdom, was paying four dollars the win and a meagre 95 cents the place.

Fuck's sake.

The atmosphere in the Queensland Racing Club Members' Bar at Eagle Farm was febrile. All eyes were on the race, except for the pair belonging to Bold Personality's former owner, Bill Naoum. With the crowd going nuts around them, The Phantom was anything but a poltergeist, his solid form adopting whatever preposterous pose was required to prevent the one man who knew what Bold Personality looked like from getting a decent view of proceedings, recognising his horse and blowing the whole scam wide open.

As it turned out he needn't have bothered, but he didn't know that then, and neither did anyone else. This was the point in proceedings when nobody knew anything for certain, but some people knew a lot more than others.

Hayden Haitana knew he was doomed, he just wasn't sure what form his undoing would take; as in, whether he'd be arrested or killed. There was a raw certainty in the pit of his gut that, even if the horse won, for him at least it would end badly. While he was a central character in the plot of this tragic drama, he felt like he was a member of the audience, watching his own fate unravel before his eyes.

He had a clear view of his ghastly future, but didn't even see the race, though not because he was wallowing in fear and regret and couldn't bear to watch. As the horses tore around the track before the baying mob, Hayden was out the back of the stables, watching his beloved horse demolish a steel float from within in an amphetamine-fuelled fury, as the bomb he'd been given to power him to victory over Harbour Gold exploded inside a metal box on wheels instead of on the Eagle Farm straight.

A thousand kilometres to the south, Mick Sayers sat alone at his kitchen table in Bronte, with only a radio, an overflowing ashtray and the last third of a bottle of Jack Daniel's for company. Marian had sensed looming disaster two days earlier and told him she was going to visit her non-existent sister for the weekend. Sayers hadn't heard her and hadn't noticed that she wasn't around. That suited them both fine.

Father O'Dwyer had got on at 20/1 at Appin, and as Gus Philpot was thrust out of the Eagle Farm barrier on the back of his demented beast of burden, he was watching proceedings on a TV in the public bar at Warwick Farm racecourse with, appropriately enough, a horse's neck in his paw – a schooner of Resch's with a double shot of vodka dropped into it in a shot glass. The barman hadn't blinked when he'd asked for it five minutes earlier – he'd served far worse things in this place.

The man of God was in two minds about the race – if he won, he stood to make two grand on his $100 bet. But to collect, he'd have to go back and find his bookie at the Appin dog track. As the screen before him oozed in and out of focus, he asked himself whether it was worth the two gorillas to return to that horrible place, and decided that on balance it probably was.

He burped, wiped the sweat off his brow, and mumbled, 'Errgle . . . c'mon, Fine Cotton . . . urp . . .' to nobody in particular.

Out on the turf, Bold Cotton was travelling well but he had ground to make up, and as they approached the turn Philpot reached for the whip and gave his mount a gentle tap of persuasion. It was enough – the creature moved seamlessly into top gear. Philpot grinned as he felt himself sway back in the saddle, accelerate and move around the tail of the field. This was all looking much sweeter now.

Terry Lewis had managed to pull himself away from his bathroom mirror and was listening to the race on the radio in the comfort of his home. The Chief Commissioner of Queensland Police was taking a keen interest in the race. It was starting to look as though the 'certainty' was going to make a decent fist of things.

Back at Eagle Farm, his mother was peering through a set of binoculars in the stands and she saw Fine Cotton make his move. Terry would be pleased.

Bert Holland from the fraud squad turned his head in amazement as Fine Cotton sprinted around the final corner and into the straight, with only second favourite Harbour Gold for company, when he heard his boss involuntarily scream, 'Go, Fine Cotton! Go, you good thing!' but the commissioner's urgings were lost in the cacophony of thousands of others roaring the same demand.

In Yowie Bay, George Freeman was lying on his gargantuan leather couch, wearing his trademark dressing gown and nothing else, the central heating keeping the winter's chill at bay, sipping on a lemon, lime and bitters and letting a middleweight shot of peth make its way from his left thigh to the pleasure centres of his brain.

His trusty wireless on the coffee table was tuned to 2KY, and he reached over to turn it up after the announcer had given the payouts for the third in Morphettville, and informed him that the nags were 'At the gate in Eagle Farm for the 1500 metre Second Division Commerce Novice Handicap, where there's been a lot of interest in Fine Cotton . . .'

He was in a very good position – physically, mentally and financially – because it didn't matter to him if the new and improved Fine Cotton won, or if Harbour Gold pinched him at the post. George had it all covered, just like he always did.

Sure, there could be a fall. A lightning strike, maybe. The earth could open and swallow Eagle Farm into a massive sinkhole, but barring catastrophe, George was as sweet as a nut. The Pope lay back, closed his eyes, and let the call of the race wash over him.

Across the country, men who should know better imitated jockeys on their mounts, riding Fine Cotton home while slapping their own arses with the flat of their hands. Others demanded the apprentice jockey, Gus Philpot, show no restraint with the persuader.

'Hit it. Fuckin' hit it, you dwarf!'

Wayne Wilson's call reached new levels of hysteria as the horses battled down the straight.

'One hundred out. Harbour Gold puts its nose in front. Fine Cotton's coming back. Harbour Gold. Fine Cotton. Fine Cotton. Harbour Gold. Fine . . . I can't split 'em. Photo. Judges have called for a developed print.'

Fine Cotton and Harbour Gold hit the line neck and neck. There was nothing in it – nothing except millions of dollars, massive fraud, flagrant corruption, sweat, tears, booze, drugs and mass hysteria.

Behind the stands Hayden Haitana heard the deafening roar of the mob, and so could the real Fine Cotton, now in the throes of extreme speed psychosis, the racket driving him nuts, metal panels flying off his float as the mayhem pushed him over the edge. Haitana couldn't watch, not the race nor the suicidal insanity of his horse. He wandered dazed into the nearest bar and screamed his order of three beers. He was the only one buying. Everyone else was going mad. He swallowed the first XXXX in two gulps.

A minute earlier Bobby North had been despondent. He'd spotted the cops around the stands and wondered which one would arrest him, but now, with Fine Personality gathering speed, he began to think what had been impossible to contemplate – triumph, riches, success.

For a brief moment, no more than a minute, there was silence, a startled hush in the crowd at Eagle Farm. And then the judges called it. Fine Cotton by a short half-head. A lip, more accurately. One of the hairs on Bold Personality's nostrils. That's how much there was in it. Fine Cotton had edged past Harbour Gold at the winning post. It was as close as you can get, but the ringer had done the job.

With the announcement the crowd roared and the volume hit a crescendo of ecstatic celebration, the tsunami subsiding just enough for the voice over the PA to be heard confirming the placings before the screaming and yelling began anew.

In Bronte Mick Sayers leapt halfway to the ceiling, slugged back the last of his bourbon and hurled the empty bottle into the kitchen wall in orgasmic triumph.

At Warwick Farm, Father O'Dwyer threw up over the back of a hysterical fellow joyously waving a Fine Cotton betting slip in the air, and who didn't notice what had happened to him.

Bobby grabbed a walloper who was jumping up and down in excitement and embraced him. They pulled apart without any awkwardness. They both clutched their betting tickets in their hands. Fine Cotton to win.

Across the nation and beyond, punters cheered and bookies had the ashen look of men who would soon have to return home to explain to their wives why little Johnny or adorable Jill would not be going to private school.

As the grandees of the Queensland Racing Club, the cops, the punters at the track and around the nation celebrated, as the bookies stared at the result in paralytic horror, The Phantom ran for the stairs to find Haitana and make good their escape. The formalities would have to be dealt with as quickly as possible – correct weight, blanket on, into the float and out the gate.

Even in the fetid air of Boggo Road Gaol, there was a resounding sense of triumph. It came from Bertie Kidd's cell. Bertie let out a shriek. Fine Cotton! That was three cartons of Rothmans right there. Bertie's cellmate, Labe, had left the jail three months earlier to be replaced by a young kid with a rough crew cut and taste for stealing cars. Bertie thought momentarily about giving the lad a dousing with the contents of the piss bucket. He looked down to see a motley turd floating in a puddle of stale piss and thought better of it. Bertie was a terrible loser, but he could win with good grace.

This was as sweet as it gets, and the ring-in's architects and those with prior knowledge began to mentally count their winnings. The glimmering moment of ecstasy felt like it would last forever. And then all hell broke loose.

In Yowie Bay George Freeman smiled quietly, nodded, and waited for the shit to hit the fan. The shit that he'd demanded from the men he'd dispatched from Sydney to Brisbane to take care of.

Gus Philpot rode back to the scales beaming like a little boy finding a bicycle and a train set under the Christmas tree. He heard it first. He thought some of the punters were booing him for kicking Fine Cotton home. But then it became clearer. And by the time he clambered off the horse, it had turned into a roar.

'Ring-in! Ring-in!' It was a chant, a mantra and incantation. Philpot had no idea what was going on. He only knew it was bad.

One large bloke looked directly at the stewards in the box and yelled out angrily, 'Come on, you bastards – wake up,' before resuming the ring-in chant.

One by one the stewards did rouse themselves from their slumber. A vet was called upon. He brought with him a plastic card the size of a small paperback novel. The vet looked at the card, then he looked at the horse. Then he looked at the card again. He peered down at the horse's fetlocks, noticed white paint dripping onto his hooves, and shuffled off back to the stewards' room.

Gillespie had made it as far as the car park when it came over the PA. It was as though God had put on his black cap before passing sentence at the Last Judgement.

Haitana was almost crushed by the mad rush to the bar, but by then he'd already swallowed two of his beers and managed to flee, with his third glass in hand, into the open air.

'Race four, hold all tickets. Race four, hold all tickets . . .'

Bobby North heard it too and, not for the first time that day, his head dropped. Then he heard the PA fire up again.

'Hayden Haitana to the stewards' room. Hayden Haitana to the stewards' room.'

'That's it. We're fucked,' he said out loud.

And this time he was right.

CHAPTER NINE
A manhunt and a horse hunt

'When you hear *Jingle Bells*, the bells are tolling for you, son.'
— George David Freeman

IT WAS A relatively simple job assembling the Queensland Fraud Squad. No phone around or APBs on police radio required. Most of the state's dedicated fraud investigators were wandering around at Eagle Farm in various states of shock, distress and wild-eyed fury. Having hurled their betting tickets away in disgust, they gathered at the Members' Stand and muttered darkly to one another.

Compared to this, defrauding the state of Queensland was a victimless crime. Scribbling out a dodgy cheque? Who gives a fuck? This time the cops themselves were victims, dupes in a dastardly deception that had lightened their wallets, extracted their own hard-earned or at least the black cash, receipts of bribes they regarded as the fruits of their hard labour.

Senior Sergeant Will Ramsey had dropped $100 on the race. Despite him still carrying several hundred more in his wallet, he viewed the ring-in as a personal affront, akin to taking food from the mouths of his children.

The Brisbane telephone book wasn't big enough. Maybe in 20 years it would be, but in 1984 Ramsey knew it lacked the mass and weight required to knock a crook around the head and shoulders in a proper, forceful manner. The old Gray-Nicolls he kept in his locker for a spot of office cricket was his preferred interrogation tool. He fancied himself playing an audacious cut shot to the back of the head of any crook involved in the ring-in. That was just for starters, to get him off the mark. Knocking the ball around before he really got started with his innings.

A hundred bucks. He planned to launch some lusty blows at some dodgy bastard's head.

As the shadows grew across the track, Ramsey and his colleagues watched the cameramen and soundies gather around their boss,

Bert Holland. The chief inspector looked gravely at the motley collection of media fidgeting around him. He'd dropped $500 on Fine Cotton. If looks could kill, everyone within his field of vision would have collapsed and died horribly there and then.

He nodded to his subordinates standing in the shadows. Ramsey noticed and nodded back. Holland growled in frustration. 'Here,' he said, pointing to a position on the turf directly behind him, in the manner of a man scolding a disobedient labrador.

The penny dropped for Ramsey, and with a murmur to his colleagues they marched over to take their places behind their boss. It was a show of strength as much as a show of solidarity. There were more coppers behind Holland than there were reporters in front of him.

Holland cleared his throat, no easy task given his penchant for smoking two packets of Winfield Red cigarettes every day. On the first hack, the phlegm merely clattered around the back of his throat before returning to its resting point just above his larynx. Holland hucked and coughed again before spitting out an enormous yellow-green glob of phlegm onto the grass at his feet.

He was ready.

'What has happened here today is an outrageous crime,' Holland pronounced, 'a despicable act played out by career criminals with intent to defraud the people of Queensland. When we find those responsible, they will face the full force of the law.'

The gaggle of Queensland reporters had questions, so many in fact that they shouted them out at the same time. Who had placed the bets? Who knew what and when? Were Fine Cotton's connections in custody? Why did it take so long for the stewards to know what had happened? Who were those men yelling out 'ring-in, ring-in' at the end of the race? And finally, and with a view to getting their copy correct for the following day's papers on what was still a baffling incident, which Fine Cotton was which? Were there two Fine Cottons? Were there more than two? Where are the Fine Cottons now?

The question that remained unasked was why on Earth were so many members of the fraud squad not just present at the scene of the crime but had been seen huddling in bars at the track for several hours, sinking middies before the crime actually occurred?

Perhaps anticipating that awkward question, Holland put his hands up, palms extended to the braying mob. 'No further questions,' he replied, stomping off to the general manager's office, apparently unaware he had not answered any.

The press conference was the easy bit. Now Holland had to speak to the boss. The good news was the fat bastard was up in Cairns and wouldn't be back until the following day. Fronting him in his office, face to face, would have been horrible. The bad news, something Holland understood at almost a cellular level, was that one wrong word from him over the phone to Russ and he'd be pulling drunks out of the Birdsville pub for the rest of his career.

He walked into the manager's office, grabbed the phone and dialled the number. After a series of reconnections and polite but firm requests from Holland to be put through to the minister, the unmistakable voice of the Minister for Everything came through loud and clear.

'What the fuck is going on there?'

'It's a ring-in, Minister.'

'I know it's a fuckin' ring-in. I'm 1000 miles away and I know it's a fuckin' ring-in. Where's Lewis?'

'He's put me in charge, Minister.'

'You pricks better not be in on this,' Hinze said. 'Did anyone see him?'

'I don't know, Minister. He wasn't in uniform.'

'As if that fuckin' matters. Listen, you get your mob to shake down every fuckin' lowlife in the caper. Start with that bastard Haitana. Pull him up and tell him he's going to get a hamburger with the lot. You blokes have got around 12 unsolved murders on the books, by my guess. Pull him up and put it right on him.'

'It's a fraud matter, Minister.'

'I don't give a fuck. Put a fuckin' murder blue on him. Charge him with the disappearance of the Beaumont children, for all I fuckin' care. But pull him up and get him to cough. Fuckin' now, if it's not going to cut into your valuable punting time.'

'No, sir.'

Holland put the phone down. All things being equal it hadn't gone badly. He walked back to the mounting yards. In the growing gloom, he spotted Ramsey and called him over.

'Get amongst it, Sergeant. Speak to every trainer, jockey, bookie and strapper still hanging around here. Tell them to get the word out to that prick Haitana that it's Martha Reeves and the Vandellas time.'

Ramsey, whose musical tastes did not extend to the Motown hits of the 1960s, looked at his boss quizzically.

'Fuck's sake, son. Nowhere to run. Nowhere to hide.'

Hayden Haitana was already on the run and he was looking for a place to hide. The Phantom had split. Vanished into thin air. Courtesy of Mick Sayers, he owed Haitana 20 large. Hayden had often wondered if he'd ever see it, but now he knew for sure he would not.

165

Haitana stepped on the accelerator and the horse float lurched behind him. It was empty now. He'd taken care of that. 'Got to get out of Queensland,' he told himself. Then he'd feel a bit safer.

His head throbbed and his eyes squinted, both in pain and in the glare of the Queensland sunset. He'd left his sunglasses at the track. Right on the bar in the Members' with a copy of the form guide. He needed a drink, just a beer or two to calm the nerves, but he knew he couldn't stop until he crossed the Tweed. Any car pulling a horse float was likely to be pulled over by the jacks.

He fumbled around with his shirt pocket and pulled out the betting ticket. Taking his eyes off the road for a moment, he looked at it and let out a laugh.

Fifty bucks on Harbour Gold at 5/1. A winner. He could do with that dough now, but there was little chance of him seeing that bookmaker to collect any time soon.

He drove on, crossing the Tweed at dusk. He flicked his headlights on and lifted the visor up off the windscreen. At least he didn't have to squint anymore. He was back in New South Wales and he felt better for it. He checked the fuel gauge again and figured he had just enough juice for the three-hour drive to Coffs Harbour.

'Don't speed. Don't give them any excuse to pull you over,' he said out loud and not for the first time.

He knew the old truck had a broken tail light, but he couldn't worry about that now. Just keep driving. He kept his foot down until he saw the Big Banana, the gigantic fibreglass fruit floodlit on the horizon. Fruit was not really his go and he never quite understood the allure of the yellow monstrosity, but this time there was something deeply comforting about it. It meant he was home.

He pulled in at the drive-through bottle shop at the Greenhouse Tavern and bought himself a dozen longnecks. He wanted to go inside for a schooner or two, but thought better of it. He took off with the box of beers bouncing around on the passenger seat beside him.

Haitana wondered what sort of refuge his home would offer and for how long. His name wasn't on the lease. It'd be a few days at least before the coppers came sniffing around. He pulled up outside the old weatherboard and sighed with a deep relief. He had a roof over his head. He had beer. Things were looking up.

He laid low at home until the beer ran out a day later, occasionally peering through curtains when he heard a car go past. No-one called. No-one came.

He needed more beer and he felt comfortable enough going back to the Greenhouse, and this time he'd go inside and enjoy a few from the tap first. Besides, he had an idea and he thought it might just work.

Haitana was concerned with protecting the skerrick of what remained of his reputation. The last thing he wanted was an arrest at the track, dragged off in handcuffs in front of the people he'd spent his life with: the trainers, the strappers, the jockeys. He may have been regarded as a person who fell into the more dismal categories of colourful racing identities, but he was a horseman first and foremost.

He pulled into the pub in his old truck. The float had long gone – yanked off the bull bar and rolled around into the backyard. Out of sight, out of mind.

He popped a baseball cap on, pulling it low over his forehead. He walked into the bar, his old local, looked around and didn't recognise a soul. Happily, there didn't seem to be anyone lurking around, looking out of place – there were only a couple of grey nomads who'd pulled their caravan into the car park and gone in for a drink and a meal. They didn't look like cops, but if they were, Hayden figured even he could outrun them.

He bought himself a schooner and asked the barman if the phone was working. The barman nodded. Haitana took a long draught on his beer, plunged a couple of coins into the phone and dialled the number.

'Hello? Yeah, I want to speak to Jana Wendt. Tell her it's Hayden Haitana.'

On exactly the same day at almost the exact same time, Queensland Independent MP Lindsay Hartwig got to his feet in the Legislative Assembly.

Hartwig was one of those political oddities who popped up all too frequently in Joh's time. The member for Callide was a grazier from Monto, a two-pub, one-horse town, three hours' drive west of Bundaberg. He delighted locals by regularly appearing on local radio, mimicking a call of a mysterious horse race that inevitably ended with a shrieking, excited cry of 'And down the outside, here comes Lind-say', thus paying homage to the fine Queensland tradition of electing barking-mad politicians from the more remote reaches of the state.

It is safe to say his politics sat deeply on the right side of the divide, but he was no fan of the premier, nor was Joh a fan of Hartwig. A few years earlier, he had dared criticise the President of the Queensland National Party, Sir Robert Sparkes, and felt the wrath of Joh for his trouble. His motives for the potentially career-ending incident were straightforward. He was neither corruption fighter nor closet socialist. Lindsay Hartwig simply did not like being told what to do by a jumped-up property developer or even by the premier.

Expelled from the National Party in 1981, he stood as an independent in the Queensland state election of 1983 and was returned to the parliament with a handsome margin. Nevertheless, he continued to vote with the Bjelke-Petersen government at every opportunity, rendering his expulsion pointless, as if the fuss with Sparkes had been nothing more than a pillow fight over who would lie on which side of the bed.

Hartwig chose Question Time in Queensland's mono-cameral legislature to make a bit of self-serving noise, asking the Minister for Everything, Big Russ, if he believed Robbie Waterhouse was 'the Mr Big of the scandal'.

Hinze replied with the straightest of bats. Police inquiries were continuing, he said, and as a result he would make no further comment.

As he parked his gargantuan backside back down on the emerald green leather seat, Hinze gave a little smile. Hartwig may have merely been putting about some gossip or maybe he had chosen to do Big Russ a favour. Regardless, the reaction was immediate and stunning.

It took the heat off Hinze immediately. Who would bring Queensland racing to its knees with this ugly caper? Who would do such a thing? Well, those flash bastards from down south. It was them. It was them who done it. Taken poor, innocent Queenslanders to the cleaners.

This was an easier tale for the Minister for Everything to sell to the public. Without saying a conclusive word one way or another, Hinze had allowed the story to flow casually through the parliament, and from there into the media. It would have been far more uncomfortable for Hinze to admit the architects of the ring-in were a bunch of pisspots and ne'er-do-wells lounging about in

Queensland, who'd hoodwinked the Queensland Turf Club and made fools of the cops. Better for him and the government that the accusing fingers and raised eyebrows turned to the south and guessed at an elaborate conspiracy driven from Sydney.

Hinze had announced that the QTC would hold a public inquiry, effectively an investigation into itself. Big Russ knew the committee couldn't find their own arses with a sextant and a well-thumbed copy of *Gray's Anatomy*. That was just fine by him. The shit wouldn't stick. Clarrie Roberts could keep munching on his party pies and dreaming of Shangri-La at Eagle Farm.

It was business as usual in Joh's Queensland.

Hours later in Sydney, Robbie Waterhouse fronted the cameras and declared his innocence. Robbie and his old man, Bill, knew about the ring-in. They had – and were later found to have – prior knowledge of the ring-in. They knew, sure, but everyone did. There were lost tribes deep in the New Guinea highlands who'd been tipped into Fine Cotton. The tote in Port Moresby was fit to burst when Bold Personality lurched out of the barrier.

However, as time went on and more details emerged, the idea that Gillespie, Haitana and a handful of their criminally stupid mates had almost pulled off a multimillion-dollar swindle began to be questioned. The guilty understood that alibis were required. A patsy was needed. And as any crook in Sydney knows, the best fall guy is one who has already fallen and isn't going to get up.

George Freeman had collected. He always collected on time and in person. The SPs came to him one by one, ringing the bell at Yowie Bay, hearing the click of the gate and walking in, heads bowed in reverence to hand him his money. George had received them all like the Pope might, murmuring blessings as the money went from their hands to his. A million and a half in total. Cash on the knocker. It wasn't George's biggest day on the punt, but it was definitely in the top three.

He was magnanimous in victory and shook his head in disbelief when the subject of the ring-in was raised. When asked, he merely explained that Harbour Gold was the best horse in the race and as it stubbornly remained at 5/1 until the jump, he just kept backing it.

'It should have been odds-on,' he said. 'Five to one. I couldn't believe my eyes. They could have thrown Rain Lover in and I still would have backed it.'

The bookies didn't mind paying George. They'd won the day. For 24 hours before the race, every mug with a bit of spare cash and a gleam in their eye wanted to back Fine Cotton. If it had been declared the winner, all the SPs would have taken a bath, some of them knocked out for good. They would have had to go and get real jobs. God forbid.

George had simply taken the cream off what was an otherwise excellent day for the bookies. Paying him was an act of fealty. Put it down to a business expense. George Freeman was the Pope of Sydney. And he was infallible.

As he piled the cash up, doing a rough count and putting portions to one side for his expenses and for his helpers who'd performed so well at Eagle Farm, he realised he had a phone call to make. It was a call he was looking forward to making and he'd bounced it around in his head back and forth for a few hours. His first instinct was to go hard, take no shit, no excuses, no more delays. But then, while he sat there with a stack of money in front of him the size of a small car, he thought he'd play it differently.

He'd won. He could crush the poor bastard, but where was the fun in that?

'Mick, how's tricks? Haven't heard from you for a while. Everything all right?'

Sayers was at home, sitting in a fog of stale cigarette smoke and cheap regret.

He had been dreading this call. There'd been times over the last few days when the phone had rung and he'd ignored it, presuming it was Freeman. But he knew that was no plan. If he kept delaying the inevitable, he'd end up with a couple of holes in the back of his head. Fully air-conditioned, as Christopher Dale Flannery would say.

'Yeah, George we need to talk.'

'How about I talk, and you listen?'

Sayers said nothing, fully expecting a tirade of abuse and threats of violence were coming his way.

'You know, Mick, Georgina told me today there's only 65 shopping days before Christmas.'

It was rare that Freeman ever mentioned his wife. Sayers knew of her only by name. Freeman was known to meticulously guard his wife's privacy. It was an odd reference and Sayers regarded it as an ominous one.

'Right, George.'

'I'm going to give you an early Christmas present, Mick.'

'Oh yeah. What's that?'

'You know you're into Bert Talbone for $120,000. He's been grizzling to me, so I've paid him, and we'll put that on your tab. Now if my maths is any good, that's one million three hundred and twenty thousand you owe me.'

'About that, yeah.'

'Good. Here's my Christmas present. You don't have to pay me until Christmas. Not Christmas Day, 'cos I'll be with Georgina and the boys. Wouldn't do for you to knock on my door then. Christmas Eve. That's the cut-off.'

'What's the vig?'

'Now what sort of gift would that be, mate?'

'No interest? No payment until December 24?'

'I like you, Mick. You're good for business. No interest, cash in my hand by Christmas Eve. But I want all of it, no fucking about.'

'What's the catch?'

'No catch, but if you haven't paid me in full by Christmas Eve, I will catch you and that's it. All over, red rover. You know what I'm saying?'

'Yeah, I get it.'

'Your luck's going to turn, Mick. I can feel it.'

'I know. I can feel it too. Any day now.'

'Just don't get involved in any more of those shit shows. Ring-ins and what have you. You're a bloody good punter. Go with your gut.'

'George, every bastard is telling me I set that one up in Brisbane. I heard about it. I told you. I had a lash on it, did my nuts. If I'd known the shit men who were running it, I wouldn't have gone anywhere near it. I just hope you didn't come to any grief on the back of my mail.'

'I didn't touch it either, Mick. Fuckin' amateur hour up there.'

'Right you are. December 24 then?'

'Yeah. Christmas.'

'Thanks, mate. Seriously.'

'No worries. Get amongst it, Mick. Get back in the ring, son. You're worth a lot more to me alive.'

'I'll do my best to stay that way.'

'Don't forget, when you hear *Jingle Bells*, the bells are tolling for you, son.'

Freeman put the phone down and stared at it briefly. For a moment he felt a sense of euphoria, the giddying power of his munificence. Life or death. He had complete control.

The elation didn't last long. It was roughly replaced by the tell-tale constriction at the back of his throat and a hacking cough that shuddered through his entire body. He had felt it coming through the day, but preferred to ignore the signs. Fucking asthma. He sucked hard for air, gasping and wheezing in turn as he fell to the floor. Georgina and the kids were out. He needed to get upstairs.

The first flight was a scramble that left him breathless. He stood at the top of the stairs, in the grand foyer of his home, all marble what-nots and expensive bric-a-brac Georgina had collected. It was like sucking air through a pinhole. The more he gasped, the worse it got. He eyed the staircase that led to his bedroom and wondered if he'd make it.

He trudged on, pulling himself up by the bannister, and staggered into his bedroom, bumping his leg on the circular bed before reaching into his bedside drawer.

100 ml wouldn't do it. He needed 150 for this one. He stuck the needle into the bottle and pulled back hard, his hands shaking until he thought he was at just the right level. He pulled the needle out and after giving his left thigh a slap, he stuck the needle in with as much care as he could summon. He pushed the plunger down and fell back on the bed.

His breathing grew shallow and he wondered if this time it would slow further until there was nothing. He couldn't care less. The panic had left him.

Although he didn't know it yet, Freeman was about to go to war. But even if he'd had the slightest inkling, it would not have mattered. The pethidine had just kicked in and George Freeman was floating away.

The Fine Cotton ring-in, a disaster, a farce and a farrago from the outset, was reaching an ugly conclusion. Haitana had always expected things would get tropical, but nothing like this.

There was a nationwide manhunt for him. Every copper in every state and territory in the land had him in their sights. He was being hunted down like a serial killer, like some madman who'd chopped his family up with an axe and hit the road before the inevitable siege and shoot-out with the law.

Hayden Haitana's face appeared on every newspaper, and almost every news bulletin on television, he bothered to look at. The bastards had used the mugshot taken after he'd been collared for fraud. He'd owed the bookies a bit of money. They started to get antsy. It got a bit messy when Haitana started pushing bad cheques around for a bit of punting money. Next thing he knew he was in handcuffs and being sentenced to 12 months in Boggo Road. He only served six. He got out almost two years to the day before Pat went away for the same crime. Paper-hanging. Kite-flying. Keeping it in the family.

He'd been on a three-day bender before his arrest, his eyes rheumy and bloodshot, his unshaven face looking like he'd fallen chin first into a box of iron filings.

The last news he'd heard was a grab from a press conference. Some Queensland copper with a 90-year-old face wedged onto a 60-year-old body had uttered words that, in the mind of the average Australian, put Haitana in the same league as serial killers and kiddie fiddlers.

'We hold grave fears for Fine Cotton,' the cop said, his voice trailing off as the camera returned to an ashen-faced newsreader, grimly editorialising with a slow shake of his head.

Grisly images from *The Godfather* were evoked, with a bodyless Fine Cotton bleeding into silk sheets somewhere in Brisbane. Hayden Haitana was missing, and the media breathlessly reported he, too, may have been callously dismembered. Three days after the ring-in was rumbled, the *Sydney Morning Herald* reported rumours of Haitana's sudden demise. Was he lying face down in a ditch, a couple of additional orifices in his head, or was he already chatting amiably with the QTC between mouthfuls of party pies? Maybe he was holed up in a cheap motel on the Gold Coast, jumping at any sudden noise.

No-one could be sure, but the worst was feared and duly reported.

Haitana despaired. He might as well have been dead. It would have made things a hell of a lot easier. He accepted the fact that anyone who had not made his acquaintance would be inclined to put him in the same vague criminal category as a whole host of violent scumbags. He wondered if the shrill cries of newsreaders combined with their grim visions of horse mayhem gave small children nightmares.

Unmurdered, he was now officially the lowest bastard in the country. The sort of man who'd calmly slaughter a horse, cut it up into bits and feed it to starving dogs.

Haitana knew he could never hurt a horse. Sure, he might sling them some performance-enhancing chemical encouragement on occasions, but beyond that he had always found a deeper sense of companionship with horses than men.

He had left Bold Personality at the track. What else was he supposed to do? Naoum could take care of it. Besides, The Phantom's cheque had bounced, and the ownership of the horse legally returned to Naoum.

Haitana had taken care of Fine Cotton. Great care. The cops had one thing right. He didn't want Fine Cotton found anytime soon, but he was no horse killer. He was not so sure about Gillespie. Perhaps The Phantom would act on the old criminal maxim that a jury wouldn't convict without a body. Anything was possible in The Phantom's world. The whereabouts of the nine-year-old gelding would remain a secret.

He knew he couldn't stay at Coffs Harbour. His days in the sun there were over. He was on the run again. Haitana spent his night at a truck stop on the Pacific Highway, grabbing a little sleep before the glare of the northern New South Wales sun burst in through the windscreen and shook him awake.

He grabbed at the bottle of cheap scotch under the driver's seat before grasping it tight. He took a couple of deep swigs, coughed and turned the key in the ignition. The old truck spluttered in tune with Haitana's rasping hack. His throat and the carburettor cleared at almost the same time. He pumped his foot on the accelerator a few times in encouragement and the truck revved into life. He wound the window down and spat a glob of thick grey mucous onto the gravel below, before taking the handbrake off and setting out back on the highway.

He had to look his best for the cameras. That bloody mugshot was not how he wanted the world to remember him.

He needed a shave, a shower and a shit, but not necessarily in that order.

*

By the time Jana Wendt knocked on Haitana's motel-room door, *60 Minutes* had been running for five years. The US format had transferred neatly into an Australian version where a clutch of award-winning local journalists, including Jana, covered every story of even the vaguest interest, from animal attacks to gushing celebrity interviews. Millions of Australians set their clocks by it. Every Sunday night at 7.30, they gathered on their couches and their Jason recliner rockers to hear the *60 Minutes* clock tick-tick-tick.

Unsurprisingly, the interview with Haitana was the show's headline item on 30 September 1984. Had it aspired to any form of superlative in the long history of the program, it was only that it was arguably the greatest shambles of an interview ever seen on Australian television screens. Sadly, the footage no longer exists, the tape destroyed in an understandable attempt to expunge it from the national consciousness, but the memory will linger for those who witnessed it.

After checking into the cheap motel in Brunswick Heads, Haitana's ablutions had gone to plan. That was not the problem. He was showered, clean shaven and unburdened of three pounds of barely processed shit that had run the roller coaster of his bowels at horrific speed before being explosively deposited into the toilet bowl in the phone-booth-sized bathroom.

That ghastly business out of the way, he'd put on the clean shirt he'd carefully folded into his suitcase. He'd even availed himself of the complimentary disposable toothbrush found in the meagre bathroom and scrubbed his teeth diligently before rinsing the detritus from his teeth with what was then a half-empty bottle of scotch.

That was not really a problem either, given Haitana's vast appetite for alcohol. His much-put-upon liver would have comfortably dealt with that. He may have reeked of booze and might even have appeared at peace with his 'wanted man' status. A television audience would be none the wiser. Haitana could easily neck a half bottle of scotch and pass a sobriety test.

The problem was that while Haitana awaited the arrival of the *60 Minutes* crew, he prowled the confines of his tiny motel room in a state of deep agitation, seeking to calm his nerves by consuming the remainder of the bottle. Then, still feeling some sense of foreboding, he opened another one and downed that too.

By the time the much-feted journalist Jana Wendt arrived with a cameraman and sound technician in tow, Haitana was as drunk as three men: those three men being himself, the former Governor-General Sir John Kerr, who became known as the drunkest man in Australia at the Melbourne Cup in 1977, and Kerr's drinking buddy on that ill-fated day, former Victorian Premier Sir Henry Bolte.

Later, Haitana would claim Wendt had supplied the whisky but that was a lie. She at least would have purchased booze somewhere higher up on the bottle-o's shelf than Haitana's slurp of choice, which bore some faux Scottish brand in a dismal attempt at authenticity. Dunlivin', it might as well have been called.

Wendt knew she had a ripping yarn on her hands. Haitana might not have been Australia's most wanted man at the time. That dubious award remained in the keeping of the prison escapee and counter jumper, Russell 'Mad Dog' Cox, and would for almost another decade. But Haitana was the most celebrated criminal on the run at that point in time. He was the gatekeeper to the ring-in that had enthralled the nation.

Once it began, the interview veered quickly into high farce. Haitana grinned like a madman at his introduction. He was momentarily distracted by the sound technician's boom mic and swatted at it as if irritated by a gigantic blowfly. The soundie stoically kept the mic in place, so Haitana clutched at it again, this time grasping it and, pulling it down towards his mouth, he began chewing on it and muttering obscenities.

After that Haitana leered at Wendt, ogled her breasts and her legs, stricken by alcohol's powerful ability to provoke and unprovoke, to paraphrase Shakespeare. Intent had loomed at the turn in first place but was ultimately overrun by the sort of libido paralysis that only comes after consuming the best part of two bottles of rotgut whisky.

Of what little sense Haitana had been capable of communicating in that interview, the audience was able to glean only that he said his life was in danger, but was unable to identify anyone who had threatened him, let alone Gillespie's bogie man, Mick Sayers. Gillespie did not get a mention, either by name or sobriquet. Haitana merely referred darkly to an anonymous chief conspirator who had priors for smuggling native wildlife.

Wendt had heard the rumours of the involvement of the Waterhouses and she asked if there were any Sydney bookmakers involved. Haitana responded with a wink and said the biggest names in horseracing were up to their back teeth in it.

When asked where Fine Cotton was, Haitana said he didn't know but that he believed the horse was in hiding, as if Fine Cotton had realised he'd become too tropical and had high-tailed it out of Brisbane, and was now peering out through the venetian blinds in some faraway hideout.

Jana Wendt asked again if Fine Cotton had come to some mischief. Was he still alive? Haitana's response was to fart, follow through and fall asleep. Interview concluded.

Wendt and her sidekicks quickly gathered their things together and fled the scene. The interview would provide a great examination of the skills of the program's video editors. Nine minutes of tape was eventually cut down to a breezy two, featuring a clearly refreshed Haitana but failing to convey how horrifically pissed he was.

60 Minutes' tilt at explaining the bizarre story of the Fine Cotton ring-in had come up short. At least the program's audience had for the first time been given a rough introduction into the almost microscopically small calibre of one of its protagonists.

Haitana didn't come to for another three hours, his pants wet front and back. When he woke he found himself wondering if the tête-à-tête had happened at all, but the haze quickly cleared and he remembered the awfulness of it.

Never mind that, he thought.

How long before the rozzers were onto him and surrounded the motel room before kicking the door in and sticking guns in his face? They could come at any minute. It was time to go, but where?

He didn't even feel safe in New South Wales anymore.

CHAPTER TEN
Princes of perjury

'I just followed the money.'
– Father Edward O'Dwyer

RUSS HINZE KNEW that Queensland punters, like punters every-where, would bet on two flies climbing up a wall, should push come to shove. But if Queensland punters ever clocked that Blowfly A was juiced up and Blowfly B wasn't Blowfly B at all, but another fitter, faster fly, Blowfly C, there'd be hell to pay.

Punters would walk away and shell their money out on other, more reliable fare. That great Queensland public institution, now National Party plaything, the Queensland TAB would suffer first. Agencies in strip malls the length and breadth of the state would be deserted with two bored attendants seated behind the counter, playing cards.

Then where would Joh's Queensland be? A couple of regional hospitals short on gaming excise for a start. Worse still, the SPs who paid the cops to stay in business would cry poor. Hinze would find that his own cut was, in fact, cut. Fuck that for a giggle.

Happily, Hinze had not appointed Clarrie Roberts to discover any uncomfortable truths. It would not do for punters to conclude that the Queensland racing industry was a deeply dodgy caper, its overseers drunk on a rancid cocktail of incompetence and corruption.

He had just the right man in Clarrie Roberts. Roberts couldn't get to the bottom of this. He'd be flat out skimming the scum off the top.

Had Roberts approached the task with any degree of vigour and intellect, he would have recalled that, in 1982, they'd sworn trainer Bill Steer off tracks for life after he'd pulled a ring-in at Doomben. On that occasion, Steer had switched Apparent Heir over for a dawdler named Mannasong. There was a betting plunge then, too, although nothing like the money that went on Fine Cotton. The ring-in only came unstuck when Apparent Heir, two or three classes above the rest of the field, decided to take the day off and finished back among the also-rans.

The connections of both horses were one John Gillespie, partnered by a shadowy figure by the name of Mal McGregor-Lowndes. Both men had a long list of criminal convictions, McGregor-Lowndes for wildlife smuggling, including a bizarre conviction where he was pulled up for trying to sell sparrows as canaries after painting the ubiquitous grey-brown birds a bright yellow.

In scenes that were only mildly evocative of the Fine Cotton fiasco but almost identical to Monty Python's Dead Parrot sketch, McGregor-Lowndes was only rumbled when the flaxen sparrows, palsied by paint fumes, began hitting the bottom of their cages, leaving aviculturists angrily seeking redress.

The QTC might also have discovered that in 1983, Gillespie and McGregor-Lowndes had acquired the four-year-old gelding, Captain Cadet. The horse had not had a run under its new owners, due possibly to the fact that Gillespie was enjoying one of his numerous holidays in Boggo Road at the time. Released on parole, Gillespie had planned a ring-in with Captain Cadet only to learn that, like Dashing Soltaire a year later, he had suffered serious injury and could not race.

In order to give the inquiry the barest whiff of credibility, the QTC had bailed up a few of the punters who'd backed Fine Cotton. They all said the same thing. They were chasing the money, and the money was all on Fine Cotton.

Chairman Clarrie Roberts even pulled in 'The Butterfly' – John Mort Green, his good mate who'd passed him a betting ticket with Fine Cotton's name on it. Clarrie didn't mention the fact he stood to win over $300,000 had Fine Cotton been given the thumbs-up by his stewards, and he knew The Butterfly had too much sense to bring it up either.

Po-faced, The Butterfly said he'd backed Fine Cotton based on the mail he'd picked up around the track. When he saw the money on Fine Cotton begin to come in, he had his betting agents back it in a big way. He'd lost over 40 grand when Fine Cotton was disqualified. Clarrie led the grimaces and the murmurs of sympathy when The Butterfly told his tale of punting woe.

The larger problem for all racing authorities who'd started poking around the Fine Cotton affair was that for years the races in Brisbane had been beset with betting plunges. It had been going on for so long that punters had learned to ignore the vagaries of form and simply sit back and watch the betting markets, ready to jump on a hot favourite that an hour beforehand had been sitting unloved at 12/1. More often than not, the horse would win.

Thus, any punter who might or might not have been in on the ring-in could offer a credible defence that they had merely had a lash on the big market mover.

It was a game of follow the leader, but the question remained – who was the leader? The QTC knew Haitana was in on it and determined, grimly, that the trainer would never set foot on a racetrack again. But even their simple minds could not be bent to the notion that Haitana had acted alone. It was all too hard. In the end the QTC decided not to decide and handpassed the lot over to the cops.

South of the Tweed, racing authorities were also confounded. Like Queensland's Minister for Racing, they understood the practical problems associated with a bent game, but, unlike Hinze, they resolved to do something about it.

The Australian Jockeys' Club, the premier racing industry body based in Sydney and cop on the beat of Australian thoroughbred racing, decided to change tack. Finding the architects of the scheme was too damned hard and might not in any measure find those who'd profited from it. Instead, the AJC decided to follow the money, and examine every large bet placed on Fine Cotton.

Ominously, those who placed them found themselves in the sights of Chief Steward John 'The Sheriff' Schreck. At the track The Sheriff effortlessly sported a trilby with the air of a man who had emerged from the womb, tried one on, liked the look of it and determined to keep it atop his bonce for good. It was rumoured that he showered in the thing.

The records showed bets had been scattered around Australia, the most peculiar being whisky priest Father Ted O'Dwyer's large investment at the Appin dogs. Merchant banker Ian Murray's lash in Tasmania was also noted as strange. Another bet, the one that led bookmaker Mark Read to publicly declare his suspicions of a ring-in and shut betting down on the race, was placed by Garry Clarke, a betting agent for Robbie Waterhouse.

The more The Sheriff looked, the more he became convinced that Robbie, and perhaps his bookmaker father Bill, were in on the Fine Cotton scam. They might not have organised it – and Schreck and the AJC made no such charge – but the big punters, ecclesiastical and secular, were issued notices to show cause why they should not be warned off racing tracks for good, along with Bill and Robbie Waterhouse.

The Sheriff hunted Murray down like a bloodhound, picking up his spore and finding him once again in Tasmania. When Schreck came across the merchant banker, he offered the predictable defence that he'd merely observed the betting plunge and, lemming-like, decided to get on.

Murray was not quite done. He claimed he'd asked Bill Waterhouse for a bet of $2800 to $40,000 but that Bill had declined the large wager, preferring a more modest flutter of $1000 at 14/1 instead.

The patriarch of the bookmaking family used this as a defence against the charge that he had prior knowledge of the Fine Cotton ring-in. If he did, why would he expose himself to a 14/1? This did baffle The Sheriff and the AJC, albeit briefly.

The Sheriff would not be denied and obtained evidence from Tasmanian racing authorities that live odds from the Eagle Farm meet were not broadcast onto their tracks on the day in question. In other words, Murray could not have known the plunge was taking place.

Similarly, Father Ted told The Sheriff that he'd merely observed the plunge on Fine Cotton and decided to jump on. His stated reasons for his special trip to the Appin dishlickers, however, were not entirely persuasive.

The stewards knew, like the rest of Australia, that no-one went to Appin dogs for a charming day out with fun for all the family. The only people who went there had a bloody good reason to.

The Sheriff persisted relentlessly with this line of questioning until the man of the cloth broke down and confessed that he'd been betting on behalf of Robbie Waterhouse.

Murray's story eventually fell apart under interrogation too, as did Clarke's. They had all been betting on behalf of Robbie Waterhouse. The bet Murray had placed with Bill was fictitious. It was a kind of bookmaker's alibi, but it had collapsed under ferocious examination.

Bill straight-batted his way through his evidence. Plonked the front foot down and gave the bowler a good look at the bat maker's brand. He stated he'd only taken one bet on the race, the negotiated wager from Murray, but sensed there was something a bit whiffy about Eagle Farm race four and decided to take no further bets on it. Robbie made the biggest mistake, declaring under oath that he hadn't had a bet on Fine Cotton.

He clambered down out of the witness box thinking he'd charmed the AJC into benevolence. He was completely unprepared for the fact that Murray, Clarke and a man of God who was sporting a priest's dog collar in the witness box declared they were doing Robbie's bidding. He might not have physically punted a single dollar on Fine Cotton, but he had a small army of lieutenants who did, and they'd done it all with his money.

At this point, Robbie was in more shit than a Werribee duck. He was not only rumbled for prior knowledge of the ring-in, but, much worse, it appeared he had given deliberately false evidence under oath and was looking at a perjury blue and possibly a holiday at Long Bay.

The perjury matter was referred to the NSW Director of Public Prosecutions, who looked long and hard at the evidence.

In the meanwhile, the AJC determined that Robbie had prior knowledge of the Fine Cotton ring-in. His bookmaker's licence was torn up and he was warned off racetracks for life. Not just Australian racetracks, mind you, but every single affiliated racecourse in the world: the US, Europe, the UK and Asia.

The same fate befell father Bill. The AJC determined that the bet he'd taken from Murray was fictitious. It never happened. Bill Waterhouse was consigned to watching the races on the telly from his couch at home. He, too, was not permitted to take another legal bet.

The AJC had put the Waterhouses to sleep.

Ian Murray and Garry Clarke and Clarke's wife, Margaret, who'd also had a lash with Robbie's dough, were sent to Coventry as well. They would never again be allowed to enter a racetrack while they remained respiring and in the vertical.

Father Ted O'Dwyer was warned off for life too. His role in the ring-in was cause for minor scandal within the Roman Catholic Church. The Church quietly considered laicising the whisky priest, the clerical version of breaking one's sword and tearing off one's epaulettes in symbolic shaming prior to a lifetime of exile, but ultimately decided against it.

They had much bigger, uglier skeletons still rattling around in their closets. Having one of theirs punting on a ring-in would pale into insignificance when those doors finally blew open.

Afterwards, Bill Waterhouse blamed George Freeman for the whole fiasco. He was about half right. Certainly, Freeman disliked Bill and thought even less of his son Robbie, but a list of names of those who don't much care for the Waterhouses in racing circles is long – so long that it could fit neatly into a leather-bound set of *Encyclopaedia Britannica* with only a little minor editing.

Freeman had ensured Robbie knew of the ring-in. George had given Robbie prior knowledge. He'd spread the Fine Cotton ring-in mail far and wide, believing Robbie's instinct would take care of the rest. If Robbie was silly enough to be tempted, well, that was hardly Freeman's fault, was it? Indeed, for him the exile of the Waterhouses from racing was what he might call a corollary benefit.

George Freeman's vocabulary didn't extend to such fancy phrases, but just quietly, he would have liked the sound of it.

*

It would take two more years for the manure to hit the oscillator in Queensland, but when it did it was spectacular.

The day after *Four Corners* went to air with their 'Moonlight State' episode on 11 May 1987, exposing corruption within the Queensland cops and at the upper echelons of the Bjelke-Petersen government, Joh was out of the state on one of his numerous goodwill tours.

It will forever remain a mystery how Joh would have handled it had he been in town. But he wasn't – by a stroke of rotten luck that sealed the fate of the government and guaranteed the Labor landslide of 1989, Joh was travelling overseas, and Bill Gunn, an honest man, was acting premier. Before Joh could scurry home and scream, 'Don't you worry about that!' at the baying press pack, Gunn had panicked, and immediately ordered a Royal Commission.

The rest is history, but the Fitzgerald Inquiry that tore Joh's empire to shreds made history itself. It hardly cleansed the state or the nation of corruption, but being a crook has been a trickier enterprise across Australia ever since. The salad days of unfettered sleaze were over.

In the end, it all got down to the sick symbiosis that allowed an intellectually and morally bereft administration to rely on a crooked and well-armed security apparatus to do their dirty work for them while looking the other way, as they convinced enough of the gullible voters in a grotesquely gerrymandered electorate that they were 'doing good things for Queensland'.

Joh was constantly distracting the citizenry, urging them to gaze in awe at the cranes towering over the Brisbane skyline, rather than peer into the gutters of Fortitude Valley. He didn't do it alone, though he certainly liked to give that impression. He had plenty of hired help only too happy to play their part, and the cops were pivotal both to his success and ultimate unravelling.

Terry Lewis was utterly corrupt, and so unsubtle about it that eventually something had to give – but it took a while to happen. It's still astonishing that this state of affairs lasted as long as it did, and the fact that Lewis effectively ran the dark side of Queensland for over a decade with minimal interference is testament to how deft the Bjelke-Petersen government was at distancing itself from the sordid truth on the streets.

Mick Sayers' luck had not turned. The bad fortune that had hung over him would continue to do so for what remained of his life.

Sayers was put firmly in the frame. Robbie Waterhouse had mentioned Mick's name in evidence and to the media at the AJC hearing. Racing commentators hinted at Sayers' involvement in the ring-in. On 2 December 1984, the *Sydney Morning Herald* described the presence of a Melbourne-born gangster now living in Sydney as the principal architect of the Fine Cotton scandal. He was being fingered for a ring-in he had nothing to do with, defamed by conmen. The AJC could summon him to give evidence, but if they did, Sayers would tell them to get fucked. All the same, he kept an eye out for process servers, eager to slap a subpoena on him. It didn't come.

He'd taken the call when Gillespie had rung him from the Courthouse Hotel in Murwillumbah. Gillespie had paid attention to instructions, firmly pronouncing that monosyllabic expression of affirmation over the telephone and then hanging up. Sayers had told Freeman with the usual caveats about price and form. Mick had offered a character reference of Gillespie to Freeman and it wasn't exactly glowing.

Sayers had backed Fine Cotton and lost. He was almost broke, and time was running out.

Mick had every right to feel agitated. A week earlier, driven by desperation and the threat of murder, he'd made the biggest mistake of his life.

It was an all too common tale from the underworld. Sayers would rob Peter to pay Paul or, more precisely, rob Barry McCann to pay George Freeman. It was the gambler's ultimate lash, a punt on his own life.

In a frenzy of poor intentions and bad decisions, Sayers hit up Sydney's biggest heroin trafficker, McCann. The plan was a simple one. He'd grab the gear, jump on it and sell it off to Sydney's new violent criminal thug with the green light from the cops, Neddy Smith. He'd done it before, usually a kilo and a half, sometimes two, and each time he'd walked away a wealthy man.

Neddy was always a welcome buyer. The high-grade China white heroin McCann was knocking out was better than the black tar shit Neddy would jump on time and time again with lactose to bring it back to a more saleable, coarse brown powder.

This time, it was a big one. Five kilograms. When Sayers gave McCann the code over the phone, like he was asking for his dry cleaning to be done, the request for five shirts and no ties (five kilograms, no halves) didn't evoke any sign of surprise. McCann was getting his smack flown into the country direct from Thailand, stored on planes by catering staff at Bangkok Airport and delicately pulled out at Mascot by a couple of maintenance guys on the take. He had plenty.

There were just two problems. Sayers owed Freeman a lot more than 500 grand and he was flat broke.

He'd decided to do it exactly the way he had before. No surprises. Get hold of McCann and agree to meet him in the car park at the Australian Youth Hotel, a pub in Glebe that, back in those days, was like a class reunion for crims.

McCann used to drink there and take care of business. His own pub, the Lansdowne, was another den of thieves and sometimes vicious crooks, but McCann thought it politic to sell his heroin elsewhere.

The two men arranged to meet at 11 o'clock in the morning. McCann had arrived promptly, a man in a hurry. Sayers had arrived 15 minutes earlier but he'd parked his car in a side street and waited. He needed to be late. Not too late but just late enough.

Satisfied that McCann was now waiting, he jogged up the street to the hotel car park. Sayers spotted the black Merc. He nodded at McCann, who was sitting in the driver's seat, and got in alongside him.

'Sorry, mate. Fuckin' parking around this place.'

'Keep your voice down,' McCann said. He turned, swivelled his body and grabbed two shopping bags from the rear of the car. 'All yours.'

Sayers peered into the bags. Three small, solid cardboard boxes in one bag, two in the other.

'Prompt, Barry. Many thanks. I'll just get the money.'

'Don't fuck around.'

Sayers grabbed the two shopping bags and headed for his car. He thought he might do a runner there and then. Not return. Just keep on going. But that was madness. It would be seen as an insult to McCann and the retribution would have been swift and conclusive. Instead, Sayers grabbed his jacket and threw it in the gutter, smearing it from side to side next to a storm water drain.

He loosened his tie and then took a breath before driving the left side of his face hard into the brick wall of the pub. He nearly knocked himself out but regained his composure with a quick shake of his head. He was bleeding from a cut above his left eye. He wiped his forehead but by then the blood was flowing freely down his face and dripping onto his shirt. Good, he thought. The more, the merrier.

McCann was not known for his patience. A minute's wait would have led to an angry scene. But here he was 10 minutes later, still sitting in his car, and he was becoming homicidal. His fingers drummed on the dashboard and he exhaled deeply, trying to calm himself down. But then he thought, 'Fuck it,' better to make use of his rage.

He looked down at the console where he kept his gun. One more minute and he'd have it in his hand. If he had to tool up, that meant he was obliged to get out of the car and make his presence felt. And if he had to get out of the car, he'd shoot someone just for the inconvenience.

While McCann was still pondering who he might shoot, he spied Sayers staggering around the corner, bleeding heavily from a head wound. Sayers approached and tried to open the passenger side door. McCann had locked it and eased the window down.

'Get away from my fuckin' car. You're bleeding like a stuck pig.'

'I've been fuckin' robbed, Barry,' Mick gasped. 'You wouldn't fuckin' believe it.'

'I don't believe it.'

'Barry, mate . . .'

'Do you think I'm a fucking mug, Mick? Is that what you think?'

Sayers could tell the ruse was failing badly at the very first hurdle. He wasn't sure whether he should press on with the story and embellish it further or just to shut up in the hope McCann would take pity and cut him a break. He chose the former.

'No, mate. I got jumped. Couple of Asian blokes blindsided me,' Sayers said, pleading.

'Get away from my fuckin' car,' McCann said. McCann gunned the motor, his Mercedes purring to life. As it did, the passenger window rose with Mick's bloody handprints festooned upon it.

'If I haven't got my heroin or my money in 24 hours, you're fuckin' dead, Mick.'

It would take longer than 24 hours. Ultimately, it took seven weeks. Just long enough for Sayers to leave his guard down and momentarily forget the danger he was in.

He jumped on the smack that afternoon, cutting the grainy product with five kilograms of icing sugar he'd pulled off the shelves at the Bondi Junction Woolworths earlier that morning, turning five keys of pure China white into 10. He knew Neddy would jump on it again and turn 10 keys into 20. By the time it got to the street and into some junkie's arm, it would be less than 10 per cent pure. That was OK. Anything stronger than that and smackies would be overdosing all over the place, the pick still quivering in their arms.

Neddy paid him a cool million. No stretch for Ned. He was making that a week. More shopping bags, this time four, stuffed with cash.

Sayers drove straight to Yowie Bay. Freeman accepted the repayment at the door, still in his dressing gown, with a grunt and a nod, like Sayers was returning a borrowed power tool.

The source of Sayers' newfound wealth did not come up but Freeman would know the dough hadn't come from a win on the horses. Freeman had his ear close to the ground. He didn't ask, and Sayers wouldn't tell, that he was one of McCann's heroin wholesale network. It would not have gone down well.

1984 was almost at an end and Sayers was still respiring. He'd invited his dad and his two brothers up from Melbourne for the Christmas break. He took them out to the clubs and pubs and got them pissed. Mick, however, remained sober, alert and on edge.

Mick had packed Marian's bag and she took off for a few days to let the Sayers boys have some fun. She went to stay at her own apartment on Sydney's Lower North Shore, returning briefly on Christmas Day to cook the turkey and dole out the almost endless supply of booze.

Throughout the week Sayers' youngest brother, Robbie, felt something was wrong. He would see his brother jump at the slightest noise and when the phone rang, Mick would panic and demand no-one take the call. He seemed to spend most of his time peering out the window, a smoke hanging out of his mouth, while he ran his eyes down the street and back again.

'What's up, Mick?' the teenager asked.

Sayers hadn't wanted to alert his family to the terrible peril he faced, let alone his youngest brother. Robbie looked up to him, the 12-year age difference making him more like a father figure.

'I'm off, mate.'

'Waddya mean, you're off?'

'I'm off.'

In that instant Robbie understood what his brother meant.

'Jump on a plane, Mick. Get out of town. Run. Hide.'

Sayers put his arm around his brother and pulled him towards him.

'There's no point, mate. In my line of work, when you're off, you're off.'

Robbie protested again but Mick cut him short.

'There's nothing you or I can do about it. The only thing you can do is keep your mouth shut and look after Dad if push comes to shove.'

Two days later, Sayers dropped his brothers and his father at the airport. The goodbyes were perfunctory. Abrupt, short. When it came time to farewell Robbie, he chucked a soft punch into his belly and smiled.

'See ya later, kid. Take care of the old man.'

'Come with us, Mick. Get away from it all. Let it die down.'

'Poor choice of words, mate. I'll see you around.'

New Year's Day 1985 came and went and Sayers was still in the vertical. Any day above ground was a good day. He wasn't silly enough to believe McCann would forget about the small matter of the half a million dollars of smack he'd lifted off him, but maybe, Sayers thought, McCann had a bit on his plate at the time.

That's how it happens. Sayers dropped his guard and incrementally began to step back on his security. He couldn't help himself. There was always one more race, one more lash.

Years later, Robbie recalled asking him during a quiet moment on Christmas Day if the rumours were true. Did he organise the Fine Cotton ring-in?

'You think I'd be involved with those mugs?' Mick replied.

Robbie believed him then and he was right.

*

Two months earlier, one of those mugs, Hayden Haitana, was arrested in the Truro pub, a town 100 kilometres north-east of Adelaide with an already notorious reputation as the site of seven murders by one of South Australia's numerous serial killers.

The moment he pulled into town, Haitana knew he needed a drink. He had a thirst he could have painted in oil. He parked the old F100, pulled his baseball cap down low and popped his sunglasses on.

The disguise fell somewhat short of ambition. There was a nationwide manhunt for him and the barman recognised him at once. He pulled a beer for Hayden with a smile and then went into the back office to call the cops.

Haitana was arrested without incident and within 48 hours was extradited to Brisbane to face the full wrath of the Queensland Fraud Squad. The Phantom was still missing, but by then the cops had lost enthusiasm for bringing the full force of the law to the culprits. He continued to hide in plain sight in Murwillumbah.

The manhunt for Haitana had its equine equivalent. The Queensland Police muttered darkly that Fine Cotton must be dead, an ugly collateral death to protect the guilty.

But as it turned out, Fine Cotton was alive. And not just alive, the gelding was in police custody and had been within an hour of the race. In the chaos that ensued in the immediate aftermath of the ring-in, Haitana had dropped Fine Cotton off at the Queensland Mounted Police stables, a stone's throw from Eagle Farm.

He figured the cops and handlers probably wouldn't notice an extra horse in the stables and he was right. No-one seemed terribly concerned that a rather lovely and lovable dark chocolate brown gelding spent his days grazing in the paddocks and made his way to the stables each evening for a feed and rest.

It was only when a vet was summoned to tend to one of the other horses a full eight weeks after the ring-in that the penny dropped. There was an extra horse at the stables. A good-looking horse too. Chocolate brown with white socks. One of the mounted policemen came down to have a look. Mystified at the unexplained presence of an extra horse in the paddock, he did a ring around. About an hour later the fraud squad arrived. The cops belted down in number to the stables to see for themselves.

As they approached, Fine Cotton looked up and then returned to grazing peacefully in the paddock. He must have wondered what all the fuss was about.

CHAPTER ELEVEN
Party time

'It's really only fraud. Just one count.'
— Bobby North

IT IS SAID there are two certainties in life: death and taxes. If it was a universal rule, an axiom for the hardship of modern existence, it did not apply to the Sydney underworld's most prominent members.

They didn't pay tax for a start. Being in the business of murder for money, or cold-blooded slayings at the barrel of a gun to improve one's status, meant the possibility of an audit at the hands of the Australian Taxation Office was not high on the list of forebodings. A violent death was an unpleasant prospect, but more an occupational hazard than an odds-on favourite.

The two great certainties in life for a Sydney gangster were jail and bent cops.

Mick Sayers was determined not to fall victim to either of these pitfalls. He assiduously avoided the company of New South Wales' finest. A good Melbourne crook kept well clear of the wallopers. Mick could still recall the words of the old Painter and Docker, Billy 'The Texan' Longley. Banged up in H Division in Pentridge while Mick cooled his heels in the marginally more salubrious confines of B Division, The Texan had taken to pontificating about crime and the vagaries of law enforcement in each state.

'In Melbourne, there's us and there's them. In Sydney, you wouldn't know the fuckin' difference.'

It was apt. Sydney was a nest of vipers and every cop had a crim in his back pocket. That meant any crim looking to get himself out of a tight squeeze would give anyone up, friend or foe. Foe first, sure, but mateship, too, had very narrow limits.

Sayers' dabbling in the heroin trade was well hidden under his persona of racetrack bon vivant and gadabout punter. The taxman didn't seem especially interested in his profit and loss statements. The fistfuls of money that went out in one hand, mainly to Freeman's SP bookies, were replaced by the revenue in supplying the burgeoning demand of Sydneysiders' hungry arms. Out one hand, up the arm of another, and a modest profit on the balance sheet at the end of the day.

The Fine Cotton ring-in had been an unmitigated disaster and he had lost plenty on it, but it wasn't the end of the world. The Queensland coppers couldn't find their own arses with an atlas and a sextant, but even if they did have Haitana in a small room being asked all sorts of awkward questions, Sayers was out of the picture. Too many steps away. Gillespie might have given him up. That prick would do anything to save his own arse, but the conman was nowhere to be found.

Sayers was still into McCann for the big lump of smack he'd pinched. He could sort that out if he was given some time, some breathing space. He needed a plan and the only one that made any sense was a ball-bursting day at the track where he'd punt his way out of a death sentence, baffle the bookies and take their dough. Then he could take care of McCann. Make everything right again. He just needed time and a turn of fortune.

The prospects of the rozzers banging on the door and a stint in jail were quickly dismissed. The biggest worry he had came in the form of a one-man crime wave, his old mate from B Division, Christopher Dale Flannery. It was only a matter of time before Flannery would come knocking.

Flannery was in Sydney. He hadn't driven up the Hume in a shiny new red Mercedes as Sayers had done three years ago, or jumped on a plane to the Emerald City. Flannery had arrived in handcuffs, extradited to New South Wales on a murder charge.

Raymond Francis Locksley was a hoon and a toe-cutter from Sydney, who thought he could stand over the brothel trade in Melbourne. The greasy punk had set fire to a couple of knock shops to make his intentions firmly understood, seemingly unaware that certain elements within the Victoria Police force were receiving additions to their salaries to ensure that the smooth and uninterrupted function of the business of the house continued apace. Rather than pay an additional stipend to Locksley, the brothel owners contacted the wallopers and were discreetly referred to the services of Christopher Dale Flannery and his murder-for-hire business, Rentakill.

That was it for Locksley. He was found face down out in the scrub in Menai. Two .357 rounds in the back of his head. Flannery had shot the extortionist in Melbourne and driven back up to Sydney with Locksley bleeding out in the boot.

Christ, Sayers thought, the boot of Flannery's car would be a treasure trove to any forensic examination. A mobile morgue for the suddenly demised.

Flannery had only just walked from another murder charge. The disappearance of businessman Roger Wilson. At the time, it was the longest running criminal trial in Australian history. Sayers had followed the reports keenly in the newspapers. The cops seemed to have the wood on his old cellmate but then a crown witness, a young prostitute who would finger Flannery and his associate for the murder, didn't turn up. Unsurprisingly, she hasn't shown up since.

They never did find Wilson's body either, although it's said that anyone who drives along the Mulgrave Freeway in the outer south-eastern suburbs of Melbourne and hears a disturbing *be-doom, be-doom* as the tyres hit two small bumps on the otherwise smooth road might be considered to have paid his remains a visit.

Eventually acquitted, Flannery walked out of the Supreme Court in Melbourne. It was the briefest taste of freedom. He only got three steps outside the courthouse when a New South Wales Homicide detective, Bill Duff, stepped forward and put the cuffs on him.

Sayers knew the fix was in after Flannery was extradited to Sydney and got bail the same day. Bail on a murder charge. It was unheard of under normal circumstances. Duff was the conduit to Roger Rogerson. Flannery was in the pocket of the most dangerous cop in the state.

Sayers kept tabs on Flannery in dispatches. A word here and there in the pub or on the racetrack. His old cellmate was doing a little quid pro quo for a flash doctor, Geoffrey Edelsten. Fuck knows what all that was about, but it was bound not to be good.

Then Sayers learned that Flannery had been hired as Freeman's bodyguard. That was like throwing water on a fat fire. Sayers had an image of a pile of bloody bodies poolside at Freeman's house after Flannery had fallen out with some of George's mates over the relative merits of placing a pineapple ring on a hamburger.

And then, on the Friday before the Fine Cotton ring-in, Flannery had turned up at the Lansdowne Hotel, a pub in Sydney owned and run by Barry McCann, and king hit McCann's missus. Broke her jaw. Barry wasn't present at the time, but as his wife lay unconscious on the ground, guns were drawn and Flannery did his party trick, biting the top off a schooner, chewing and swallowing the jagged glass with a bloody smile.

One thing was certain. Flannery's arrival in Sydney was not going to end well. Sayers knew the phone call would come with a cheery Flannery on the other end, suggesting a meet, a drink and a walk down memory lane. He didn't have much choice but to agree. A polite decline was not an option.

The two men were joined together by the awful shared experience of jail, as young crooks staking their reputations among some of the most violent men in Australia and living to tell the tale.

Sayers was reading the paper at his home in Coogee, paying attention to the announcement of the Fine Cotton trial which was scheduled to kick off in a fortnight. He'd noted Gillespie was still at large but had been charged in absentia.

Perhaps it was because he was on his fourth cup of coffee and his fifth cigarette of the day that when the phone rang, he jumped. Perhaps it was because the only calls Sayers received after the Fine Cotton ring-in were dark threats and ominous warnings. But when he finally picked the phone up, Sayers was almost relieved to hear Flannery's voice, full of vim and mateship.

''Bout time you and I played up, Mick. A big one. A fucking huge night on the tiles.'

Sayers couldn't say no. But he didn't feel he wanted to either. Flannery was right. There was only one way to do this. A bender, a relentless, reckless episode of wretched excess – replete with booze, strippers and a head full of cocaine.

It had to be done. The sooner, the better.

Sayers was able to keep tabs on the wash-up of the ring-in because the news ran in the papers almost every day. There were regular updates when Haitana was arrested and when Fine Cotton was found. In October, Haitana, Bobby North and Tommaso di Luzio were all charged with conspiracy to defraud the public by affecting by deceit the result of a race conducted by the Queensland Turf Club. Gillespie was also charged but was doing his best impression of the Invisible Man at the time.

The Fine Cotton ring-in was, sports editors universally declared, a day of shame for the racing industry. Once they settled on this, the reports were a mixture of confusing facts and less than subtle hints that the conspirators – Haitana, di Luzio, North and Gillespie, who remained happily at large – could not have acted alone.

There were suggestions of dark forces at work, the sinister hand of organised crime at the highest level running interference and officials at the back of the stands collecting backhanders to look the other way.

It was true, to a point, but the more journalists dug into the story of the ring-in, the more confused they became. The fact that three drunks and a manipulative fantasist had almost pulled off a multi-million-dollar scam under the noses of racing authorities and their overseers and regulators in government, as they stumbled from crisis to crisis, was considered too obvious and not nearly juicy enough.

But for all the convoluted theories, no-one asked why Eagle Farm was full to the back teeth with coppers who were clutching Fine Cotton to win betting tickets, a number of whom were members of the Queensland Fraud Squad who were subsequently entrusted with investigating the farce.

Above all, no-one asked how many ring-ins might have taken place with a slightly more sober and better organised outfit pulling the ring-in and getting away scot-free. To do so would have ignited a much wider scandal, of the common or garden punter being fleeced by forces beyond his or her ken on an all too regular basis.

In Australia in 1984, there were only a few lawful means for a punter to enjoy having a lash and, at the time, betting on horse-racing made up almost 90 per cent of all wagering in the country.

If the whole show was rigged, with the outcome of this particular game of chance known in advance by a few, the whole industry could have collapsed there and then.

Happily for racing in Australia, the reporting in the wake of the ring-in added to the overall impression that the Fine Cotton switcheroo – a fraud, a farrago and a fiasco – was one out of the box, a oncer, never to be repeated.

However, it left one important question unanswered: if the Fine Cotton ring-in was ostensibly such an easy thing to (almost) pull off, was the racing industry, at least in Queensland, so poorly regulated that any clown with a glint of criminality could drive a Leopard tank onto a racecourse, call it Phar Lap's great-grandson, and drive off with the cash and prizes?

The QTC remained stoically in denial. The stewards complained they were too hard pressed to keep an eye on every drippy horse that staggered into the barriers. For all the shame and outrage, the preconditions for another ring-in remained in place.

The Queensland government, like all state governments around the country, understood the practical realities of the punt. Revenues from gaming put kids through schools, applied fresh bitumen on road surfaces and had the trains running more or less on time. If the punters walked away and left their money in their wallets, where would it all end?

No stranger to financial self-improvement by fair means or foul, Russ Hinze was happy to work the conspiracy theories or give them some volume. He was happy to point a finger at the Waterhouses. He had no proof but that didn't bother him. It was more important to create the illusion that the only way to crack Queensland racing was by an elaborate conspiracy that involved ne'er-do-wells from down south.

In other words, it was standing room only on the grassy knoll, the magic bullet replaced with a bucket of hair dye and a spray can of Dulux hi-gloss. A lunar landing mocked up in a Hollywood studio with Bold Personality clambering out of Apollo 11.

Racing writers and sports journalists generally are not, for the most part, aware of the principle of Occam's razor, otherwise known as the first law of parsimony, which broadly speaking says that the simplest solution is almost always the correct one. Conspiracy theories make for better newspaper sales and no-one commenting from within the industry wanted it known that racing in Australia and specifically in Queensland was a free-for-all of corruption, race rigging and market manipulation.

Some racing writers offered their explanations while failing to acknowledge their trackside allegiances. Many owed the winnings of a successful quadrella punt to George Freeman and carefully excised his handprint from the scandal. Others were cosy with the Waterhouses and ran interference. Sayers' name was mentioned as a distraction.

In these moments of great tumult, it was decided not to decide, or, more properly, leave the miscreants to the courts and pretend the whole fuck-up was a distant memory.

Sayers had arrived first and chose a seat where he could keep an eye on both entrances to the public bar. Flannery had chosen the location, the Botany View Hotel in Newtown in Sydney's Inner West, but Sayers knew it as a good and humble pub with a passable counter lunch and a working TAB at the end of the bar. He'd only had a sip of his beer when Flannery walked in.

The grin, the swagger, the pale blue eyes of a violent man who enjoyed his violent reputation. Nothing much had changed except Flannery's outfit. He wore an expensive grey suit and a blue polka-dot tie. A bit of a change from the prison greens.

The hit man also sported a man bag, a black leather carry-all. Sayers watched the dandy-ish killer toting his bag and knew at once what its contents were: a stack of bogus credit cards, a pile of cash, several small snap-lock bags replete with Flannery's drug of choice, and a .38 snub-nosed revolver. It was only the crazy brave or those with a suicide lust who would have cajoled Flannery for his man bag.

Sayers remembered Flannery had picked up a taste for expensive clothing and accoutrements when he got a job at David Jones in Perth while he was on the run for a couple of armed robberies. Sayers imagined the hitman dressed in his finery, tape measure in hand, taking the inside leg measurements of the hoi polloi before he had a change of heart, quit and went back and robbed the joint.

'Chris, you look like a pox doctor's clerk, mate.'

'Doin' better than you, mate. Fine Cotton. What the fuck were you thinkin'?'

'Ease up, mate. That had nothing to do with me.'

'That's not what George says. He reckons you were all over it.'

'You workin' for him now?'

'Five hundred cash in hand and I'm on call if he wants me to pay someone a visit.'

'Is that what you're doin' here?'

Flannery glared at Sayers, the mask slipping for a moment.

'If I was here on George's orders, you'd already be on the floor with a couple in ya.'

Sayers stared back.

'Come on, Mick. Just fuckin' kiddin', mate. I wouldn't clip you unless the price was right.'

'I'll get you a beer. Resch's?'

'Fuckin' cat's piss, mate. VB or I will put a couple in ya.'

Sayers returned with the beers to the sight of Flannery racking up two long, broad lines of cocaine. Sayers could see the shards of rock Flannery had lazily attempted to crush. This was going to be tough on the sinuses.

Flannery handed Sayers a rolled-up $50 note with a grin.

'Age before beauty, mate.'

Flannery then raised his voice in a mock boxer's call.

'And now the one, the only. The pure, the unadulterated. Weighing in at two grams plus, all the way from Medellin, Colombia, the heavyweight champion of the world . . .'

In the background, the barman looked up and shrugged. It was not the worst thing that had happened in the public bar. It was hardly down to him to put a stop to it. Besides, the bloke in the suit looked like a real handful. Best to turn away and pretend he hadn't seen any of it. The two other patrons in the bar looked up briefly and returned to stare gloomily into their beers.

Sayers bobbed down on the smallest of the lines, at least a gram in weight, a line the size and width of an HB pencil, and inhaled deeply.

'Go, go, go, go!' Flannery exhorted. Sayers stopped breathing for a moment, looked up and fell into a coughing fit.

'Fuck's sake, Chris. I can't finish that.'

'Aw, come on, mate. Weak as piss.'

Sayers handed the uncurling note back to Flannery, who looked Sayers in the eye while he rolled it back taut.

'Let's get ready to rum-ballllllll!'

Flannery devoured his own larger line, and without a moment's rest attacked the remainder of Sayers' line, before finally sticking his head back up and clearing his throat with a guttural clatter.

'Ah. Breakfast of fuckin' champions, mate.'

'Nature's pick-me-up, mate.'

For more than an hour the two men ranted at each other in drug-addled earnestness. If either man afterwards had been asked to give their accounts of the conversation, they would have been unable to, but the cocaine had applied an ersatz sense of wisdom to their every word, as if two astrophysicists had been brought together to discuss the secrets of the universe.

They both felt what they were saying was very important and had to be expressed at once, but anyone listening in – at least anyone not in the middle of a cocaine frenzy – would have no course but to declare the conversation a great, steaming pile of bullshit.

At one point, Flannery resumed his role as commentator, shouting out a call of the final minutes of the 1979 grand final, when his beloved Carlton had bettered the old enemy, Collingwood.

'Harmes goes and chases his own kick. He slaps it back into the goal square. Kenny Sheldon picks it up and goals. Did it go out? Did it go over the boundary line? No way, you fuckin' Collingwood filth. Stick it up ya arses. We won. We fuckin' won. Suck on that, you fuckin' toothless turds.'

Almost at the same time, Sayers had begun loudly offering an editorial on the talents of the great racehorse, Kingston Town. He, too, reverted to commentary, reciting, in part, Bill Collins' famous call of the 1982 Cox Plate, adding a bit of colour of his own.

'Kingston Town can't win. Like fuck he can't, cos here he comes down the outside. He gets past Grosvenor and sticks his head in front at the line. Peter Cook, what a fuckin' ride. Three Cox Plates to the champ.'

Sayers took a breath and gulped on his beer. 'Three Cox Plates. That'll never be done again. Not in our lifetime, Chris.'

'I'm not into the horses like you, mate,' Flannery replied. 'But I'm prepared to take your advice on that. I mean, fuck, we could both be off before the next grand final.'

It was only after Sayers returned from the bar with their seventh schooners that the cocaine fog started to lift and a semblance of continuity and sense resumed.

'You want someone knocked, Mick? I'll give you a discount for old times' sake.'

The old Rentakill was back, armed and dangerous. His piercing blue eyes scanning the horizon for a fresh kill.

'Jesus, no, mate. We're just having a drink.'

'I'll knock anyone if the price is right.'

'I don't want anyone knocked.'

'What about that prick, Haitana?'

'He's in the jug, mate. He's got nothin' on me. I've never even met the bloke.'

'What about the other bastard? What's-his-name. The fuckin' con artist.'

'Gillespie. Shit man. He's legged it. Don't worry about him.'

'Fuckin' hate con men,' Flannery philosophised. 'If you're goin' to rob a bloke, what's wrong with stickin' a shooter under his nose and telling him to hand over the cash? That's what missing these days, Mick. The personal touch.'

There were more beers and more cocaine, which Flannery tracked out on the dunny seat in the gents. They snorted, laughed and talked over the top of each other again back at their table.

The ashtray filled with Viscount butts. Sayers noticed they smoked the same brand. *That's what two years in stir together will do to you*, he thought. Another year in the same 12-foot cell with Flannery and he might have ended up a hit man.

He could still remember Flannery's words all those years ago back in B Division. Remarkably, Flannery had got off the DJs' payroll job. God only knows how. But he still had the two armed robs in Victoria to answer for. The judge gave Flannery six years, like he was handing out a speeding fine.

Not long after he unrolled his mattress on the top bunk above Sayers, Flannery had mused on his career prospects.

'I'm no good at counter jumping. Always gettin' fuckin' pinched. I think I'll kill people for a living.'

'Good thinking, mate,' Sayers replied. 'It's a growth industry.'

They both laughed but Sayers sensed Flannery wasn't kidding. He had the antecedents for the gig – armed robbery, crimes of violence, plus a profound sense of entitlement and a furious temper. Sayers had seen the ugliness rise in Flannery sharply, without any apparent reason, and wondered where it all came from.

One day in B Division, when they were both walking up and down in the exercise yard, he found out.

Flannery's name was roughly called by one of the guards. He had a visitor. Midweek. Most unusual. It might have been his brother, Peter, the lawyer at the Trades Hall Council with some news or other on his sentence, but that didn't seem likely as Flannery had copped the armed rob convictions sweet.

Flannery walked off but was back within minutes.

Such mundane events raise the curiosity of prisoners. Anything that breaks the terrible monotony becomes a talking point.

Sayers clocked the look in Flannery's eyes. He was pink-faced and fuming with rage. Sayers watched Flannery walk up and down the yard again, muttering and swearing to himself. Finally, curiosity got the better of him and he approached Flannery at a safe distance.

'Who was your visitor?'

Flannery looked Sayers in the eye. He was trembling with anger.

'Father Leo.'

'What did he want?'

'He wanted me to forgive him.'

'What did you tell him?'

'I told him to get fucked.'

From that, Sayers gleaned enough not to ask any further.

The Old De La Salle boy had heard the whispers. No priest had ever touched him, but the rumours were everywhere. In the schools and the churches, priests, Christian Brothers and boys. If they weren't beating the shit out of kids, the men of the cloth were up them over a table behind the pulpit. Sometimes they did both, often at the same time.

Flannery was no Catholic. He was just a light-fingered kid who'd had a few pinches as a juvenile. On his third or fourth conviction he'd been punted to the Morningstar Boys' Home, south of Melbourne. He would have been no older than 14. The Franciscans ran it and answered to nobody. They did what they liked to the kids. And Flannery was just one of hundreds to be subject to their vile indignities.

Sayers knew a few who'd been through the Mick Wringer. Bashed by cops and fucked by priests. Some had the thousand-yard stare of the truly lost, their lives destroyed from the moment their bodies were invaded. Bearing a victim's guilt, they descended into a life of booze and drugs. The walking dead.

Others, like Flannery, burned with rage. The experience had taught him the salient lesson that while he had been a victim, now it was someone else's turn.

Yeah, Flannery had all the makings of a stone killer, a rough cocktail of a brutish environment as a kid, finely tuned by regular bashings in H Division and polished to a sharp edge by the pointlessness of prison.

Flannery got out while Sayers was still waiting for parole, and by that time he was raring to go. He broke his cherry six months later: Roger Wilson, the businessman who found himself short of money and out of time.

The two men staggered out of the pub. It was three o'clock. The plan to enjoy a counter meal had been forgotten. Their lunch was limited to a mix of liquids and powders. Sayers felt his empty stomach rumble. He hadn't eaten for more than 12 hours but still the cocaine ruled. Food was off the menu. Unnecessary. A stroke over par.

Flannery flagged a cab and they both jumped in. He gave detailed directions to Tony's Bar in Double Bay while Mick lounged on the back bench seat. Some of the larger snap-lock bags in Flannery's man bag had been set aside for the bar's owner, Spaghetti 'Tony' Eustace, a quick-witted British crook who found himself at home among Sydney's wealthy, doling out dodgy cordon bleu and jumped-on cocaine in equal parts to his cashed-up clientele.

As the taxi drove down Bay Street, Flannery urged the driver to pull over.

'We'll get out here, mate,' Flannery said, flipping the driver a $50 note. 'Come on, Mick. I should buy me mum some flowers. And you should do the same.'

The two men entered the Double Bay florist. Flannery strode inside with the air of a man comfortable among the blossoms, sights and scents, while Sayers lurked uneasily outside, perusing the fare that had been plunged into buckets. He'd always given his mum a call on Mother's Day but he'd never bought her a bunch of flowers. He never bought flowers for anyone, including Marian.

Sayers grabbed meekly at a bunch that were close at hand. Flannery looked at Sayers' selection with disdain.

'They're shit, mate. Come on. This is for your mum. The poor old bird's probably still getting over the armed robbery squad kicking down her door, coming to arrest her little boy.'

Sayers dumped the flowers back in the bucket and stood back, observing Flannery walking around the shop, peering into vases and sniffing bouquets. Flannery asked for two posies and by name requested they both include carnations in pinks and yellows, cornflowers in blue, gerbera daisies, alstroemerias, tulips and hydrangeas, wrapped in a light cover of angel's hair.

Still startled by Flannery's intricate botanical knowledge, when it came time to step forward and give his old address for delivery, the family home in Caulfield, Sayers couldn't remember the street name and stared blankly into the distance until at last it came to him.

Flannery put $200 in 50s down on the counter and the florist, a middle-aged woman pleased at serving a male customer with such an extensive awareness of floral arrangements, beamed. Satisfied, Flannery turned and walked out of the store clutching his man bag, his drugs and his gun, with Sayers still mouth agape, tagging along.

Flannery, the professional killer and florist. It was an odd combination, but when Sayers thought about the large number of wreaths that would arrive in the wake of a visit from Rentakill, it almost made sense.

Neither Bobby North nor Tommy di Luzio had spent more than one uncomfortable night in the lock-up. They were both roughly shoved out of the Brisbane Police Headquarters armed with their charge sheets and told to go home. Bailed on their own recognisance. Tommy went home to lament to his girlfriend.

By the time Bobby got home, the spare bed was all set up for him. The conjugal rights were officially over. His wife was a sullen, silent, forbidding presence in the home. When she felt her anger subside, she would stare out through the lounge-room window at the ruined lawn decaying under the force of four litres of hair dye and she would return to despising her husband anew.

Glancing at the charge sheets which detailed North's role in the ring-in, for the first time her husband had been charged 'with conspiracy to defraud the public'.

'Conspiracy,' she said out loud to herself in horror.

Bobby, who was just a few metres away watching the cricket on the television, had not heard his wife's voice in days and thought it politic to respond.

'It's really only fraud. Just one count,' he said hopefully.

His wife burst into tears and stormed off to the bedroom, slamming the door shut behind her.

Haitana had been remanded in custody. It was a fair cop. Doing the dash to South Australia as a wanted felon would necessarily attract that kind of response to any bail application.

His solicitor, Ralph Devlin, had dutifully made the attempt, offering the not totally absurd suggestion that Haitana was at risk behind bars from banged-up cons who could spot an easy mark and go the bash on a promise from other crims higher up the ladder.

Haitana would, Devlin promised, hand in his passport. There would be no flight to New Zealand or anywhere else. His client had been the subject of death threats. He had been duped to join the criminal enterprise. The prosecution's case was thin. Devlin rolled on and on until almost breathless. He fell silent and looked at the magistrate for a hint of mercy.

The magistrate wasn't having a bar of it and threw the application out. Haitana was shuffled off into a prison van.

He found himself in the one place he'd promised himself never to return to. Boggo Road. The remand section was a little easier. He wore his own clothes instead of the prison greens that were either too hot during the day or, when the bluestone walls seemed to radiate, too cold. As an inmate awaiting trial, he had an almost unlimited number of calls he could make at his own expense. He didn't have to share a cell. He was allowed more visits and his lawyers could call in on him anytime.

The likelihood of a serious quilting in the shower block turned out to be a furphy. Bertie Kidd had put the word out that Haitana was hands off. Everyone listened to Bertie and when he cleared his throat and spoke with the authority of Boggo Road's most powerful inmate, his word became law.

It must have been quite a spray involving the grisly details of violent retribution should anyone be silly enough to ignore the decree, because Haitana found that all prisoners in the remand section looked the other way whenever he walked by. Kidd's word had preceded him. They were too frightened to speak to Haitana, let alone give him a touch-up in the showers.

One morning at breakfast, a young bloke in front of him reached for the last banana in the bowl and placed the rotting brown fruit gently onto his tray. Haitana had had his eye on the banana too, but the kid had got in first. *Oh well, never mind*, he thought. The kid clocked Haitana and was immediately aghast.

'I'm sorry, Mr Haitana,' he said and gingerly placed the banana onto Haitana's tray.

Haitana didn't even have time to accept the apology with a casual wave, because the kid had turned and fled, taking up a seat in the furthest corner of the prison mess.

By the time Haitana stood with his breakfast tray and his banana, looking for a place to sit, the other inmates stared nervously back at him. When he took a seat and smiled at the diners next to him, they became horrified and got up and sat elsewhere. It was better than a bashing, but Haitana longed for some human contact, some sign of empathy.

In his first week in remand, the only moments when Haitana felt some semblance of humanity was when he was sitting discussing his case with his lawyer. His lawyer made all the right soothing noises. The Crown case against him was weak, he said. Hayden had only continued with the conspiracy after Dashing Soltaire was injured, because he feared reprisal from angry Sydney gangsters. Haitana, his lawyer said, had acted under duress. Furthermore, it would be argued that Hayden received no financial benefit from the conspiracy, besides a promise from Gillespie of a payment that never eventuated.

Haitana was impressed but he remained convinced he'd be found guilty. The system, the government, the racing industry, the coppers and the bookies would want a head to roll. And as Gillespie's head wasn't handy, Haitana's would have to do.

Back in his cell for the best part of 20 hours a day, the piss bucket at the foot of Haitana's bed sat in mocking vigil. Every time he had to empty his bladder, sending a steam of hot piss into it, he thought, *This is my life now.*

Boggo Road's remand section offered some privileges not extended to the convicted crims in the adjoining cell blocks. One of these was a colour television in the communal lounge. Corrective Services staff had determined that fixing the set to an external antenna was a huge waste of money and resources, so the TV sat with a coathanger jutting out of it that inmates would pull to and fro in order to get not a decent picture but at least an image that was vaguely watchable. It helped if someone stood next to the set holding the coathanger when the footy and the cricket was on. Or *60 Minutes*.

Haitana missed most of it. He had no inkling his interview with Jana Wendt was being beamed into the remand section, but his fellow inmates had watched it all, enthralled, turning to rowdy cheers at the blurry vision of a drunk Haitana leering at the glamorous interviewer.

Haitana was drawn to the noise and as he entered the communal lounge to find out what was going on, he saw himself on television for the first time. He was struck firstly by how overweight he appeared, that the old adage of television adding 10 kilograms to any human being seemed, if anything, understated.

Then, as the dreadful memory of the interview came lurching back into his mind, it became a simple reminder of his guilt and how the interview placed him as the central figure in the ring-in. Gillespie would never be silly enough to be caught up in this exercise in vanity. Even if the rozzers did pinch him before the trial, Gillespie could point to the *60 Minutes* interview which showed Haitana, as pissed as 10 men, relaxed in his role in the ring-in.

Haitana feared, too, that his fellow inmates would see him as a cartoon, a derelict pisspot and a buffoon. Bertie Kidd's decree might be pushed aside.

He needn't have worried. In prison no distinction is drawn between fame and infamy. One equals the other. They are, in effect, the same thing. And so it was in Boggo Road Remand.

Many of the inmates had been on television for the briefest second or two doing the perp walk with their jumpers pulled up over their heads. But this was different. Their man Haitana was being interviewed by Jana Wendt, a confirmed good sort, and what's more he came on to her and got away with it. He'd become famous, or was it infamous? It didn't matter. Their fellow prisoner was a celebrity who'd gotten a whiff of the high life and possibly a whiff of Jana Wendt after she'd got up off her chair. That's what mattered.

As the story ended, the entire room gave Haitana a standing ovation. He noticed the good people at *60 Minutes* had edited out the moment when he'd shit his pants in that motel room and gave a silent blessing to their skills. He'd come out all right. Shit faced, yes. Stupid, definitely. Dumb as fuck, you betcha. But he'd been on *60 Minutes* and that meant he was a hero.

The ice had thawed at Boggo Road Remand. Haitana was no longer a man to be feared. He was a man to be admired.

The following day, in the exercise yard, the kid who'd almost pinched his banana came up to Haitana and thrust a biro into his hand. He shoved an old copy of the *Courier-Mail* at Haitana.

'Can you sign it? Please, Mr Haitana.'

Haitana was wary, wondering what sort of scam the kid was up to. An older bloke, who appeared no stranger to incarceration, turned his head.

'He wants your fuckin' autograph.'

Haitana had never been asked for his autograph before. He grabbed the *Courier-Mail* and scribbled his name with a flourish.

He was famous.

CHAPTER TWELVE
Killing time

'He's not a protected species. He's not a koala bear.
I'll shoot him like a dog in the street.'
– Chris Flannery

MICK SAYERS AWOKE with a Force Nine hangover. His sinuses were clogged with cocaine residue and snot. His mouth was a desert and his throat the texture of number five emery paper.

He looked at his watch. It was a quarter past three. The sun streamed through the venetian blinds of his bedroom. Using what logic was available to his fractured brain, he figured it was 3.15 pm. The middle of the afternoon. But what afternoon?

The hands on his Seiko Chronograph offered only the whisper of an answer. He knew what time it was but what fucking day was it? He knew it was 1985. Still alive in '85, he'd mused when the New Year rolled around. But beyond that his mind was a blank.

He needed a calendar not a clock.

He raised his head from his pillows and his temples throbbed. He sniffed and coughed for a moment, screening the bedroom for further clues.

His wallet was at his bedside table. He reached for it and examined its meagre contents. He had precisely $27 in cash to his name. He remembered he'd had the best part of a grand on him when Flannery had marched into the Botany View. It was, he lamented, the cost of socialising with Chris Flannery and he'd paid a considerable price.

Placing his wallet back, he saw Marian had left him a note. He gathered it and held it close to his face, his left hand trembling slightly.

'You were in quite a state last night. Drink water. Take Panadol. Have an MM day. Love Mxx.'

MM. Minimal movement. Wise counsel from his partner and he immediately concurred. Water, yes. He needed gallons of it, but Panadol would be like pissing on a bushfire. He needed the valium

226

he kept in the bathroom drawer. A couple of those would do the trick. Get rid of the shakes for a start.

Stumbling into the en suite with its lurid flock wallpaper, he clutched at the top drawer of the vanity, pulled it open and peered down at the pill bottles and packets strewn around inside. *Christ*, he thought, he could start his own chemist shop with this lot alone.

Grabbing an orange bottle, he muttered reading its contents. Diazepam. That sounded about right. He screwed the top off and clumsily scattered one, then two, and finally three pills into the palm of his left hand.

He slapped the pills into his mouth and turned the cold faucet on. He knew the water would take time to run cold and clear but he didn't care. Slurping away he washed the pills down, felt them clear his throat and make their way to his stomach. He kept on gulping as the water grew colder, rinsing the remnants of a dismal cocktail of beer, red wine, champagne and some awful mint liqueur he remembered he'd consumed in shot glasses with Flannery.

He took three neat steps to the toilet and began pissing in a long, unbroken stream.

God only knows where they were when he and Flannery got stuck into the top shelf. The thought of Flannery colossally pissed and heavily armed made Sayers shudder.

His engorged bladder emptied, Sayers blew his nose into a wad of toilet paper and peered at its contents. Clear snot mixed with a brown substance he assumed was a mixture of cocaine and blood. With all the coke he'd consumed, he could have dried it out, cut it up and sold it on the street. Cocaine. One user only. Get stuck in.

Still in his underwear, replete with a brown stain that ran the length of the gap between his arse cheeks, he plodded into the living room and saw the *Daily Telegraph* on the dining table. Another clue.

Fuck, it was Thursday. He'd been on the piss and the charlie with Flannery for two days.

He flipped the paper over and glared down at the sports section. Rugby league shit. He considered the possibility of flipping to the horseracing section but thought better of it. His head still hurt and the words on the page were a jumble of blurry hieroglyphs. This was not a time for reading but a time for quiet reflection.

He sat down on the couch. What the fuck had happened? Had Chris pulled his shooter? Were they both wanted by the wallopers for questioning? What about Barry McCann?

The last thing he could recall was walking into Spaghetti Tony's in Double Bay, just minutes after Flannery had revealed his strong opinions in flower arrangement. Eustace had pulled them into his office at the back of the restaurant. More cocaine. Eustace had a penchant for French champagne. The expensive stuff. Sayers remembered belting it back by the bottle.

He lit a cigarette and inhaled deeply. The nicotine calmed his jangled synapses and it slowly started coming back to him. Nothing specific. Just odd details dangled together in no certain chronological order.

He remembered that Flannery's missus, Kath, had turned up at some point. Chris and Kath were two inert compounds – on their own potentially lethal, possibly toxic in large doses, but when put together they became ferociously combustible, often downright explosive.

Sayers had a vague memory of Kath shrieking at Chris over some slight, real or imagined. Chris had pulled his gun and stuck it in his own mouth, fiddling with the trigger. Christ, what a scene.

It had happened, Sayers recalled with a start, when they were in the backyard at Flannery's home in Arncliffe out by the airport. Aside from having a quiet beer at the Lansdowne with McCann acting as the barman, it was the one place on Earth he didn't want to be.

He sucked down hard on the Viscount butt. At least he was still alive. McCann hadn't caught up with him during the journey. He rose from the couch with a groan and peered through the blinds out at the street below. All was quiet.

Perhaps it was the valium that unscrambled his brain, but the memory, the worst one of all, came flooding back. It started as an audio fragment. Two words, repeated over and over. 'Danny Chubb.' 'Danny Chubb.' 'Danny Chubb.'

Chubb had been popped before Christmas, brought down at Millers Point, a parcel of fish and chips he'd bought for his mum still hot in his hands. It was a classic two-man hit. The first gunman brought Chubb down with a shotgun, the other performed the coup de grace with a .38.

Chubb was a merchant seaman who ran heroin and guns into Sydney. Everyone had a Danny Chubb special. Sayers had a .25 Ruger in his bedside drawer courtesy of Danny Chubb. He'd done a bit of business with him. Chubb had the face of a weasel and the morals to match. But he sold his black tar heroin on tick and that suited Sayers fine.

The sun was coming up and Flannery and Sayers were drinking long necks. Victoria Bitter. Flannery's sip of choice.

Why Flannery had taken 36 hours to mention Chubb's murder, why he'd waited until both men were heavily intoxicated and deep in the midst of a cocaine psychosis, was something Sayers couldn't comprehend. Perhaps Flannery thought the booze and the drugs would act like a truth serum and Sayers would blurt out every-thing he knew, which, as it turned out, wasn't much.

'What do you know about Danny Chubb?' Flannery asked.

'He was a cunt. Now he's a dead cunt.'

'You were into him, weren't you? Couple of hundred large, I heard.'

'Four, I think.'

'Got yourself a motive to have him knocked right there, mate.'

'Chris, if I knocked everyone I owed money to, half of Sydney would be lying face down in the gutter.'

'The talk is it was you. You did your nuts on the fuckin' ring-in and that's how you got back in the black.'

Sayers shook his head dismissively.

'The goss goes a bit further, mate. You and me. You with the shottie. Me with the .38.'

'Now you know it's bullshit.'

'Mate, you should know how this town works. It doesn't matter who took him out. If the wrong people think it was you and me, then it was you and me. Perception is reality in Sydney.'

Sayers took a large gulp from his bottle. There it was. Another reason for him to be put off. Flannery put an arm around him and took a deep breath.

'There's a war on, mate. McCann and his shit men are up against the old team. George, Len, Stan. They're veterans. Done the hard work, kept the cash rolling in for years. No-one would dare start a stink with them a few years back, but now they're all old blokes. Past it.'

'Waddya sayin', Chris?'

'I'm sayin' if we play our cards right, we could end up on top. You run the punt. I do the law and order.'

'That's the charlie talkin', mate.'

'I got Roger behind me.'

'Rogerson is psycho, Chris.'

'I got shit on him and he knows it. I go down, he goes down with me.'

'Never trust a cop, Chris. A.C.A.C., remember?'

'You had anything to do with that piece of shit McCann?'

'No,' Sayers lied. Flannery's truth serum had some flaws.

Sayers didn't want anyone to know he'd ripped off McCann. He didn't want The Team to know he was moving heroin around. That would have been deadly on its own. And if Flannery knew Sayers was tapping into McCann's seemingly inexhaustible supply of heroin, his old cellmate would have taken umbrage. Umbrage with Flannery meant guns, blood and death. Sayers had enough enemies without adding Chris to the list.

Flannery tightened his grip around Sayers' shoulders. The sun was rising and was peering through the branches of the blue gum growing lonely in the backyard. The light shone through, right onto their faces, causing Sayers to blink while Flannery stared straight ahead.

'I'm going to kill them all, mate,' Flannery said. 'McCann and his duds first and then I'm coming after The Team. We're going to run this fuckin' town.'

Freeman and The Team had been at war since August. McCann had pulled the Pearl Harbour in Enmore, just two weeks after Bold Personality had stuck his nose in front at Eagle Farm. One of McCann's boys turned up at the club with a few large lads in tow, and encouraged the manager to remove the poker machines that Len McPherson had leased to the club on agreeable terms. Agreeable to Len, anyway.

The bloke who ran the club rang McPherson straightaway in a panic. Len saddled up the horses, grabbing his hardest men: Milan 'Iron Bar Miller' Petrocevic and Brnko Balic. Even Flannery came along for the ride, just to add some extra crazy.

By the time they got there, McCann's boys had gone. McPherson stomped into the club, grabbed the phone and called the upstart.

'I'll fuckin' blow you up, son.'

McCann didn't reply. He didn't really get a chance. McPherson slammed the phone down so hard, he broke it. Once he broke it, he pulled it out from the wall and hurled it out the front door where it came to rest on top of the pile of broken poker machines on the street.

Like Freeman, McCann had a fondness for horseracing and he, too, was a short man with a violent temper.

The Team had had a run-in with McCann in 1978 when he started a casino and abruptly declined to pay their protection money. The place, an upstairs joint in Newtown, was burned to the ground. The Team's enforcer, Stan Smith, had a quiet word in McCann's ear: 'Dead or out of town'.

McCann chose the latter, setting up a casino in Wollongong, out of the spotlight, and bided his time. The Team knew he was on the rise but they thought they had his measure. They didn't fully appreciate the extent of McCann's ambition. He wanted to be the Pope of Sydney, and as there was no vacancy for the position, McCann would make one.

McCann regarded his Wollongong self-exile as a chance to expand his criminal networks and build his reputation. He used up Chubb, bought his dark brown smack, jumped on it and shovelled it around Sydney. The money was good but when he created his own contacts in Thailand and developed a trafficking network that allowed his more potent China white heroin to be casually flown in through Sydney Airport, he started making big money.

He had so much of it, he used it as carpet underlay in his week-ender in the Hunter Valley. By the time Bold Personality jumped at Eagle Farm, Barry McCann had $10 million squelching underneath his toes.

At Yowie Bay, Freeman's mind turned back to the last war. It was little more than a skirmish. Maybe that's all this would be. Take a few upstarts out. Sort it all out over a coffee in the Cross. Get on with business.

George, Lennie McPherson and Stan Smith had run Sydney like they owned it for 20 years. There hadn't been a serious challenge to The Team for more than a decade. They had revelled in their power and amassed fortunes.

George got on the blower and told Stan what had happened at Enmore. Stan had been poncing around in the US, hanging out with the Chicago mob. Underboss Joe Testa liked having Stan around and comped him a room in Vegas.

But skylarking with the Mafia would have to wait. It was time for Australia's most prolific hit man to come home and do what he did best.

George was still counting his Fine Cotton money when Flannery had turned up. George was having a sauna in the eastern suburbs with a mate. A schvitz, his mate called it. George often took visits from friends and allies in the sauna. They had to clamber in wearing only a towel. No bugs, no wires. A perfectly safe way to conduct frank conversations.

Freeman was astonished to see a semi-naked Flannery enter the schvitz uninvited.

'There he was blowing his bags, telling me how many people he'd put off,' Freeman said later.

Clearly the two men felt some rapport, because within weeks Flannery went on the Freeman payroll. Freeman didn't need the protection as he rarely left the house, but Len and George had decided it was a good idea to keep the killer close. He was just the sort of violent man they needed on their side. Better with 'em than agin 'em.

Flannery had no boundaries. Rules of engagement meant nothing more to him than hit hard whenever, wherever, whoever.

Two weeks after the Enmore incident, Flannery dropped McCann's missus at the Lansdowne. No-one had told him to front McCann's joint and start a stink. When Freeman heard, he sighed.

It would be fair to say that by this stage any attempt at a diplomatic solution had come and gone.

Sayers nursed his hangover on the couch at Coogee. The awful memories of the previous 48 hours had taken some amorphous shape, and all things being equal he believed he was in a stronger position than he had been before the Flannery bender.

If Flannery could pull the Rentakill job on McCann, Sayers would be sitting pretty, his list of creditors wiped blank. Maybe he'd take Flannery up on his offer.

Lighting one more cigarette, he thought it sensible to lie low. Wait for the shooting to stop before poking his head up. He'd stay indoors, keep himself safe. Maybe just a day out at the races here and there. No-one was going to knock him at a racetrack.

If Flannery was going to go on a murder spree, the best place to be would be right on that couch. It was a good plan. Flannery could kill anybody. Now he was planning to kill everybody. It might just work out.

But McCann's boys got in first.

On 20 January 1985, Flannery pulled into the driveway of his Arncliffe home in Sydney's south in his Ford LTD with his wife and two kids. They'd been dining with Flannery's new best mate, Roger Rogerson, at the Scots Club just around the corner. A spot of Sunday lunch. A schnitty for The Dodger, Kath had the prawn curry, bowls of chips for the kids, and a medium rare T-bone for Chris.

It had all started very amicably and even Kath had concealed her loathing of Rogerson for long enough for Flannery to get a bit of business done. On the pretext of sliding some dough into the pokies, Flannery and The Dodger made their excuses.

'How's George?' Rogerson asked quietly.

'He's toey, mate.'

Rogerson nodded. Everyone was on edge. Lennie had locked himself in his Gladesville home and was refusing to come out. He stayed there all day and all night, peering through the blinds at every car that drove past. Sometimes he wrote the plates down and would ring Rogerson for details. Roger had checked. A couple of them were dodgy. McCann's boys almost certainly. Lennie blew up over the phone.

While Flannery cranked the handle of the one-armed bandit, Rogerson regaled him with a story of Lennie's Gladesville cabin fever.

Australia Post had an advertising campaign going. Help your postie. Make sure you have your street number clearly marked on your letterbox. Lennie lived at 22 Pearson Street, but he was not inclined to advertise the fact. Help the postie? He could get fucked.

The Gladesville post office then sent Lennie a letter, politely requesting he make things easier. They'd meet him halfway and included in the letter were two 2s, in silver adhesive. Could the resident at 22 Pearson Street simply peel off the backing and stick the numbers to his letterbox? Help your postie, the letter urged.

The resident at 22 Pearson Street felt intruded upon and got on the blower. The postal clerk at Gladesville copped it. Lennie made his displeasure known. There was no way he was putting the numbers on his letterbox.

'What is the problem?' the clerk inquired.

'Listen. I've got people runnin' around tryin' to fuckin' shoot me. I'm not givin' them a walk-up start.'

'But,' the postal clerk demurred, 'if these people go to number 20 and then go on to number 24, they're going to know where number 22 is.'

'Yeah, but by then I'll be fuckin ready for 'em.'

Lennie never did get a number on his letterbox.

Rogerson and Flannery laughed like lunatics. The thought of the Big Man wearing his living-room carpet thin striding back and forth, a dribbling paranoid, was deeply amusing to them both.

Flannery drained his glass of beer as Rogerson leant in and whispered to him.

'I'm starting to get a bit of heat over that other matter.'

Flannery looked at Rogerson. Amusement quickly turned to anger. It didn't take much to set Flannery off.

'I thought you said it was sweet, Roger.'

'Black Angus is taking care of things. But the bloke is telling him I offered him money to run dead on the business in Melbourne.'

'Black' Angus McDonald, the acting head of New South Wales CIB, had been inquiring into the shooting of NSW detective Michael Drury. Rogerson had put it about that Drury was bent and got popped by an angry drug dealer from the Central Coast. That was good enough for the investigative half-wit McDonald, but Drury, who'd been shot twice in the chest with Flannery's .38, had survived. Drury was now conscious and insisting his shooting was linked to Rogerson.

Flannery cranked the handle one last time. Fifty fuckin' bucks and no feature, not a skerrick. Fuck.

'I told you I should have put him off in the hospital,' Flannery replied, rising from his stool and marching off. 'You better tell me if I'm hot. I ain't goin' down for this one alone.'

'Chris, Chris.'

But Flannery was back at the table, telling his wife to grab the kids and get in the car.

Rogerson caught up with him at the club door.

'Our man in Melbourne is the only loose end. Once he's gone, they've got nothing, Chris.'

'Do I have to deal with him?'

'No, no. Leave it with me.'

Flannery was helping his daughter out of the car when a green Jaguar drove slowly past. The passenger leaned out of the window and let rip with a burst of Armalite fire. Bullets smashed in to the brickwork of Flannery's house. Flannery sheltered his daughter, pulling her tight and covering her body with his. He was hit while he held her. One shot grazed his ear and another pierced the webbing between thumb and forefinger on his right hand.

On 20 February 1985, Sayers enjoyed a good day at Rosehill Gardens. He'd had a win in the first and never looked back. By the last, he'd pocketed almost $100,000. Money in his kick and a lot of it. Perhaps his luck had finally changed. On the long drive home, he joked and told his best racing anecdotes, amusing Marian and delighting an old retired jockey who sat in the back of the red Merc.

He pulled the car into the driveway. Marian and the jockey were still laughing at one of Mick's stories when he leapt out to pull up the garage door. That was when he saw them. Two blokes dressed from top to toe in black and sporting balaclavas. At first, he thought he was going to be robbed. The not insubstantial contents of his pocket deftly removed at gunpoint.

Then he knew.

It was rentakill with a small 'r'.

It wasn't Chris. Flannery was in the Gold Coast having a bite to eat. He had the credit-card receipt to prove it.

For a bloke carrying a few pounds over the odds, a few schooners over his fighting weight, Sayers could still move swiftly when he had to. He didn't see the gun. Didn't even hear the shot, but it smacked into him like a sledgehammer blow to the right shoulder. He staggered back onto the rocks of the front garden, almost losing his footing.

Then he was up again and on his toes. He ran down the driveway and across the road, almost colliding with the third gunman standing in his neighbour's garden. He saw the gun this time, the long barrel swivel and turn directly towards him. Sayers was no gun nut so he wouldn't have known he was facing a .225 Winchester rifle, enough gun to bring down a bull elephant. All he knew was it was enough to take him out.

He felt a searing pain in his chest like someone had doused him with kerosene and set him on fire. He staggered, but this time he didn't get up.

For a moment he lay there, hearing Marian's screams as she ran towards him. He saw the three men jump into a panel van parked down the road. He even thought he could make out the registration plate. McCann's men, maybe. Maybe The Team.

By the time Marian got to him, he was gone.

The old axiom that dead men tell no tales is true. In the underworld the enforced silence of the dead has many additional corollary benefits. Dead men also provide uncheckable alibis. Dead men wear a lot of blame the living would prefer was not their due. Dead men were very handy not to have around.

Within days of his violent murder, Sayers was the prime suspect in the murder of Danny Chubb at Millers Point. Never mind that it didn't make any sense. Sayers was dead and that was enough.

It didn't matter anymore. Mick Sayers had been shot like a dog in the street. It might have all come unstuck if Flannery had lived to tell the tale, but by the second week of May, 1985, Flannery had disappeared. Like Sayers, he was more valuable to the underworld dead than alive.

There was a Melbourne Cup field of suspects. Seventeen years later, the New South Wales Coroner, Greg Glass, handed down findings that Flannery had disappeared on 9 May 1985 and was killed on or shortly after that day by person or persons unknown. Rogerson was named as a person of interest but there were many others. This was a gangland murder and there were so many red herrings and fanciful theories explored, the craziest of which was that Flannery had made it out, grabbed a lift and blew Sydney just as the walls were closing in.

But he did get into a cab. Years later, a taxi driver came forward who said he recalled picking up Flannery. Flannery was toting his man bag. The driver described him as agitated and ill-tempered and, on one occasion, Flannery opened up his bag and the cabbie spied a handgun and a large amount of cash. The driver told the inquest he dropped Flannery off at Sydney Airport.

The cabbie's story was dismissed by many because it implied Flannery jumped on a plane, fled Sydney, and that he's been sitting on a banana lounge sipping cocktails on a beach somewhere ever since.

However, Flannery went to the airport, not to catch a plane and get out of town, which might have been the only thing that would have saved his life. He went there to rent a car. Flannery was in the habit of renting cars at the airport with a credit card he used under a false name. He had done so many times when he and Kath were living in Arncliffe.

Fitted out with a rental car, Flannery drove to his meeting with George Freeman at his Yowie Bay home. Flannery was excited. He wanted a look at this new gun Freeman had for him. He did get to see it, and when he did, Stan Smith was holding it and pointing it at him.

Freeman's ground-floor bar had a number of alcoves and hidden closets, perfect for a gunman to hide. Within minutes of Flannery's arrival, Smith emerged from his hiding place and sprayed Flannery with automatic weapon fire, killing him instantly.

Flannery was then rolled up in a carpet and his body placed on Freeman's boat. His body was weighed down and dumped at sea.

With Flannery out of the way, The Team could get back to business. They might have to concede some ground to McCann, flick a bit of business his way just to keep him sweet, but giving a little ground was a whole lot better than living under the threat of a violent death.

When Flannery didn't show up back at the Connaught later that day, Kath started calling everyone. She called George who said Flannery hadn't turned up. Then she called Rogerson, but Roger told her he hadn't seen him. Flannery had disappeared.

The cops went to Freeman's house the following day. Stood at the gate and pressed the buzzer. The two Rottweilers went ballistic so the cops remained outside. One detective who'd been around the traps a while drove over to a local butcher and bought a kilo of rump steak. When he got back, he hurled it over the fence, and the dogs jumped all over it, ripping the meat apart in a ghastly reminder of what they might do next if the cops didn't get into the house once they'd had a feed.

Freeman finally came to the front gate, offering his apologies. He'd been in the pool. Hadn't heard them.

It was almost exactly 24 hours after Flannery's disappearance. Freeman didn't seem terribly bothered they were there. He took a seat in his bathrobe and watched them poke around. They found nothing. They didn't have the forensic kit at the time to test for blood, but there were no visible signs of blood splatter anywhere in the house.

The rental had gone the previous night. Dropped off back at the airport.

With Kath screaming blue murder, the cops went back to Yowie Bay four days later, this time with the forensic blokes who splashed the phenolphthalein about. There was no sign of blood, although they did notice the carpets in the basement looked brand new and the place was sparkling clean.

Freeman was off scot-free. Stan had done the business. Now at last Lennie could stop marching up and down his living-room and get some fresh air for the first time in four months.

There would be a negotiated ceasefire and a lasting peace. The Team let McCann off the hook for now. They'd catch up with him soon enough.

When it did happen, two years later, it was spectacular. McCann was found face up in a park in Marrickville. Even before the media had cottoned on, the cops had already pulled in Stan Smith to see if he had an alibi.

Smith didn't know McCann was dead, but was not entirely unhappy to hear the news.

'How do you know he's dead?' Stan asked.

One cop with an especially dry sense of humour replied, 'He's been shot 25 times in the face, Stan. How do you reckon he's getting on?'

Stan had a cast-iron alibi. He was back up the coast watching the dope-laden boats come in. The story goes that The Team hired two Chinese assassins on a fly in, fly out. They knew what they were doing, firing point .22 calibre rounds into McCann's face in an almost circular pattern. They seemed to enjoy themselves.

By the time the forensic blokes turned up and started counting the rounds discharged around the children's playground, the two blokes were in a plane and on their way back to Hong Kong.

The Team was back in charge. What was left of McCann's mob shit themselves and scattered. Some went into retirement, others chose new career paths or hit the road. Dead or out of town.

When the cops raided McCann's horse stud in the Hunter Valley, a luxurious homestead and stables paid for with the receipts of his heroin trafficking, they noticed their feet squelched under the carpet in the master bedroom. They pulled the carpet up and saw McCann had used $20 and $50 notes as underfelt. A tick over $10 million's worth.

They searched the stables and found a .225 Winchester rifle.

In turn, even The Team would discover the inescapable reality of mortality. They would all go, one after the other. The price they paid for the life they led was that the grim prospect of a violent death at the end of a gun went with the territory. Only the smart, the brutal, the calculating and the bloody lucky would avoid it.

When Sayers was buried after his body was flown back to Melbourne, there were just a few family members present. Marian Ware could not bring herself to go. A motley crew stood, heads bowed, at his grave site in Springvale Cemetery, proving that crime doesn't pay but you can save a few bob on the catering.

CHAPTER THIRTEEN
Trial and error

'Justice is like beer. You don't buy it, you rent it.'
— Hayden Haitana

HAYDEN HAITANA KNEW that the sorts of men who might pop large-ish patches of sunshine into his head had other, more pressing issues on their minds – like trying to stay alive and how to murder the men who were planning to murder them.

The killers Hayden thought might come from Sydney to knock him were too busy shooting themselves to worry about the ring-in. He kept an eye on reports of the uproar while The Team and McCann's mob went to war. Despite Gillespie's ghastly predictions, no-one ever did get knocked over the Fine Cotton ring-in.

Haitana knew he was going to carry the burden, the odium and virtually all of the guilt over the scandal. The cops had dragged him in and threatened to charge him with other offences he hadn't even heard of. Murder and violence. He stuck to his 'No comment' tactic throughout all three police interviews, even the one where Senior Sergeant Will Ramsey had burst into the room, wielding a cricket bat, the Old Gray-Nick. In the end, all they could charge Haitana with was fraud. Sixteen counts of it at first, but by the time he was standing before a beak, it had been trimmed back to a neat one.

Haitana had spent a month in the remand centre at Boggo Road. His solicitor, Peter Jones, had visited weekly and the two men went through the case in the type of detail Hayden thought initially was pointless.

Jones, a bespectacled, balding fellow, looked more like an accountant than a solicitor. He was not a racing man and Haitana had to give the solicitor a crash course in the racing caper, from the intricacies of breeding and horse ownership to the vexed business of betting.

The first two meetings left Haitana despondent. His lawyer seemed not to know the first thing about the ring-in and in the absence of Gillespie, Hayden had become convinced he was going to become the fall guy.

'What sort of time am I looking at?' he asked Jones not more than 10 minutes into their first chat at Boggo Road.

'We're going to get you off, Hayden.'

'Yeah, but worst case.'

'Worst case. First offence. A year. You'll do six months.'

'It's not my first offence.'

'Ah,' Jones replied. 'What are your antecedents?'

'What?'

'Your record. Your criminal record?'

'I did nine months for fraud in 1980. Kite-flying. Bad cheques to the tune of a few grand.'

'Anything else?'

'Not in Australia.'

Jones cleared his throat. 'Two years tops, Hayden, but we are going to get you off.'

Haitana had rolled out the ring-in story in minute detail to Jones over the course of their next two meetings. The solicitor took copious notes, scribbling away on his yellow pad, head bowed, stopping only occasionally to ask the odd question.

Haitana returned to his cell, certain he was looking at the worst-case scenario and perhaps even more. Two years, maybe three, pissing in a bucket at Boggo Road. When his bail application got the tick with the Supreme Court and he emerged from the gloom of prison, Haitana believed it was only a brief respite from incarceration and the piss bucket would be his companion again soon.

His next meeting with Jones took place at the solicitor's plush office in George Street, Brisbane. Haitana was generally uncomfortable around the trappings of wealth, but the sight of the comfortable chairs and pretty secretaries dispensing cups of tea and biscuits to the client as he waited for his brief to arrive gave him a renewed sense of optimism.

Jones stepped into the conference room and offered Haitana a cursory smile.

'Did you have a bet on the race, Hayden?'

'A lazy 50 on Harbour Gold.'

'You didn't bet on Fine Cotton?'

'No.'

'You didn't think it would win?'

'By the time Bold Personality jumped, I'd virtually given up on the whole show.'

'No other bets on race four that day?'

Haitana shook his head.

Jones smiled.

'In order for fraud to be proven, you, Hayden, had to benefit from consideration – money. You had to make a profit and you did not. There is no fraud.'

'What about the 10 grand Gillespie promised to flick me?'

'Do you have that $10,000, Hayden?'

Haitana shook his head again.

'The promise of money from a convicted conman does not amount to consideration.'

In time, Haitana would come to enjoy his meetings with his solicitor. Jones only occasionally took notes, preferring to outline the strategy at trial. Jones told him the *60 Minutes* interview would be played to the jury. Haitana immediately cringed.

'Jesus, I was pissed as a cricket.'

'That is not a crime, Mr Haitana. Your story then, as now, has not changed. You fell into John Gillespie's trap and you feared for your life. His relationship with violent Sydney criminals, including this Michael Sayers character, was something he hung over your head. The tape shows that you believed you were acting under significant duress. The unsolved murder of a fellow trainer, George Brown, created a terrifying prospect for you. And Mr Gillespie went out of his way to build the possibility that you, too, would be murdered if you failed to follow his instructions. That is what we will be telling the jury.'

On Monday, 7 October 1985, Hayden Haitana, Tommaso di Luzio and Robert Roy North stood trial, charged with having conspired with John Patrick Gillespie to defraud the public by affecting by deceit the result of a race conducted by the Queensland Turf Club. All three men stood in the dock in Court 5 at the Brisbane District Court and entered pleas of not guilty.

When the trial began, the media swarmed around, a few journalists making their way into the courtroom to report directly from the trial while a gaggle of cameramen set up their gear outside the courthouse.

Hayden, Tommy and Bobby arrived at the courthouse at different times and had to make their way through the throng with microphones pressed to their faces, demanding comment and expressions of guilt.

There was an expectation the trial would be over quickly. Perhaps just a day. A nice quick trial and the media would hang Haitana, North and di Luzio in the morning.

Once underway, it became clear that the trial was going to run for some considerable time. Haitana, North and di Luzio had separate defences. Di Luzio maintained he was completely unaware of the ring-in and had been duped by Gillespie all along.

North's defence ran along similar lines. He would acknowledge in court that he was up to his bicuspids in the Fine Cotton-Dashing Soltaire ring-in, but once that had gone tits up he was merely along for the ride.

Haitana relied on the Jones defence, presented by barrister John Copley, that he had not made a cracker from the race, overlooking the betting slip Hayden still carried in his wallet for a $250 win on Harbour Gold.

On the first day, it became obvious the trial was going to run a while. The media quickly grew bored. The prosecution case, led by barrister Ralph Devlin, delved into the intricacies of horse breeding and the ownership papers of Fine Cotton under the bogus name of Lee Falk, who he took as an alias for di Luzio.

At the end of week two, Devlin was still droning on, clutching at exhibits that included betting slips made out in North's name for significant sums. North, he told the jury, stood to win almost $200,000 if Fine Cotton had been declared the winner.

As suspected by Haitana, Gillespie's non-attendance (Justice Loewenthal issued a bench warrant for Gillespie's arrest on sight within minutes of the trial commencing) cast Hayden into the role of architect, or co-conspirator, along with the invisible Phantom.

Haitana, North and Gillespie had dyed the horse, claimed Devlin, and the discovery of a spray can of Dulux Hi-Gloss white paint in Hayden's car proved that he was a key player in the conspiracy to defraud punters of their hard earned.

By the time the three defence barristers presented their case, the media was almost gone, save a couple of journalists from the *Courier-Mail* who scribbled their accounts of proceedings in shorthand.

Di Luzio's partner, Sarah Giannelli, took the stand and gave evidence under oath. Part character reference, part angry harangue on the stupidity of her boyfriend, she offered evidence that Tommy was an unwitting dupe, a witless yes-man, ripe for the plucking when the inveterate con artist John Gillespie came along.

Asked to explain di Luzio's role in the transport of Bold Personality to Brisbane on the eve of the race, Giannelli replied with a question of her own.

'Who would pull a horse float with 1000 pounds of horse on board with a Toyota Corolla?' Her defence counsel could see she was on a roll and left her to continue. 'He completely stuffed that car up. I had to take it down to the tip. Cost me $70 to tow it there. I mean, what idiot would tow a horse float for 300 kilometres, or whatever it was, and think they were going to get back to Brisbane in one piece?

'Have a look at him,' Giannelli concluded, turning to the jury. 'He's not exactly Lex Luthor, is he?'

The jury tittered. Tommy bowed his head in shame. His defence, properly summed up, was one of gross stupidity. He could not have planned a complex conspiracy to defraud the public because he was deeply struck in the realms of incomprehensible idiocy. It was a bridge too far.

The defence for Tommaso di Luzio rested.

Neither North nor Haitana took the stand in their defence. That would have been too risky. To Hayden's chagrin the *60 Minutes* interview ran as if on a loop. Copley argued time and again that Haitana's fears were real. He had been in fear of his life, that he would go the way of trainer George Brown.

Often in the trial the tape would be stopped at a certain point, leaving Hayden to dwell uneasily on a frozen image of his outrageous drunkenness. It made him uneasy, embarrassed and often thirsty.

A free man at least for the duration of his trial, Haitana had taken to enjoying a counter lunch at the Public Service Club. His barrister had signed him up as a guest on the second day of the trial, urging him to try the chicken parmigiana. It was the cheapest, best lunch in town, Copley opined, and once he'd tucked in, Hayden found it impossible to disagree. Every day, Haitana washed the economical feast down with four schooners and waddled back to the dock.

Where was Gillespie? In the first few days of trial, Hayden had taken to swivelling his head around every 10 minutes or so to see if The Phantom had wandered in to keep an eye on the trial's progress. He was certainly capable of that type of arrogance, but Gillespie would remain a notable absentee.

Years later, Gillespie would claim he'd received a phone call from Russ Hinze, who had warned him not to turn up. Freeman was after him, which meant Flannery would come a'calling. According to Gillespie, Hinze had said he'd be put off outside the courthouse under a hail of gunfire.

It was another piece of Gillespie delusion. The conman must have been having a bad day, or, perhaps, was not in front of a working copy of the Gregorian calendar. By the time the trial commenced, Flannery was sleeping with the fishes.

In more recent times, Gillespie has stepped forward to claim he didn't back Fine Cotton at all. Rather, he boasted he'd put all his money on Harbour Gold, and it was he, rather than George Freeman, who pocketed over a million in winnings.

The real story is that Gillespie was not inclined to sit with Haitana and bear the brunt of the judge's opprobrium. He'd been charged under summons. He hadn't even seen the blue. The Queensland wallopers had sent it out in the mail to his last known address at the Gabba.

Rather than have to deal with an eight-week-long trial and a much longer jail term, Gillespie took off to Thailand for a few years R&R. He set up a couple of bars in Phuket and made himself a nice little earner, ripping off sex-starved sex tourists. Easy money. How he got there with a little folding stuff remains a mystery, but perhaps some wealthy Queensland dowager had her bank account drained by Gillespie before he took off.

A year earlier, the nation had been enthralled by the story of the ring-in, but by the time it went to trial, public interest had waned. The rumours that had abounded of high-level political corruption, with gun-happy gangsters pulling the strings in the background, fell away at the sight of the three men in the dock.

The trial was into its seventh week when closing arguments were offered. Copley for Haitana claimed it was the QTC who should have been on trial for officiating over a dog's breakfast of racing events. His client, while foolish, had not benefited from the ring-in.

The jury retired to consider their verdict on Monday 11 November, shortly before 3 pm. They remained sequestered for four days until they finally emerged with a verdict at 10.30 am on 15 November.

Tommaso di Luzio was acquitted. Robert North and Hayden Haitana were found guilty. Justice Loewenthal excused di Luzio from the court. He was free to leave. Tommy turned and strode out of the courtroom at a pace, before remembering his manners and turning to bow to the judge. Giannelli embraced him outside.

'You're an idiot,' she said, 'but you're my idiot.'

Back inside the court, Justice Loewenthal handed down the sentences. Haitana and North stood.

'I accept that Gillespie conceived the idea and arranged for the purchase of the three horses, Fine Cotton, Dashing Soltaire and Bold Personality. He was instrumental in organising substantial betting and must have had a large stake in the outcome.

'Mr Haitana and Mr North, you both agreed to some sort of ring-in at an early stage, but did not know the details and did not even know what horse was to be substituted. You became willing parties without knowing what it was you were involved in. As the prospect of detection became greater, particularly when the dyeing of the horse failed, your willingness grew less. But you felt too involved to withdraw and the possibility of a vague threat might have played a part in the state of your minds. There was no evidence Mr Haitana had backed Bold Personality and the most you stood to gain was a sum from Mr Gillespie if he honoured his obligation.'

Justice Loewenthal drew breath, then announced, 'I sentence you both to a term of imprisonment of no more than 12 months.'

North declined to comment. Perhaps his thoughts had turned again to a life of cans of tuna in socks, with *Penthouse* centrefolds taped to his back.

Haitana, however, thanked everyone from the judge and the prosecutor to the Queensland Police for the 'fair way they have conducted themselves'. 'I would also like to thank my friend and barrister, John Copley, and Peter Jones for their hard work.'

Hayden had thought to add a bit of cheekiness, a little bit of humour. He'd prepared a sentence that he thought apt: 'Justice is like beer. You don't buy it, you rent it.'

But when he looked at Justice Loewenthal smiling back at the trainer, he decided to keep his joke to himself.

'Be at your best behaviour, Mr Haitana,' said Justice Loewenthal, 'and put this matter behind you.'

Eight weeks earlier, the media had huddled en masse in the courtroom, eager for a snippet of evidence that might take the ring-in beyond these three unfortunates and the missing Gillespie. To the Waterhouses perhaps. Maybe even to the door of the Minister for Everything, who remained a powerhouse of Queensland politics.

Now it was done and dusted, though, the story that had screamed page-one headlines 14 months prior was shuffled off to the *Courier Mail*'s inside pages, next to the ads for discount booze and jeweller's shop watch sales.

Haitana could hardly believe his luck. He'd never really expected to walk away, but a year wasn't the worst thing that could have happened. He could do 12 months in the slammer on his ear. Hayden knew enough about the vagaries of the Queensland justice system to know he'd probably be out in nine.

He was off to Boggo Road again, that terrible place, but he would get through.

When he got there for the health check, he stood in line, dropped his strides and felt a latex finger slide up his date. A kindly doctor spotted him from a distance and placed a stethoscope over his heart and then his wrist.

Haitana's years of booze and greasy food were about to pay off.

'Hypertension,' the doctor told the guards. 'Better get him off to the farm.'

The farm was a minimum-security prison at Palen Creek, in the Gold Coast hinterland near the New South Wales border. It was a working farm where inmates tended to crops and livestock. No piss buckets and no horrifically violent crims to deal with.

You beauty, Haitana thought. *They might even have a few horses.*

AFTERWORD
The wash-up

'When you're off, you're off.'
– 'Melbourne Mick' Sayers

Hayden Haitana

After his release from prison, Hayden Haitana returned to South Australia and took up residence in Goolwa, a coastal town 80 kilometres south of Adelaide. Sworn off racetracks for life, Hayden muddled along, eking out a living from odd jobs and the punt.

Bearing his trademark disguise of a pair of sunglasses and a baseball cap, he managed to slip through the turnstiles at a number of racecourses in Australia – Morphettville and Gawler in South Australia and Mornington in Victoria. No-one seemed to notice or, if they did, they didn't seem to mind.

Haitana's exile from the turf endured 11 years longer than that of Bill and Robbie Waterhouse. In 2011, 27 years after the Fine Cotton ring-in, he successfully appealed his lifetime ban and was permitted to enter racecourses again.

He spent the remainder of his years as a virtual recluse, drinking heavily and lending a hand to the trainers who ran out of the Gawler track. Whether it would be his heart that would give out first, or his liver that would drop him, was a matter of ferocious conjecture among his racing associates. The two organs were regarded as equal-price favourites, but the heart put its nose in front at the post. Hayden Haitana had a massive coronary occlusion and died at his home in December 2017. He was 72.

John Gillespie

The Phantom failed to appear at his trial over the Fine Cotton ring-in and the magistrate subsequently issued a bench warrant for his arrest.

But Gillespie denied the Queensland Fraud Squad the pleasure of making a rough arrest. He eventually wandered into a Brisbane police station, only after he was good and ready. Denied bail, Gillespie was returned to the confines of HM Boggo Road.

He pleaded not guilty to three counts of dishonest dealings, but was unable to convince judge or jury of his innocence and was sentenced to three years' imprisonment. He served two.

Gillespie has now over 300 convictions, the most recent involving the fraudulent sale of a fake Monet.

In 2016, he again made headlines, this time for being named as a client of Panamanian law firm Mossack Fonseca, which handled the 'grey areas' of offshore financing and the establishment of dubious tax minimisation schemes, until a disgruntled former employee of the firm downloaded their secretive client list and forwarded it to the media.

Among the roster of vicious despots, Russian mobsters and dodgy politicians looking to reduce their tax liabilities, there was one John Patrick Gillespie.

He is believed to be living in northern New South Wales, but don't take our word for it and certainly don't take his.

Robert North

The man who had his zealously maintained lawn ruined under a shower of cheap hair dye and several steaming piles of horse-shit was charged with one count of intent to defraud. North was sentenced to 12 months in prison. Despite his fears, he served his time without incident or complaint. Well, a bit of grizzling early on but that soon passed.

When North's wife got home and saw the state of the lawn, she divorced him on the spot.

He moved away from Brisbane in the late 1980s and was last heard of selling real estate in Cairns.

Tommaso di Luzio

The Corolla-driving horse transporter stood before a judge alongside Haitana and North. The judge immediately understood di Luzio was a gormless dupe incapable of understanding the complicated criminal conspiracy he had wandered into. He walked away a free man and never went near a horse again.

Gus Philpot

Years after the infamous race, Philpot reflected on the event. 'I was still a bit dazed when I got back to the jockeys' room and some of the older blokes were pointing at me and my ride, saying, "You've just ridden a ring-in." And I pulled one of them aside and said, "What's a ring-in?"'

The QTC stewards cleared him on the spot within an hour of the race. At least they got that bit right. But Philpot remained in the spotlight and the subject of innuendo for years afterwards. He was dragged into a criminal court case and was a witness to the QTC and AJC inquiries, where he gave the same evidence over and over.

There was never any adverse finding made against him, but the mud stuck and the apprentice found he couldn't get a ride in Queensland. Owners saw the name and thought only of Fine Cotton. The shame, the laughable disgrace of it all. If he wanted to remain in the racing business, Philpot had to move interstate. He eventually wound up in Victoria and trains from stables in Ballarat.

Mick Sayers

While alive, Mick Sayers was used as a bogeyman. After his murder, he became a patsy, an easy go-to dead guy to lay all the blame upon. Even Robbie Waterhouse picked up the line that Sayers was the architect. Mick was lying in the deepest repose in a Melbourne cemetery. He could hardly argue.

The gun they found at McCann's property was an instrumental piece of evidence used in the 1991 trial of Sayers' murder. A New South Wales police detective seconded to the National Crime Authority had some concerns about the way the murder investigation had been conducted. Two years after Sayers was murdered, the NCA cop decided to poke around the crime scene. Lo and behold, he discovered a spent round from the Winchester .225 rifle in the neighbour's front garden.

Tom Domican, Kevin Theobold and Victor Camilleri, all McCann's men, were charged with murder. The cops had an informer, Roger Ford, who pointed the finger at the accused. But Ford was an inveterate liar, a heroin trafficker and a noted horse-race fixer to boot. The jury chose not to believe him. The three men were acquitted at trial in the New South Wales Supreme Court in 1991.

Sayers' murder remains unsolved.

Robert 'Bertie' Kidd

Bertie Kidd won the chocolates (and the cigarettes) when Bold Personality saluted at the ledger as Fine Cotton in 1984. Despite some grumbling in B Division at Boggo Road, Kidd called *force majeure* on the ring-in. There were no refunds.

A career criminal for more than 60 years with almost 30 of those served in prison, at 71, Kidd was convicted over a series of violent home invasions and aggravated burglaries in the Manly area in Sydney. He was sentenced to 15 years imprisonment in 2004. Upon his release from Goulburn, Kidd was served with a deportation order, to send him back to his place of birth, the United Kingdom. He'd arrived in Australia from England as a

14-year-old and had never returned. At the time of writing, Kidd is 87 and still considered dangerous by police. He is fighting his deportation in the courts.

Pat Haitana

Pat Haitana, who had studiously avoided Gillespie's crazy scheme, knew The Phantom was trouble and warned his older brother of the perils of associating with him. Pat might have been present when Gillespie cooked up the ring-in in Boggo Road, but he could hardly be called a conspirator. Nevertheless, he was shunned by the industry. His ambition to ride in the city meets was never realised.

But then again, he never spent another night in prison either. Despite being involved in racing and having the name Haitana, the inevitable attempts by police, clutching at whatever straws were blowing in the wind, to somehow link him to the conspiracy led nowhere. Which is fair enough, as there is no evidence that he had anything to do with it.

Pat Haitana's current whereabouts are unknown.

Father Ted O'Dwyer

Father Ted was the well-irrigated man of the cloth who travelled down the Hume Highway from Sydney to 'help out a mate' by placing some rather large wagers on Fine Cotton at the greyhound track in Appin on the morning of the race. In *The Gambling Man*, racing journalist Kevin Perkins' study of the Waterhouse clan, he wrote: 'FOD [Father O'Dwyer] surely would have been the most unlikely commission agent ever to step on the turf.

'Listening intently to proceedings at the AJC hearing into the debacle, his hands clasped across his ample gut, it could well have appeared to be the pose of the confessional – "Forgive me, Father, for I have sinned." Indeed, after his solicitor declared it scurrilous to suggest he was knowingly betting on a ring-in, he walked out.

'Transferred to Wallangarra, not even a one-horse town, on the NSW border, he returned from a thirst-quenching visit from Goondiwindi to find his neighbour's bovine ruminating on his shrubs . . . he borrowed a shotgun and let the beast have both barrels in the southern end.'

The remarkable Father Ted O'Dwyer died in February 2016, and a revealing report on his funeral in St Patrick's Cathedral in Toowoomba appeared in *Horizons*, the monthly magazine of the local Catholic diocese.

It reads, in part, 'Despite a controversial life, Fr O'Dwyer was also remembered as a devoted, faith filled man who, by the end of his life, had conquered his personal demons. Fr Hal Ranger delivered a sincere and heartfelt eulogy at the Funeral Mass. "Despite the passing of 91 years and hundreds of colourful, risk-filled, often outrageous ventures and adventures, the daily Rosary and daily Mass remained central to Fr O'Dwyer's life right up to his death," Fr Ranger said.'

Marian Ware

Being Mick Sayers' girlfriend must have been a rather hairy ride. The resulting murder trial of Domican, Theobold and Camilleri heard that Marian had told police that, in the weeks before his death, Sayers had met with Chris Flannery and that the meeting had not gone particularly well.

As for the ring-in, in 1985 she told AJC stewards that John Gillespie had owed Sayers a good deal of money, but had come up with 'some sort of idea'. However, she professed to not knowing what the idea might have been. Mick didn't say and she didn't ask.

Wendy Smith

The woman who trained Dashing Soltaire for John Gillespie didn't have her day in court, because there was nothing she could be charged with. She had committed no crime and had no prior knowledge of the ring-in. It was all guilt by association.

However, the horsewoman and trainer, one of few in the industry at the time, received her marching orders courtesy of the QTC and she was warned off racetracks for life in 1985 for giving 'misleading evidence'. It all happened quietly. The newspapers made no mention of it. But the QTC records that she was handed a life sentence, cast out of the sport she loved for her trouble. Wendy didn't appeal. She didn't have the money or the energy to take the QTC on. Later, she married and, as Wendy Fahey, pulled up stumps and moved to the Northern Territory in the 1990s.

Bill Naoum

Bill Naoum put Bold Personality in a big paddock and ensured the gelding lived a full and happy life. He continued as a trainer, still training winners until his retirement in 2012. He remains active and enjoys golf, but whenever the words 'Fine Cotton' are mentioned in his earshot, his brow furrows and he emits a low growl and the odd swear word.

Russ Hinze

When the dust settled on the Fitzgerald Royal Commission, Russ Hinze faced charges of receiving corrupt payments of over

$500,000 and certain prison time. Hinze's digestive system, a gigantic rat's maze replete with more unprocessed shit than is regarded as healthy, finally gave way, bringing relief to corrective service officers and inmates alike. Hinze died of bowel cancer on 29 June 1991.

There was no piss bucket at Boggo Road big enough for Big Russ.

Labor Deputy Premier Tom Burns perhaps summed it up succinctly by way of backhanded eulogy when he said, 'The best cartoon of him was the one that showed him as a bulldog. He'd been on television describing why he would rather be a bulldog than a mouse, but he was shown as a bulldog with dark glasses and a white cane, outside a casino and brothel in the Valley that had a flashing neon light, saying he did not know there were any there.'

Joh Bjelke-Petersen

In 1991, Joh was tried for perjury in relation to evidence he had given at the Royal Commission, regarding a rather large sum of money he had trousered from a Chinese property developer.

Ultimately, a young lad on the jury who had been a member of the Young Nationals, a sort of Hitler-Jugend version of the then Queensland National Party, remained stubbornly unconvinced as to Joh's guilt, resulting in a hung jury and a mistrial.

Queensland prosecutors deemed that Joh, at 81, was too old to be re-tried.

Twelve years later, Joh would show he had more front than a Russ Hinze polo shirt when he lodged a claim against the then Queensland Labor government for $338 million over what he said were 'missed business opportunities'.

The Queensland solicitor-general dismissed the claim and reminded Joh that if he was fit enough to enter into a protracted legal dispute with the Queensland government, he might just be fit enough for the old perjury matter to be placed back on the court lists. Joh's claim ended there and then.

Joh died at Bethany in Kingaroy in 2005 of Parkinson's disease.

Terry Lewis

He got the knighthood he lusted after in 1986, but Sir Terence Lewis would not be referred to as a Knight of the Realm for very long.

The former Queensland Commissioner of Police was not lucky enough to have a member of the National Party on the jury when he stood before a District Court Judge in 1991 charged with 23 counts of perjury, corruption and forgery. The jury did find that Lewis had not perjured himself at the Royal Commission, but had received bribes totalling somewhere north of $700,000 and had forged Joh's signature.

He was sentenced to 14 years' jail with a non-parole period of nine and a half years.

After his release from prison he, too, showed a bucketload of spunk by demanding the return of his police superannuation, worth almost a million dollars.

His efforts in the courts failed; the last of his outrageous attempts to have his convictions overturned lapsed in 2005.

He lives in Brisbane and turned 91 this year.

Glen Hallahan

It had all started so well. From the day a young Constable Glen Patrick Hallahan arrested triple murderer Raymond Bailey in

Mount Isa in January 1958, until the day he left the police force three decades later, criminals who crossed his path in Queensland often came to a sticky end. He found Bailey's DeSoto sedan and his concealed .22 pistol under the driver's seat, the gun used to wipe out a family in remote South Australia a month earlier. Extradited to Adelaide, Bailey was hanged in June.

Then again, a lot of miscreants did very well out of their acquaintance with Hallahan. He would sell them guns, counterfeit cash and drugs. He would, for a price, protect his pet 'dogs', only euthanising the squealers. Perhaps the most dangerous and corrupt of a very dangerous and corrupt mob of evil coppers, his CV of conveniently unsolved homicides is long and impressive. But justice was never served upon Glen Hallahan. Not, at least, until he died in 1992 of cancer.

Tony Murphy

Detective Tony Murphy was a very successful sleuth. Many villains felt his wrath and consequently wound up in Boggo Road and a host of other horrible hoosegows, but his methods were unconventional, to say the least. A member of the tricky troika of top cops known in the '80s as The Rat Pack, he was assistant police commissioner to Terry Lewis, and his boss's involvement was made pretty clear when bagman Jack Herbert told the Fitzgerald Inquiry that Murphy had asked him, years earlier, if they should include Terry Lewis in The Joke – the organised network of corrupt officers who effectively refereed the shenanigans of Queensland's underworld for fun and profit.

Murphy sailed very close to the wind, especially after the drug overdose 'suicide' of Shirley Brifman, who was due to give evidence against him in court, but was a deft hand when it came to covering his own arse. From the mysterious murder of waterside worker 'Norman the Doorman' back in the 1970s, to the forensic examination of the Fitzgerald Inquiry, he never once graced a prison cell with his presence. He died peacefully in Brisbane in December 2010, aged 82.

Fine Cotton

The horse that stopped a nation was bought by film producer John Stainton in 1985, the idea being to star Fine Cotton as himself in a feature movie about the ring-in. It never got off the ground, Stainton explaining that the whole thing was 'a legal minefield'. He had a point – in 1985, it certainly would have been a minefield, legal or otherwise.

Stainton nicknamed the horse 'Satchmo', after Haitana told him that 'If the horse could talk, he'd blow the trumpet on all those involved'.

Fine Cotton died on 20 February 2009, aged 32, after a long and comfortable retirement on Stainton's farm north of Brisbane.

Bold Personality

Left at the track by Haitana and Gillespie, Bold Personality was returned to its owner, Bill Naoum, after Gillespie's cheque bounced. It never raced again and was sold to a Brisbane family who renamed it Percy. Percy spent the remainder of its life in a big, verdant paddock. Happily, it never moved at anything faster than a slow trot ever again.

Dashing Soltaire

The horse that was intended to be the horse that replaced the horse that wound up kicking its float to bits while yet another horse won the Second Division Commerce Novice Handicap on that fateful day is, without doubt, dead. But all attempts to find out where it eventually wound up and what happened to it have proved fruitless, largely because of the spelling of its name. Most reports on the event refer to the beast as Dashing Solitaire, which is quite understandable, but no help to researchers.

The animal was innocent of any crime. So, for that matter, were Bold Personality and Fine Cotton, which is more than you can say about most of the human beings involved.

Len McPherson

McPherson continued his life of crime, standing over other less physically overbearing criminals and assorted members of the public. He became a star witness at various judicial inquiries, royal commissions and gangster coronial inquests, where his performances were enjoyed by almost everyone – with the exception of those in the big chair at the front of the room.

When he took his seat in the witness box at the coronial inquest into the disappearance of Chris Flannery, he glared at Coroner Greg Glass, and asked, 'What did you have for breakfast this morning?'

A bemused Glass declined to respond, so Len went on.

'I had a fuckin' cold sausage roll. That's it.'

Glass cautioned Len for his outburst and his off-colour language but the rant continued.

'I got to have a knee operation. The bastards will probably cripple me.'

Glass threatened to have McPherson returned to Cessnock Prison, which suited Len just fine. He was always uncomfortable about giving evidence under oath. Len continued offering his counsel on the provision of health care and nutrition in NSW Corrective Services until Glass had had enough and sent him packing back to his cell.

In 1994, at the age of 73, McPherson was sentenced to a maximum four-year jail term, after telephone intercepts revealed he conspired to have the legs of a business partner broken over a dispute regarding the distribution rights of a popular brand of bourbon whisky.

He died in Cessnock Prison in 1996.

Stan Smith had always warned him about talking on the phone.

Stan Smith

Stan 'The Man' Smith was arguably the most successful criminal of his generation. Police believed he was involved in 15 murders and 25 shooting incidents. In his later years, he turned to large-scale trafficking of marijuana and cocaine. However, for his significant criminal reputation, he spent just three months in prison from the time of his 21st birthday.

Some five years prior to his death in January 2011, Stan found God and became a devout follower of the teachings of Christ. It appeared to be a sincere enough conversion, although not quite so earnest that Stan felt the need to walk into a police station and confess to all the murders he'd committed.

Stan, the hit man and mass murderer, was often seen doling out a hot feed to the homeless in Sydney and stuffing religious agitprop in the letterboxes around his neighbourhood.

Young wannabe gangsters seeking Stan's approval for some criminal enterprise or other would find themselves asked to kneel and bow their heads while Stan offered prayers to the Almighty for their safe passage and blessings that a divine hand would keep them free from interference from the criminal justice system.

Unlike so many of his associates, he died in his own bed and in his own time in 2010.

George Brown

The phrase 'Don't forget Georgie Brown' pops up in this story from time to time. It translates roughly to 'The consequences of not doing what you're told are too fucking horrible to contemplate.'

George Brown came to a very grisly end just months before the Fine Cotton ring-in, but the crime remained unsolved. In 2019, the NSW police offered a one million dollar reward for information that 'will lead to a conviction or convictions for those responsible'. A million bucks, after 35 years. A lot of money for a very cold case.

As to who these murderous men were, well, the NSW cops have a big bag of money waiting to be collected if you should happen to know.

The Waterhouses

Oscar Wilde wasn't renowned for spending much time at the track, but he did once make the wry observation that racecourses are 'sunny places for shady people'.

The Waterhouse clan have been titans of the Australian turf for over a century and, like any famous racing family, have had their moments of basking in bright sunshine and dodging dark clouds.

'Racing really is a hard, tough business, tougher than any other,' wrote Waterhouse patriarch Bill in his 2009 autobiography *What Are the Odds? The Bill Waterhouse Story*. 'But there's more money in it than any other business. It's bigger than BHP, and that's why I'm involved in it.'

The part played by the Waterhouses' bookkeeping operation in the events of 18 August 1984 has been examined so forensically by so many that further analysis is pointless. Charges of everything from conspiracy to idiocy have been hurled at them from every quarter, and while what they knew, when they knew it, and what, if anything, they might have got in their kick from the wash-up, it's pretty clear that everyone in the Waterhouse family wishes to this day that the bloody race had never been run.

But hey, they're still around, in 'a hard, tough business'.

And they're doing OK.

ACKNOWLEDGEMENTS

THE AUTHORS WOULD like to thank a lot of people, people who were pushed up against bars in hotels and forced to listen to tedious anecdotes spewed out in their presence.

We are grateful to them for their time and, despite their status as captive audiences, that they still managed to laugh in the right places. They know who they are.

We salute the good people of the Australian thoroughbred racing industry for their time and efforts in helping distinguish fact from fantasy, truth from myth, and for taking us straight to the heart of this incredible story.

Our special thanks go to Richard Fidler, who understood the Fine Cotton story's important role in Australian social history and demanded that it be told.

We are indebted to the late, great Mark Colvin, who raised an eyebrow and told the authors to stop messing about with bar-room recitals and get to work writing.

The authors are also deeply grateful for the cautious enthusiasm of writer, journalist and historian Paul Ham, who put us in touch with our literary agent, Jane Burrows. Jane has become a confidante, defender and friend.

We also raise a glass to former *Courier Mail* journo Phil Stafford of Brisbane, for his research into the events of Race Day.

Kylie Seretis must be mentioned in dispatches for her endless patience in printing out working copies of the manuscript, discovering the odd howler through careful proofreading, and making crucial contributions through her encyclopaedic knowledge of everything from women's hair care products to the NSW highway system.

Peter would like to thank his wife, Jenni, and his two daughters, Emily and Jessie, who regarded the many hours his home office door remained closed with endless patience and good humour.

Pat would especially like to thank Tilly the cat, for only walking across his computer keyboard once during the final frantic editing process.

Finally, our thanks go to Patrick Mangan, our wonderful editor, who moulded the vast piles of text heaved into his email into the book you have in your hands.

ABOUT THE AUTHORS

Peter Hoysted

Peter is a columnist at *The Australian* where he writes under a nom de plume, Jack The Insider, on politics, sport, true crime and whatever else takes his fancy. He wrote and produced *Tough Nuts: Australia's Hardest Criminals* for Foxtel's Crime and Investigation Channel in 2010: a two-series, 16-episode examination of Australia's most notorious gangland figures. In 2013, Peter co-authored *Unholy Trinity* with former Victoria Police detective Denis Ryan, exposing police corruption and the protection of paedophile priests in Victoria.

Pat Sheil

Pat is a Sydney writer and journalist. Since first being published in student magazines in the late '70s, and the music magazines *RAM* and *The Edge* from 1980, he has written for, and edited, many and various publications, written for radio and stage, and authored or co-authored several books. Pat edited the *Sydney Morning Herald*'s popular daily dose of frivolity, Column 8, for 12 years until 2016. He was also a founding member of the notorious shock/rock band Jimmy and the Boys, with Ignatius Jones.

Discover a
new favourite

Visit **penguin.com.au/readmore**